DATE DUE

D

PRINTED IN U.S.A.

Democratic Humility

Reinhold Niebuhr, Neuroscience, and America's Political Crisis

Christopher Beem

LEXINGTON BOOKS
Lanham • Boulder • New York • London

Published by Lexington Books
An imprint of The Rowman & Littlefield Publishing Group, Inc.
4501 Forbes Boulevard, Suite 200, Lanham, Maryland 20706
www.rowman.com

Unit A, Whitacre Mews, 26-34 Stannary Street, London SE11 4AB

British Library Cataloguing in Publication Information Available

Library of Congress Cataloging-in-Publication Data

The hardback edition of this book was previously catalogued by the Library of Congress as follows:

Beem, Christopher.
Democratic humility : Reinhold Niebuhr, neuroscience, and America's political crisis / Christopher
Beem.
pages cm
Includes bibliographical references and index.
1. Political culture--United States. 2. Democracy--United States. 3. Political psychology--United
States. 4. Mass media--Political aspects--United States. 5. Niebuhr, Reinhold, 1892-1971. I. Title.
JK1726.B44 2015
306.20973--dc23
2015010638

ISBN 978-1-4985-1142-1 (cloth)
ISBN 978-1-4985-1144-5 (pbk.)
ISBN 978-1-4985-1143-8 (electronic)

Contents

Acknowledgments

This project would not have come to fruition without the support (and indulgence) of many friends and colleagues.

Tom Ellis pushed me to go beyond analysis to offer some prescription. Anne Summers encouraged me at important stages. Terry Madl read every chapter as I finished it and was positively unbalanced in his encouragement. All three remind me what it means to be a good friend and a good democrat.

Lawrence Mead read an early precise. As he has been on many occasions, he was generous with his time and offered helpful advice. Chip Morris reviewed the chapters on neuroscience. Jane Hampden Daley read the chapter on the media. Reverend Seth Dietrich read the chapter on religion. Peter Levine and Diana Hess read the chapters on civic education. Franklin Gamwell, Bishop Ed Leidel, and James Benton read the entire manuscript. To all, my sincere thanks. The book is much improved for their time and thoughtful attention.

Pattie, Rachel, Connor, and Sam all generously accepted the hours that I spent writing when I should have been doing other stuff. Their love and encouragement means everything to me. Henry was an agreeable and unobtrusive writing companion (except when another dog would walk by).

Milwaukee County Library was an indispensable resource. The German Socialists who founded Milwaukee left a legacy that continues to sustain an informed and intelligent public life. I think about them with admiration.

I am extremely grateful to all for their support, generosity, and expertise. The errors that remain are my responsibility.

Introduction: Things *Are* That Bad

Given the condition of our political culture, it is comforting to point to our common belief in democracy as something that transcends our current disappointment. Being democrats, little d, means that whatever else we believe, we are committed to a fundamental set of ideals about how people should best organize themselves politically. It means embracing the idea that by virtue of our common humanity we are equal, both in our desires and our innate dignity. Within wide limits, we therefore have the right to live life the way we see fit, and to go as far as our abilities and drive will take us. More, equality means each citizen has a right to have a say in the decisions that affect our lives. We cannot achieve justice without that right; with it, we all take on some measure of pride and responsibility in its achievement.

These ideals unite us, Republicans and Democrats. In fact, it is our shared commitment to those ideals, more than ethnicity or religion or class, which identifies us as Americans. They orient our efforts, political and otherwise, give us a something to shoot for, and make it clear when we have fallen short. Finally, we find nobility in this enterprise. A democracy allows people to stand up for themselves and embrace the dignity of self-rule. "As I would not be a slave, so would I not be a master." That is how Abraham Lincoln defined democracy. And despite it all, we continue to hold tight to that ideal.

So far, so good.

Of course, no matter how well things are going, far more often than not we fall well short of these ideals. Democracy is never perfect, and most of the time, it is a long way from it. Anyone who has spent time doing the day-to-day work of democracy—the school boards, the church councils, the zoning commissions—already knows this. In our idealized world, these are the places where civil society reaches its zenith—where good men and women come together to argue and discuss, bringing their unique experiences to bear, finding a common good through the crucible of their enlightened self-interest. In the real world, democracy in action often means killing yet another perfectly good evening, sitting on metal folding chairs, drinking bad coffee, and listening to some yahoo who has nothing better to do than drone on and on about his own private stalking horse, all the while knowing that when the whole enterprise finally comes in for a landing, his vote is going to count as much as yours. All too often, democracy takes too long to get not very far and the trip is a uniquely unpleasant combination of contention and tedium.

A similarly depressing tale can be told about electoral politics in a democracy. Because all votes count the same, the lowest common denominator sets the standard for a discourse that easily gravitates toward the vicious, the vacuous, or both. Candidates and their acolytes regularly say things about their opponents that they know to be unfair, if not completely untrue. And when someone has a question for them, the successful candidate knows to spin rather than to say what he or she really thinks. (Sometimes, despite their internal and external controls, they do it anyway; this kind of truth-telling is what is known as a gaff.) Campaigns today cross-reference reams of consumer data and then package their message down to very specific, even tiny marketing subsets. But that just means that contemporary campaign managers are better equipped than those who came before. For a long time, candidates have quite literally been packaged and presented like soap. If there is a difference, it is that now the folderol of campaigning has become practically permanent and inseparable from governing.

It has also become more expensive. Of course, the quest for money has always been the politician's pre-eminent task and both the giver and the recipient keep a straight face while insisting that this exchange in no way undermines good public policy. Here too, the present is different (that is to say worse) only as a matter of degree. Campaign costs are rising prohibitively, and thereby rises the power of money in politics. In 2008 the average Congressional election cost $1.1 million; in 2012 (after the Supreme Court's decision in *Citizens United*) that number was almost $1.7 million (a 54 percent increase in four years).[1] Finally, because of the regularity of campaigns, politicians rarely have any incentive to consider, let alone act upon, the long-term best interests of the nation. Five years from now might be here before you know it, but for politicians it is two or three election cycles away.

For any democrat, much of this simply has to be accepted; short attention spans and the fictions of campaign finance go with the territory no less than the lost evenings. Most of the time, democracy is merely a mechanism for muddling through. And quite frequently, it is awash in corruption and mindless blather. But it is worth recalling Winston Churchill's assessment: "No one pretends that democracy is perfect or all-wise. Indeed it has been said that democracy is the worst form of Government except for all those other forms that have been tried."[2] Churchill knew the failures of democracy as well as anybody. But he nevertheless thought it superior to any possible alternative.[3] Though it may rarely produce greatness, and often fails to escape mediocrity, democracy is the best means we have for securing a genuine measure of freedom, justice and equality. It therefore remains a great achievement and it is our fortune that we Americans can claim it is our birthright.

So even still, so far so good.

But for Republicans and Democrats, there is a growing sense that right now, we are not able even to muddle through. More troubling than the cost and slick marketing associated with contemporary campaigns is the condition of everyday politics. Political parties are more ideologically separate than they have been since around the time of the First World War. So too are American voters. According to a 2012 Pew Report, "America's values and basic beliefs are more polarized along partisan lines than at any point in the last 25 years."[4] In sum, Democrats are growing more liberal, Republicans more conservative, and moderates more scarce. What is more, the phenomenon appears to be growing. According to the authors of the Pew Report, nearly all of the increases in partisanship have occurred during the presidencies of George W. Bush and Barack Obama.

It only stands to reason that given this condition, partisan conflict will be both constant and more extreme and our politics desperately unproductive. Congressional scholar Norm Ornstein recently said, "I've been in DC since 1969 and I have never seen it this dysfunctional."[5] Former Senators Trent Lott and Tom Daschle agree: "In recent years, Washington has become deeply polarized and far less civil. Dysfunction has become the status quo."[6] In a column for Bloomberg View, Ezra Klein called the 112th Congress "The Rottenest Congress in History."[7] As for the 113th Congress, Klein said in September of 2013 that it was "a complete and total train wreck."[8] The headline for Chris Cillizza's Washington Post column on October 31st of that year was no less adamant: "Worst. Congress. Ever."[9] Leaving aside the question of which Congress was worse, the operative point is that both were very bad indeed. (The 112th set a record low for number of laws passed in modern history, the 113th was through some last minute scrambling able to avoid setting a new record by passing three more bills.)

This state of affairs is lost on no one. Everyone has heard the comparisons: "What's more popular than Congress?" (Three answers: head lice, colonoscopies, and traffic jams.)[10] But not only are approval ratings historically low, so is distrust of Congress. In 1973, the year before Nixon resigned, 42 percent of Americans expressed confidence in Congress. In 2012, a long decline has brought the figure to 10 percent.[11] (At the end of 2014, the figure had rebounded to the dizzying heights of 15 percent.) Even more disconcerting, a Gallup poll conducted in January of 2014 found that 65 percent of

Americans say they are dissatisfied with the nation's system of government and how well it works.[12] That is, Americans are not only dissatisfied with the occupants of the current Congress, they are dissatisfied with the system itself. One shudders at the question: what does it mean for the future of our nation when almost two-thirds of Americans are dissatisfied with their democracy, and what would they want in its place?

Of course, it is possible that none of this is as bad as we might think it is. American politics has always had its shadow side. It is easy to lose sight of the fact, but scurrilous attacks were made on Thomas Jefferson, Andrew Jackson, Grover Cleveland, and many others. The idea that there is some idyllic past for us to return to is naïve and a little pathetic. In sum, we may not be living up to democracy's ideals, but those democrats in our nation's past were no paragons, either. They got through okay, and so, we like to believe, will we. More than that, some pundits embrace this state of affairs. They argue, quite correctly, that a more polarized electorate has created a citizenry that is more politically active than at any time during the past half century.

To many Americans, these rationalizations just don't cut it. Indeed, they sound like whistling past our own graveyard. For them, the current state of our democracy constitutes a crisis. It calls into question our ability, even our capacity, to govern ourselves. Like every age, we are confronted with grave problems, none of which can be successfully addressed without some sense of our common ideals and purposes. And yet the likelihood that we might manifest such a sense, and deal forthrightly with any of these serious and complicated issues, appears to be ever receding. We have separated into Red and Blue worlds. The places we live, cars we drive, our hobbies, entertainment, news, and places of worship all reinforce this ever more fundamental distinction. All this has created a standard for a discourse where the answers are sure before the conversation begins and where the only sin is weakness. Partisans use rancid language (Libtards, Rethuglicans) to describe their opponents. And all sides can find plenty of red meat to both legitimate and abet this kind of behavior.

If you've stayed with me even this long, I expect you are uneasy as well. For my part, I don't know how anyone can claim to be a democrat and *not* be uneasy. Short of a blithe conviction that these things are cyclical and sooner or later work themselves out, I don't know what one could point to as reason for optimism. For the future of our birthright, what Lincoln called the last, best hope on earth, we need to account for our grave condition, and begin the hard work of improving it. We need to think about more than the next election or the next news cycle. We need to think our way out of this.[13]

In what follows, I turn to Reinhold Niebuhr to help us in this effort. For some, the name might be obscure. For others, they know him because he is the author of the Serenity Prayer, used by Alcoholics Anonymous and other such groups: "God grant me the serenity to accept the things I cannot change; the courage to change the things I can; and the wisdom to know the difference." Niebuhr taught Social Ethics at Union Theological Seminary in New York for decades, and he never strayed from his roots as a Christian pastor and teacher. But what many Americans do not know is that Niebuhr was also one of America's greatest political theorists.[14] Niebuhr was a thoughtful analyst of American history, the Cold War, and democracy. He was a colossus in American intellectual life, and a prophetic voice that made no one comfortable, but gave some measure of hope and courage to all. More, Niebuhr did not just write and talk and think. He also had the courage to act, to operate within the messy and ambiguous world of politics, to make hard choices and try to foster the proximate good. For a democracy in the midst of a crisis, his is a voice worth heeding.

Of course, for many, any such an enterprise is bound to fail. Our culture is not nearly as Christian as it was during Niebuhr's lifetime, and many American citizens have moved on from organized religion, let alone the Protestant Church down the street. Niebuhr requires metaphysical prerequisites from our culture and from us as individuals that we can no longer provide. Just so, the world has changed. The Great Depression, World War II, and the Cold War are all long past. Our enemies are different; they are not just willing to kill, but willing, even eager to die. And their weapons are not missile silos but IEDs. We have to think differently. Finally technology, too, has transformed society in ways that he could have imagined. The world is smaller, more immediate, and dramatically more connected. Niebuhr might have been a formidable resource in his own day, but we have moved on, thanks. We'll have to look elsewhere.

On the contrary, I will show that Niebuhr gives us both the terms for understanding our present condition as well as a sense of how we might address it. Far from being mired in his own time, Niebuhr lays out terms that are resonant with the most recent research in how we human beings think and act. Niebuhr said that Christianity makes the most sense out of the most facts. At least as far as the condition of our politics goes, my analysis affirms that assessment. Niebuhr's Christian-based analysis of democratic politics ably conforms to what modern scientific research shows us to be. Indeed, I want to show that his thought provides us the best chance we have both to understand and move beyond a politics that is rigid, self-righteous, and mean. In short, Niebuhr shows that democracy requires a specific form of humility to counter our natural inclination to self-delusion and self-righteousness, and points to ways by which our society might reclaim it. His thought therefore serves as a kind of the armature for everything that follows.

There is another objection that bears addressing immediately. For most of his life, and regarding the vast majority of issues, Reinhold Niebuhr was left of center. Some will therefore question whether Niebuhr is an acceptable choice for my objectives. How can someone whose life was so closely asso-ciated with the Democratic side of American politics serve as some kind of North Star for a democratic restoration? Niebuhr once ran for office as a Socialist for God's sake! If I were to add that Niebuhr's political leanings are quite similar to my own, I suspect that many would declare that the jig is up. This book may claim to be for democrats, but it is really for Democrats.

As for Niebuhr, there are two things to say. First, in what follows, I do not recount his position on any single policy matter. To be sure, those arguments are there for the making. Niebuhr's case against libertarian economics is one example of an argument that I believe is most assuredly worth recounting. (Go watch Mike Wallace's contemporaneous interviews with both Ayn Rand and Reinhold Niebuhr and see who you think comes off better.)[15] But I don't reference those arguments here. I am out to describe and utilize Niebuhr's analysis of the human condition, his justification for democracy, and his prescription for how we must work to preserve it. If someone can point out how Niebuhr's partisan politics belie the trans-partisan character of the Nie-buhrian arguments that I do propose to use, then I may have to change my mind about this. But I simply don't see the connection. The second point is that it is facile to box Niebuhr into our over-the-top partisan categories. Because Niebuhr insists that all of us operate with the same inadequacies, nobody emerges unscathed from his analysis. Niebuhr found fault with eve-rybody, and was perhaps most scurrilous in his condemnation of liberals, both in and out of the church. As a result, many contemporary conservatives claim Niebuhr's mantle.[16]

As for myself, I do not claim that I am above the partisan acrimony that envelopes our nation. (For that matter, I do not see myself as some kind of paragon of humility.) In what follows, I present an analysis and prescription that strives for objectivity. But it is true that my analysis can frequently be summarized with the phrase "Democrats are bad, but Republicans are worse."[17] In terms of the very argument I present, I must admit that such a conclusion might well be compromised by my own biases. If and to the degree that that is so, it would undermine the book's objective. But it would also to that degree confirm the very Niebuhrian insight that all of us are guilty of self-deception. Which way things end up is for the reader to judge.

OUTLINE OF THE BOOK

In chapter 1, I describe Niebuhr's theologically-informed understanding of humans beings and why we act the way we do. We human beings are animals who know we are going to die, and our inescapable anxiety leads us—inescapably—to sin. In chapter 2, I take up Niebuhr's understanding of de-mocracy. In *The Children of Light and The Children of Darkness*, Niebuhr presents what he says is "a vindication of democracy and a critique of its traditional defense." Children of Light are decent but misguided. They foolishly think that there is a once and for all solution to the problems of human history and their naïveté opens the door to disaster. Children of Darkness know how the world really works, but are without a moral compass. They are therefore evil, but also cunning, far better able to achieve their self-interested aims. In order to function adequately, democracy must operate between these extremes.

I want to show how Niebuhr's diagnosis helps us understand our own hyper-partisan context. In chapters 3 and 4, I turn to neuroscience and psychology to show that both with respect to human behavior and its implications for politics, Niebuhr's analysis is supported by contemporary scientific research. My objective is to show that whatever you believe, there are good scientific grounds for taking Niebuhr's analysis seriously. In fact, I use Niebuhr's category of "Children of Light" in ways that Niebuhr would not. I argue that science shows that all of us are "Children of Light." We are all indeed saturated by pride and self-deceit, far too eager to see the best in ourselves and the worst in those with whom we disagree, and not just naïve, but fundamentally unable to see that the failures of our opponents are present in ourselves, as well. Niebuhr says that the unreflective, unchecked operation of the Children of Light constitutes Democracy's internal peril. And using this expanded definition, I argue that that is a very good account for our present condition.

In chapters 5 and 6, I show how talk radio, cable television news, and partisan websites—what I call partisan infotainment—have given free rein to what Niebuhr would call our sinfulness and psychology would call our innate human inclinations for self-deception. I argue that the new business model understands how we human beings operate very well. Whatever we believe, partisan infotainment reinforces our understanding of ourselves as smarter and more moral than those who believe otherwise. This reinforcement is very entertaining and therefore very lucrative. Because it gives all of us what we all want whenever we want it, partisan infotainment serves and emboldens the Children of Light in all of us. As a result, our democracy is imperiled to a daunting, and heretofore unprecedented degree.

In the midst of our nasty and unproductive politics, we must simultaneously try, together, to make our democracy better. In part II, I present Niebuhr's prescription for defending democracy from its internal peril. These prescriptions demand leadership from those social institutions that lead and instruct: government, religion and education. I call these democracy's bulwarks. In chapter 7, I argue that there are reasons to doubt the power of government to help us address our problems. People point to a myriad of solutions to help us transcend our political pathology. But these solutions, whatever their potential efficacy, must come through legislation. That means a broken politics must fix itself. Without some change in the condition of our broader political culture, that is, at best, an unlikely scenario.

More to the point, the primary reason why Congress is unlikely to stop fighting, work together, or even consider a good beyond partisanship is because for all their professed dissatisfaction, the majority of the people who elect them do not want them to. We citizens are polarized too. If we really want to change our politics, we have to find ways to constrain the Child of Light within each one of us. We have to find ways to develop democratic humility.

In chapter 8, I take up Niebuhr's critical distinction between profound and profane religion. Profound religion does not let us forget this truth: that we are not God. We are merely creatures, and sinful, benighted, and contingent ones, at that. Profound religion thus serves, in Niebuhr's words, as "a constant fount of humility." I argue that on both the Right and Left, Christianity has lost this profound dimension and become profane. Not only does religion not help us, it serves to abet our prideful delusions, and thus exacerbate our present morass. I appeal to the example of Martin Luther King Jr. to show how one can affirm the profound dimensions of the Christian faith and the Christian call to humility, and nevertheless engage the political arena.

In chapter 9, I turn to education, specifically civic education, as an institution that can foster humility for the rest of us. Rather than being content that our children learn the basic facts about our government, they also need to learn what it means to be a democrat, and how to behave like one. That means they need to know about the inescapable features of the brains we have. St. Bernard said that Christian humility comes from knowing ourselves "as we truly are." *Democratic* humility likewise is born of that knowledge. Indeed, all of us must better understand ourselves as we truly are, and then learn how we must all strive to accommodate that reality within a democracy. I argue that teaching our children about those challenges represents our best chance to help our nation move beyond our contemporary failures, to embrace a more objective accounting of the facts of the matter, and thereby move toward developing a better democracy.

None of this ought to be understood as simple or easy. On the contrary, it presents us with a serious dilemma: we need humility in order to constrain our undemocratic inclinations. But humility corrodes the will to power upon which democratic politics depends. Democratic politics requires that we be more committed to our cause than the facts warrant, and that we see the opposition as worse than they probably really are. This is a very Niebuhrian problem and there is no getting out of it. I conclude that we must act as Niebuhr did, striving to understand the present condition, and then finding the balance that best responds to it. Right now, our democracy is in peril because of a polarization that bleeds into enmity and overwhelms the very possibility of governance. Right now, our politics needs to work to restore democratic humility.

As this short accounting makes clear, this is an unusual book. It covers theology and church history, neuroscience, group theory, political psychology, and media studies all in one. If one were inclined to be generous, one would call that approach synthetic (literally putting things together); if not, one would dismiss it as all over the map. I cannot dispute that the map here is pretty extensive. Certainly the subject matter covered here extends well beyond any expertise I can claim. But if we do indeed need to think our way out of our condition, then bringing together pieces that are normally kept separate might be one way to start. In any event, to my mind, the condition of our democracy right now is bad enough that it is worth a try.

NOTES

1. Costa, "What's the cost of a seat in Congress?"
2. Winston Churchill, *Churchill by Himself*, 572.
3. Reinhold Niebuhr affirmed Churchill's assessment. See Reinhold Niebuhr and Paul E. Sigmund, *The Democratic Experience* (New York: Frederick A. Praeger Publishers, 1969), p. v.
4. Pew Research Center for the People and the Press, "Partisan Polarization Surges in Bush, Obama Years: Trends in American Values: 1987-2012." Twenty-five years is a long time ago, but that doesn't mean that things were worse in 1987. It's just that 1987 was the first year they asked the question.
5. Ornstein, "Ending the Permanent Campaign."
6. Daschle and Lott, "Prescriptions for comity in government," *Washington Post*, Saturday, November 23, 2013.
7. Klein, "Good Riddance to Rottenest Congress in History," *Bloomberg View.*
8. Klein, "John Boehner's Congress is a Train Wreck," *Wonkblog, Washington Post.*
9. Cillizza, "Worst. Congress. Ever. The case in 7 charts," *Washington Post, The Fix*, October 31, 2013.
10. Public Policy Polling, "Congress Less Popular than Cockroaches, Traffic," News Release, January 8th, 2013.
11. Gallup Polls, "Americans' Confidence in Congress Falls to Lowest on Record," June 13, 2013. See http://www.gallup.com/poll/163052/americans-confidence-congress-falls-lowest-record.aspx.
12. Gallup Polls, "In U.S., 65% Dissatisfied With How Gov't System Works," January 22, 2014. See http://www.gallup.com/poll/166985/dissatisfied-gov-system-works.aspx.
13. Consider these words from Marilyn Robinson: "My point is that our civilization has recently chosen to identify itself with a wildly oversimple model of human nature and behavior and then is stymied or infuriated by evidence that the models don't fit. And the true believers in these models seem often to be hardened in their belief by this evidence, perhaps in part because of the powerfully annealing effects of rage and indignation. Sophisticated as we sometimes claim to be, we have by no means evolved beyond this tendency, are deeply mired in it at this very moment, and seem at a loss to think our way out of it." *When I Was A Child I Read Books: Essays*, 154.
14. On the other hand, Niebuhr is by no means some dusty and obscure academic. Many public figures are well aware of Niebuhr's writings and their importance. Columnists David Brooks and E. J. Dionne, for example, are both very familiar with Niebuhr's writings and regularly cite him in their work. What's more, in a 2007 interview with Brooks, then-candidate Barack Obama said that Niebuhr was one of his favorite philosophers.

15.   Niebuhr's interview is at http://www.hrc.utexas.edu/multimedia/video/2008/wallace/niebuhr_reinhold.html. The Ayn Rand interview can be found on YouTube.

16.   To note one recent example, see Loconte, "Obama Contra Niebuhr," *The American: The Online Magazine of the American Enterprise Institute,* January 14, 2010. The most famous example is probably Michael Novak, "Reinhold Niebuhr: Model for Neoconservatives," *Christian Century,* January 22, 1986.

17.   See Mann and Ornstein, *It's Even Worse Than It Looks: How the American Constitutional System Collided With the New Politics of Extremism.*

I

Democracy's Peril

Chapter One

Moderating our Pretensions: Niebuhr on Being Human

Reinhold Niebuhr (1892-1971) was born in Missouri and raised in Illinois, in a community of German immigrant farmers where his father served as pastor. That fact is merely biographical, but it is worth noting because there is a Midwestern matter-of-factness that colors much of his writing. It makes him readable (if not always easy), imminently quotable, and certainly unusual among academicians. The other relevant biographical fact is that he started his professional life as a pastor. Niebuhr began his career as an ordained minister in the *Deutsche Evangelische Synode von Nord-Amerika* and pastor of a middle-class German congregation in Detroit, Bethel Evangelical Church. In that role, he confronted—and he helped his congregation confront—the political issues of the time. This effort set the tone for all that was to follow.

THREE EARLY STRUGGLES

Almost immediately upon his arrival in Detroit, the First World War finally engulfed the United States. This was no small problem for Niebuhr. His background, and that of most of his congregation, was linguistically and culturally German.[1] All German-Americans were feeling the sting of anti-German sentiment. Neutrality, even one grounded in Christian pacifism, meant risking friends, and perhaps businesses. But embracing American patriotism meant turning their back on their heritage, their homeland, and perhaps family members. At the tender age of twenty-three, he was the leader of this flock and they were looking to him for guidance.

Overwhelmed and anxious, his diary of this early pastoral work shows him trying to work out his proper role: How was a German-American Christian supposed to respond to this war between one's adopted and one's ancestral home?[2] How would God want him to position himself in this conflict? Was anything clearer than Jesus' own commitment to nonviolence? How then should the Christian respond to the call for young men to sacrifice, die, and kill for the state? At what point does patriotism become idolatry? And how was one to respond to the brutal fact of the war itself? To the unprecedented slaughter wrought by gas and aerial bombardment? To the hopeless stalemate of trench warfare? Could a Christian condone such a war? But could a Christian sit out such a struggle? Perhaps there was no perfect side, but surely there was a better and worse side, and given the stakes, could one remain indifferent? Was God indifferent? Niebuhr struggled with all these questions, both in his sermons and his diary, but never really settled them. He recoiled from many of his peers, German-American pastors who were wholly committed to the German side of the hyphen. "The German propaganda is so hysterical among many of our ministers that largely by reaction I am getting to be a violent American patriot."[3] Yet this patriotism only went so far. The war's spectacle of suffering and waste led him for a time to give up on "the war business" and embrace pacifism.

After the war, another defining social issue captured Niebuhr's attention. The war's end meant unleashed economic demand. The prospects of factory jobs led to a large migration of, in Niebuhr's words, "both Southern Negroes and 'cracker' Whites" to the auto industry.[4] As in most northern cities, prior to this influx, Detroit's black population was confined within one neighborhood. Almost overnight, however, waves of immigration pushed Detroit's black population beyond that neighborhood's capacity. The Ku Klux Klan exploited this "not in my neighborhood!" tension to build support for its Protestant candidate for mayor, Charles Bowles. The Klan singled out blacks, as well as Catholics and Jews, as the corrupters of a Detroit society buttressed by upstanding white Protestants. In fact, the Klan's mayoral candidate was counting on votes from people just like the members of Bethel church to win the election. The incumbent Mayor John W. Smith was part of the Detroit machine and a Catholic to boot. It was not easy for Niebuhr to support him. But there was no avoiding the choice, and in the end, no question about which side to support.

In print and from the pulpit, he also directly raised the question: "Where shall the Negro Live?" and after the election worked with Mayor Smith by chairing a community interracial committee. In his diary, he recounted the commitee's hard slogging, writing, "I wish that some of our romanticists and sentimentalists could sit through a series of meetings where the real social problems of a city are discussed. They would be cured of their optimism."[5] Ultimately, the committee advocated the increased hiring of black policemen, firemen and postal workers. For his part, Niebuhr came to admire the mayor, calling his views on race relations "superior" to that of most church people, the "saints" who "develop their private virtues and let the city as such fry in its iniquities."[6]

Finally, toward the end of his tenure as pastor, Niebuhr took on the local demigod Henry Ford and the question of labor rights. Ford had an international reputation as someone who paid good wages. In 1914, five dollars a day was a lot of money, more than other factories paid, and the story was that Ford offered this kind of wage so that his workers could afford to buy his cars. Ford was considered by many to represent the ideal of the socially-enlightened capitalist. But knowing many of those workers, and seeing their working conditions first hand, Niebuhr knew that the truth was, at best, more complicated. Those high wages had remained stagnant; since the end of the war, any wage advantage to working at Ford had effectively disappeared. What's more, even as this was happening, the speed of the assembly line had increased.[7] Niebuhr saw that new young hires were replacing those who could no longer keep up. The Ford plants "junks the aging man" and offered no system of pensions to "offset this ruthlessness."[8]

Niebuhr took the battle to Ford himself and learned a style of engagement that would define his life's work. "My own political, religious and moral convictions were formed by the obvious contradiction between the power realities in the [automobile] industry and the sentimentalities which obscured them."[9] In 1926, in an article for the *Christian Century*, "How Philanthropic is Henry Ford?" Niebuhr wrote, "Detroit produces automobiles, but is not yet willing to admit that the poor automata who are geared in on the production lines have any human problems."[10] He also allowed union organizers to hold meetings at his church and he preached on the question of labor rights.

Years later, Niebuhr would reminisce, "I cut my eyeteeth fighting Ford."[11] But this is true not just in terms of his combative style or his drive to connect the demands of his faith with the world around him. From his encounter with Ford, he also developed the categories that would ground his political writings. In "How Philanthropic is Henry Ford?" Niebuhr concludes: "It is difficult to determine whether Mr. Ford is simply a shrewd exploiter of a gullible public in his humanitarian pretensions, or whether he suffers from self-deception."[12] With these words, it is clear that Niebuhr is already developing categories that will inform his later and more mature works (and which will take center stage in this book); in effect, Niebuhr is wondering whether Ford is a Child of Darkness or a Child of Light.[13]

These stories are fascinating from a historical vantage point, but I bring them up not to assess Niebuhr's choices. Looking back from the safety of one hundred years, such an effort could easily be banal and trifling. Rather I bring up this history because of how these problems thrust themselves upon Niebuhr and demanded his attention. Whatever his inner inclinations, his role as pastor and the very times in which he lived forced him to engage these issues and develop a theology and politics that was up to the challenge. Niebuhr acknowledged as much: "Since I am not so much scholar as preacher, I must confess that the gradual unfolding of my theological ideas has come not so much through study as through the pressure of world events."[14] For Niebuhr, the effort to take seriously the challenges that history threw at him developed into a driving disposition that would define his life's work. In short: how does Christianity help us understand and respond to what is going on right now? This question would accompany him as he engaged the threats associated with the Great Depression, World War II, and the Cold War. It would bring him into conversation with central figures in religion, of course, but also in politics, journalism and the academy. And in every response, to just about every issue, one finds Reinhold Niebuhr reflecting on this underlying question. Because it grounds his entire thought, and much of what I want to say, I want to make sure that this foundation receives a just if brief accounting.

ANXIETY, FREEDOM, AND SIN

Niebuhr insisted he was not a theologian. (He usually referred to himself as a professor of Social Ethics or simply as a preacher.) And it is true that frequently in his writings, there is not as much talk about God or quoting from Scripture as one might expect. But while Niebuhr's theology is not always front and center, it is never absent. As Larry Rasmussen has said, "His characteristic turn of mind assumed theological convictions as background and framework, and his reflection on Christian symbols was essential to . . . the basic structure of his thought."[15] Niebuhr's political thought is grounded in anthropology and that anthropology rested, in turn, on his conception of Christian theology.

Figuring out what we human beings should do, how we should respond to the world, requires that we strive to understand what is going on. But it also requires that we strive to understand ourselves: what we are doing and why we are doing it. For Niebuhr, the most accurate understanding of human beings comes from the Judeo-Christian tradition. The prophets of the Hebrew Bible and the Christian worldview that comes from them provide the most accurate description of who we are; better than liberalism, capitalism, or Marxism could possibly offer. Christianity, Niebuhr says, "makes more sense out of more facts."[16]

Throughout his writings, Niebuhr returns again and again to the Genesis stories of Creation and, in particular, the Fall from the Garden of Eden. Now Niebuhr did not regard Genesis as a historical account, i.e., he never thought that there was some point in time in which a naked person named Eve took fruit from some serpent. But he did maintain that the stories of creation and the doctrine of original sin communicated essential truths. In this case, the truth is that knowledge is at the root of our humanity. This knowledge of our own nakedness (our defenselessness, metaphorically speaking) generates the anxiety that both consumes us and drives us. The Bible is therefore worth our consideration not just because it is the avenue to our salvation (though Niebuhr certainly believes that it is) but because it provides a more complete, more correct accounting of who we really are, why we think and act the way we do, and what we can realistically expect from ourselves and our future. Set on this foundation, we can better understand how we should act in history, respond to worldly events, and organize ourselves politically and economically.

In *The Children of Light and the Children of Darkness*, Niebuhr considers the lion that has just "filled his maw."[17] Having chosen, attacked and killed his prey, the lion tears into the flesh content that it has everything it wants. The lion does not consider that soon he will need to eat again. Nor does he wonder about the health and condition of the herd he just culled, or the fact that one day his skills and speed will diminish. But we are different. We *know* that there are things that we must have in order to survive; we know that securing those things is a constant struggle; we know that the deprivation of those things is painful, and we know that there is no guarantee that we will always have them. Finally, we know that there is no way out of this game. We know that sooner or later, either our needs will not be met, or our bodies will give out, and we will die.

This knowledge does more than set us apart from all the other animals; it is the *core* of who we are. We know our existence is precarious and finite and that it can never be otherwise. This knowledge creates anxiety, the most fundamental feature of human existence. No lion lies awake at three o'clock in the morning stewing about the failures of yesterday or the fears for tomorrow. For us humans, though, anxiety is a fundamental and inexorable part of our existence. Nagging thoughts can be drowned out now and then, and are even forgettable for a time, but as we all know, they never really go away.[18]

But there is more to our knowledge than just anxiety. Yes, Niebuhr says, like all animals we are creatures born to struggle, suffer, and die. But our knowledge of this, our self-consciousness and our ability to think also give us the freedom to be more than just creatures. We have the ability to imagine something better and to strive for it. For Christians (and really all theists), this freedom to imagine and create a different future is captured by the idea that we are *imago dei*, made in the image of God. We are creatures, but, like God, we are also creators. We cannot escape our fate, but we can alter it, that is, create new conditions within it. (Niebuhr says that humans can break "the forms of nature.") We can imagine a different way of doing things, a more beautiful place to live, a better life, and we can work to achieve these things.

Just so, we can imagine a more just society, a more productive economic system, and we can work together, in concert with others, to make these happen, too. Everything we can point to that makes life better, from Mozart's *The Magic Flute* to indoor plumbing, results from this freedom.

But this freedom does not, cannot, take us as far as we want. It does not eliminate our creatureliness, though we hope and think and act as if it does. We try to deny that there are fundamental features of this existence that we can neither change nor escape. The human is, after all, "only a little animal living a precarious existence on a second-rate planet, attached to a second-rate sun."[19] Just so, compared to the known age of the universe, human history, let alone our own individual lifespan, is almost imperceptibly brief. We know all this to be true—Niebuhr calls it "a darkly unconscious sense"— but we very much prefer not to think about it.

We want to make ourselves safe, and ever more safe. We know that we will need to eat tomorrow, so we strive to position ourselves for a better paying job; we know that there are people who will want to take what is ours, so we install locks on the windows; we have all driven by plenty of accidents, shuddering at the flashing lights and mangled metal, so we religiously buckle our children into their car seats. But even as we do these things, we know that we can get downsized at any moment, that locks can be broken, and that children in car seats still sometimes die in accidents. "It is possible to soften the incongruities of life endlessly by the scientific conquest of nature's caprices, and the social and political triumph over historic injustice. But all such strategies cannot finally overcome the fragmentary character of human existence."[20] While we can influence our fate, we cannot master it, and that means we cannot escape our anxiety.

Our drive to overcome this anxiety leads us to deny the contingent character of our existence, to pretend that we are safe and important. And this denial leads us inexorably into sin. We are consumed by the desire to escape, so we misuse our freedom in ignoble ways, toward unachievable ends. The same creativity that leads us to develop central air or the internal combustion engine also leads us to create biological weapons and Ponzi schemes. Anxiety thus creates sin, and sin thus begins, paradoxically perhaps, with pride.[21]

This pride is not self-love; it is *inordinate* self-love, a self-love that transcends the bounds of reality. Pride is thus fundamentally tied to injustice, of not giving things their due: we do not acknowledge God's standing in the cosmos and we do not acknowledge the limits of our own. But pride produces injustice as well. Most relevantly, this injustice is expressed in our relations with others. "The ego which falsely makes itself the centre of existence in its pride and will-to-power inevitably subordinates other life to its will and thus does injustice to other life."[22] Because we want to believe that we are more important than others, we therefore work to create a world in which that belief is reflected in reality.

Pride leads us to construct a world where we are on top, where we control others rather than one in which we are controlled. Pride is therefore also, perhaps even primarily, a story that we tell ourselves to tamp down the gnawing sense of our own insignificance.[23] Sin is always connected to a lie, and it is a lie we tell, first and foremost, to ourselves.

> Man loves himself inordinately. Since his determinate existence does not deserve the devotion lavished upon it, it is obviously necessary to practice some deception in order to justify such excessive devotion. While such deception is constantly directed against competing wills, seeking to secure their acceptance and validation of the self's too generous opinion of itself, its primary purpose is to deceive, not others, but the self. The self must, at any rate, deceive itself first. Its deception of others is partly an effort to convince itself against itself.[24]

We need to try to prove to ourselves that we are right to hold ourselves in such high regard. We think of ourselves as significantly more important than the facts warrant, and our lies confirm that belief. Our lies tell us that we are different, special, better; we are more moral, more intelligent, more comprehending of the way the world works. "Moral pride is the pretension of finite man that his highly conditioned virtue is the final righteousness and that his very relative moral standards are absolute."[25]

Let me sum up: Niebuhr says that we know both our fragility and our fate, that awareness of our condition causes anxiety, and that this anxiety in turns leads us to pride. This inordinate love of self "infects our thought," and is at the root of our sinfulness. Pride makes us see ourselves as more important than we really are. It causes us to think our needs and desires are more important than those of others. In ways that conform fully with Christian doctrine, Niebuhr says that our sinfulness is inescapable: we cannot not sin. Nevertheless, we are fully accountable for it. In Niebuhr's well-known formulation: sin is "inevitable but not necessary."

SCIENCE AND ANXIETY

Now except for the sin part, this description conforms very closely to that presented by science: psychology and neuroscience especially. Affirmation of Niebuhr's anthropology does not require that one affirm his religion. Because, at least in this regard, Christianity does indeed "makes more sense out of more facts."

Experimental evidence is overwhelming that we humans hold opinions of ourselves that are unwarranted by the facts. "People tend to have impressions of themselves that are just too favorable to be justified by objective criteria."[26] We are all, in David Dunning's words, "self-flattering." People believe themselves to be more ethical than average, more honest, kinder, smarter, better looking, better employees, better leaders, and on and on.[27] Now, we can't all be correct about all these beliefs. Not everyone can be above average, of course. And that is the reason why this condition can properly be called vanity. For vanity implies a self-opinion that is higher than is warranted by the evidence. Thus, all of us, in one way or another, are vain. What's more, all of us work hard to maintain this vanity. And we do so by telling lies, by coming up with ways of discounting evidence that undermines our self-opinion, and searching for every scrap of evidence to maintain it.

We know, for example, that there are skills that we do not have. We may not be great at math, or eye-hand coordination, or remembering names. But not to worry, we tell ourselves, these things are not really all that important. It's the things that we are better at that are really significant. When we hear health advice that happens to conform to our already established behavior ("red wine is good for your heart" seems to be one that most everyone is aware of), we will remember it and helpfully pass it along, reminding others and ourselves that we are on the right track. If, on the other hand, the advice tells us that we must stop doing something that we don't want to stop, we will find ways of discounting the evidence or come up with reasons why this evidence does not apply to us. Alternatively we might simply (and conveniently) forget. When we fail at a test or a job interview, we come up with reasons to account for this as an anomaly: the test was unfair; the interviewer was a fool; and so on. We may even be willing to tell ourselves that we did not prepare as much as we should have. The self is quite more ready to accept this venal sin over the alternative explanation that we are stupid or undesirable.[28]

It's not that we don't see evidence of self-deception and vanity. As I will show, we readily recognize that other people are engaging in rationalizations about what the evidence means to *their* self-image. But we will continue to do everything in our power to convince ourselves that the same evidence does not apply to us. In the words of Dan Ariely, "We're storytelling creatures by nature, and we tell ourselves story after story until we come up with an explanation that we like and that sounds reasonable enough to believe. And when the story portrays us in a more glowing and positive light, so much the better."[29]

So what does science say about why this is the case? What accounts for the fact that our brains appear to have these built-in systems for self-deception? In short, why are we vain? Well, it appears that we do so because it's good for us. According to Timothy D. Wilson, "just as we possess a potent physical immune system that protects us from threats to our physical well-being, so do we possess a psychological immune system that protects us from threats to our psychological well-being."[30] Just like antibodies roaming through our blood stream pouncing on any microscopic intruder, our brain similarly strives to pounce on any stray piece of evidence that makes it harder for us to feel good about ourselves.

Those of us with fewer antibodies are at greater risk for sickness. Just so, consider the condition of those of us who lack the capacity for self-deception. According to Fine, there is

> a category of people who get unusually close to the truth about themselves and the world. Their self-perceptions are more balanced, they assign responsibility for success and failure more evenhandedly, and their predictions for the future are more realistic. These people are living testimony to the dangers of self-knowledge. They are the clinically depressed. [31]

Thus, science finds the explanation in evolution. There has to be a reason why things are the way they are, and that reason has to be that the predominate behavior or attribute gave those who had it an evolutionary advantage over those who did not. Indeed. "People who have positive illusions are likely to persist longer at difficult tasks, and are more likely to succeed on difficult tasks." [32] On the other hand, people who are depressed are less healthy, they get sick more frequently, they take longer to heal, and hence, they die earlier. Optimism, even if it is less grounded in reality, is a ticket to a long, healthy life. On the other hand, while the truth may indeed set you free, scientifically speaking, it will also kill you.

But there are theorists who go farther than that. If this is indeed a cold, meaningless universe, if we are all idiots telling tales, then self-deception is a very prudent and effective evolutionary strategy. In terms that directly recall Niebuhr, the "Terror Management Theory" argues that we humans are unique among animals in that we have the same drive to self-preservation, but we also know that we are going to die. This causes anxiety, and, well, terror. Not sugarcoating things, the theory's founders say that "given such awareness, humans could not function with equanimity if they believed that they were not inherently more significant and enduring than apes, lizards, lima beans." [33] Vanity may well represent a willful and pathetic disconnect from reality, but it might also be one good way to control the terror. Perhaps these tales we tell ourselves make us less likely to check out prematurely, and therefore more likely to get on with our day, and, not incidentally, more likely to exist to the point where we will be able to pass on our genes.

I trust you can connect the dots as well as I. Just as Niebuhr recounted, science presents strong evidence that we are all of us vain, that we are given to routine deception of others and ourselves so that we can preserve our vanity, and that one quite plausible reason for that vanity stems from our anxiety about both our insignificance and our fate. And even more distressing, nothing about this entire anxiety-escaping enterprise has any hope of succeeding. Not for a single one of us. We will never be safe enough. We will never fully quiet the little voice. Yet neither can we stop trying.

MORE THAN MERELY SELFISH

I wouldn't blame you if you find all this a little depressing. It is. Niebuhr warns that we must never forget this because it is the truth. However, it is not the whole truth. Niebuhr's view is more complete. It is also somewhat less depressing, and, not incidentally, more accurate.

To start with, Niebuhr believes there is more to our strategy than staving off existential terror. In line with the old adage that hypocrisy is the homage that vice pays to virtue, Niebuhr believes that we need to deceive ourselves because in some natural and elemental way, we want to be good. This, too, is part of what it means to be created in the image of God. Several pages above, I quoted Niebuhr from his most theological work, *The Nature and Destiny of Man*, regarding our need for self-deception. That quotation continues:

> The fact that this necessity [of self-deception] exists is an important indication of the vestige of truth which abides with the self in all its confusion and which it must placate before it can act. The dishonesty of man is thus an interesting refutation of the doctrine of man's total depravity. [34]

In typically Niebuhrian fashion, there is good in evil and evil in good. [35] Our desire to deceive ourselves is evidence of our desire to take the place of God. It is at the heart of our sinfulness. But it is also evidence that we are not without hope. We have to deceive ourselves because otherwise we can't live with ourselves. And this is a sign, a tiny flicker of a sign, that we are not all bad. In Richard Crouter's words: "We are not evil per se, just sinners, and they are not the same." [36]

It is also reason for hope that we don't like to think of our lives this way. We like to think of ourselves as honest and don't want to act in a way that forces us to admit that we are not. Dan Ariely summarizes his work on dishonesty this way: "Essentially, we cheat up to the level that allows us to retain our self-image as reasonably honest individuals." [37] We are similarly pulled to justice and mercy. However superior we feel, we know that other people have the same needs we do. This knowledge gives us a vague but inescapable concept of justice. All of this is part of who we are, too. What's more, here, too, there is biological support for Niebuhr's characterization. Joshua Green uses the phrase "minimal decency" to describe the apparently innate and nearly universal reluctance to "directly and intentionally harm others and (to a lesser extent) to allow others to be harmed." [38] These tugs toward decency, even if they are minimal, and even if they come in the midst of depravity and self-deceit, make it possible for us to live together and to realize some of that justice that we already implicitly understand.[39]

It remains to be said that for Niebuhr the complete story transcends human beings entirely. Anxiety and sin are inescapable dimensions of human existence, and that means that our existence is fundamentally tragic. But human existence, and thus human history, cannot be fully understood outside of God's love and mercy. Jesus' victory in the very heart of failure serves as shocking evidence of this: "The Christ upon the cross is the point of illumination where the ultimate mercy is apprehended."[40] Because of that mercy, humanity has the promise of deliverance; our history is taken "beyond tragedy."[41] The cross provides a frame and direction that gives hope and meaning to all human striving. Christians (well, Christian Saints anyway) are able to accept the anxiety, and to work through the cynicism and despair that creeps into every life, because they believe they already know the end of the story.

NO MORE THEOLOGY

There is much, much more to say about Niebuhr's theology, of course, but it is not germane for my purposes. Indeed, you might already be wondering what all this could possibly have to do with raging partisanship. Fair enough. I will endeavor to get to the point.

The point is that the best, most useful conception of human beings is one that understands us in all our complexity. We are made in the image of God, yet unable to escape sinfulness; creatures yet creators; free yet constrained. We are enchanted with our own importance, see ourselves as better and more deserving than others, even as we are haunted by the knowledge that we are insignificant and that our lives are fragile and transient. We tell ourselves lies about this, and these lies create a fabric of sin from which we cannot escape. Yet in the midst of all this, we still both hear and echo a whisper of decency.

Both sides of this reality are inescapable, and therefore we must adjust our expectations accordingly. We can be neither too hopeful about our prospects, nor can we allow ourselves to be incapacitated with despair. We cannot truly solve our problems, nor can we legitimately resign ourselves to a mean and meaningless fate. And this goes for politics as well. In sum, just as Christianity offers the best, most accurate accounting for the human condition, so too does it help us understand why democracy is the best way we have for organizing ourselves. Outlining the connection between Niebuhr's conception of human beings and democracy is the objective of the next chapter.

NOTES

1. During his childhood and adolescence, the dominant language at home, in church and in social life was German. Niebuhr later recalled being embarrassed by his accented English when he studied at Yale. According to Fox, the congregation at Bethel Evangelical was about three-quarters German. See Fox, *Reinhold Niebuhr*, 42.

2. See Niebuhr, *Leaves from the Notebook of a Tamed Cynic*, 1.

3. On Being with Krista Tippett, "Moral Man and Immoral Society: Rediscovering Reinhold Niebuhr, Advanced Learning Guide for Educators and Students," October 25, 2007, Reinhold Niebuhr, "Correspondence with Professor Samuel Press," http://www.onbeing.org/program/moral-man-and-immoral-society-rediscovering-reinhold-niebuhr/extra/reinhold-niebuhr-timeli-4.

4. Ibid.

5. Niebuhr, *Leaves*, 143. All three discussions of early dilemmas in Niebuhr's pastoral career also draw from Fox, *Reinhold Niebuhr*, 91-93.

6. Niebuhr, *Leaves*, 144.

7. Fox, *Reinhold Niebuhr*, 95-98.

8. Niebuhr, "How Philanthropic is Henry Ford?" 101.

9. On Being with Krista Tippett, "Moral Man and Immoral Society: Rediscovering Reinhold Niebuhr."

10. Niebuhr, *Leaves*, 112.

11. Quoted in June Bingham, *Courage to Change*, 129.

12. Niebuhr, "How Philanthropic is Henry Ford?" 102.

13. See chapter 3.

14. Niebuhr, "Ten Years that Shook My World," 546.

15. Rasmussen, "Introduction," *Reinhold Niebuhr: Theologian of Public Life*, 4.

16. Reinhold Niebuhr, *The Essential Reinhold Niebuhr*, Robert McAfee Brown, ed., xvii.

17. CLCD, 61.

18. Niebuhr says that the faithful Christian is no different in this regard. "It is not to be supposed that the faith, hope and trust which eliminate anxiety are simple possibilities of human existence, not even for those who have some knowledge of God in Christ" (NDM1, 289). The only difference is that Christians know they are not supposed to be anxious. They know that their anxiety denies God's sovereignty and therefore it is a sin.

19. NDM1, 3. (The title for this chapter comes from this quotation.) "Man is advised and advises himself to moderate his pretensions and admit that he is only a little animal living a precarious existence on a second-rate planet, attached to a second-rate sun."

20. IAH, 62-63.

21. Niebuhr also talks about the sin of sensuality, another strategy by which the individual looks to escape the weight of anxiety and burden of freedom. This is less important to Niebuhr's thought, and less germane to my purposes.

22. NDM1, 179.

23. Another quotation from Winston Churchill comes to mind: "We are all worms, but I do believe I am a glow-worm." (Though in Churchill's case at least, he was probably right.)

24. NDM1, 203.

25. NDM1, 199.

26. Dunning, "Motivated Social Cognition," 1.

27. See chapter 3.

28. This paragraph draws from Fine's *A Mind of One's Own* and especially a chapter entitled, appropriately enough, "The Vain Brain."

29. Ariely, *The (Honest) Truth About Dishonesty*, 165.

30. Wilson, *Strangers to Ourselves*, 38.

31. Fine, *A Mind of One's Own*, 23.

32. Wilson, *Strangers to Ourselves*, 198.

33. Solomon, Greenberg, and Pyszczynski, "A Terror Management Theory of Social Behavior," 96.

34. NDM1, 203.

35. See, for example, ICE, 64. "The dominant attitudes of prophetic faith are gratitude and contrition; gratitude for Creation and contrition before Judgment; or, in other words, confidence that life is good in spite of its evil, and that it is evil in spite of its good."
36. Crouter, *Reinhold Niebuhr*, 52.
37. Ariely, *The (Honest) Truth About Dishonesty*, 23.
38. Joshua Green, *Moral Tribes*, 60.
39. How that happens is the subject of the next chapter.
40. Niebuhr, "The Power and Weakness of God," in *The Essential Reinhold Niebuhr*, 29.
41. This is the title of a book of Niebuhr's sermons.

Chapter Two

Between Sentimentality and Pessimism: Niebuhr on Democracy

Imagine yourself as your own long lost ancestor. Very long lost. Say about 40,000 years ago.[1] You are walking along the savannah, minding your own business, when you spy on the horizon a group of people you do not know. They are not part of your tribe. Immediately, your brain goes on high alert. Your blood pressure and heart rate rises. You scan for signs of threat, determine whether you have been seen, consider how far away your tribe members are, and review possible escape routes.

From our earliest days, we have needed the security that a tribe provided. Our ancestors were preyed upon by animals that were bigger and stronger than we. So too for the animals for whom we were the prey, a coordinated hunt was far more likely to be successful. But for that matter, other people, other tribes, were a serious threat as well. Groups that were innately distrustful of the intensions of those other groups far away on the savannah were more likely to survive. Even when those other groups meant no harm, they could have possessed unknown pathogens. Either way, distrust was a good survival strategy. And because these distrustful groups survived, they have passed on their inclinations. Just so, those groups that were cohesive enough to stand together against threats, to seek to protect their own when one of them was isolated, were likewise better able to meet the threat and survive. These inclinations, as well, were passed down. As a result, among us human beings, amity within groups and enmity between them is almost universal.

But it's not just about survival; we also *want* to be together. Like other mammals, Niebuhr says, "Man is endowed by nature with organic relations to his fellow men."[2] The desire to be part of a group—to form emotional bonds with others—is part of our nature. For us and all mammals, the infant is helpless and will die without their mother's milk and protection. The children whose mothers' brain was rewarded with a feel good chemical for mothering behavior were more likely to survive. These same reward systems (notably, the chemical oxytocin) appear to be implicated in the development loyalty to one's social group.

So groups are natural: we crave the companionship and need the protection. But according to Niebuhr, there is another reason why we need them: it is hard to maintain our illusion of significance all by ourselves. Any one of us can feel awfully small amidst the crush of a morning commute or the opulence of a night full of stars. Groups—merging our egos and identities with others—therefore offer us a better way to create the illusion that we are special and powerful, and to fight off the nagging sense that we are not. In Niebuhr's words, "collective egotism does indeed offer the individual an opportunity to lose himself in a larger whole; but it also offers him possibilities of self-aggrandizement beside which mere individual pretensions are implausible and incredible."[3] By forming groups, we do more than just become more powerful than we would be on our own. We also thereby find a way to maintain the delusion that we are something special and important.

Consider this quotation from a man recalling his basic training just before World War II:

> Words are inadequate to describe the emotion aroused by the prolonged movement in unison that drilling involved. A sense of pervasive well-being is what I recall; more specifically, a strategy sense of personal enlargement; a sort of swelling out, becoming bigger than life, thanks to participation in collective ritual.[4]

Anybody who has put on a uniform can understand this feeling. There is a sense of pride, identity and purpose that comes from being part of something bigger than the self, of having committed to others and to a common set of objectives. We give the group our loyalty, and in return we get its power, its security, and (we hope) its ability to dominate competing groups.

For all these reasons, we are therefore inclined to absorb the interests of our group into our own. But if our objective is to overcome our anxiety and confirm to ourselves our sense of self-importance, there is something fundamentally paradoxical about this strategy. For by putting on that uniform, we give up much of our individuality. Our identity becomes subsumed, overwhelmed, by the identity of the group. The fact that we would accept such a tradeoff only speaks to the extent of our desperation. "Collective pride is thus man's last, and in some respects most pathetic, effort to deny the determinate and contingent character of his existence."[5] The effort is pathetic because it is ultimately no less successful in overcoming our anxiety. But to be part of something bigger, even if only a part, is still a way to become something bigger. It is therefore a trade that most of us are only too willing to make.

But almost *because* groups are a good strategy for combating human anxiety, they thereby also compound all the sinful aspects of human nature. This is the central point of Niebuhr's early work: *Moral Man and Immoral Society*. By joining a group, by subsuming our ego within the group, we thereby lose contact with our innate sense of decency and justice. All the ways in which individuals are able to diminish our sinful tendencies: our conscience, feelings of sympathy toward other human beings, and the use of our reason to see past our own self-interest and imagine a more just outcome—none of these are as operative in the world of groups. "In every human group there is less reason to guide and to check impulse, less capacity for self-transcendence, less ability to comprehend the needs of others and therefore more unrestrained egoism than the individuals, who compose the group, reveal in their personal relationships."[6] Compared to the individual, groups are inevitably less moral.[7] "The pretentions and claims of a collective or social self exceed those of the individual ego. The group is more arrogant, hypocritical, self-centred and more ruthless in the pursuit of its ends than the individual."[8]

The nearly all-consuming orientation of self-interest, the quest for power, the tendency to see all others as obstacles to our goals, and, most relevantly, the exquisite ability to delude ourselves about our moral superiority, all of this is more pronounced in groups than in individuals. In fact, the difference between us as individuals and as members of a group is so profound that our natural sympathies—loyalty and charity—are given to the group, taken over by the group, and thereby turned into a conditioned version of morality. We are all of us very generous to those who are in our group (our block, our office, our church). When one of our own needs help, we readily pitch in. When we do this, we make note of our behavior, and therefore consider ourselves good. But we ignore the fact that for outsiders with the same needs, we possess less loyalty and therefore manifest less charity.

More, by taking on the group's identity as our own, we adopt a notion of morality and justice that is itself group-centric. And that is almost inevitably a recipe for injustice. For Niebuhr "the ethical attitude of the individual toward the group easily obscures the unethical nature of the group's desires."[9] Nobles and slaves, priests and traders, different ethnic and religious groups, all were identified by their place within the society's power structure, and the goal of each group was (and is) to defend itself in the context of that structure. In that struggle, there is no room for cool consideration of the facts, no possibility for nuance or grey. Rather, there is the bald oversimplification of world into good and bad—the good of one's own side and the evil of the other. Niebuhr's colleague John Bennett described his thought this way:

> The moral impulses of the individual are often satisfied by this loyalty to the group and he easily becomes uncritical of the group's behavior. Put beside

these factors the endless capacity to cloak group behavior with false idealism, with all manner of rationalizations and ideologies, and we have an adequate explanation of the aggravation of moral problems in the relations between groups. [10]

This lack of self-criticism, this disconnect from reason, makes groups scary (if you have ever been in or near a mob, you know what I mean), but it is also what makes them powerful. Indeed, this rational disengagement is also what makes groups successful. Nobody storms the barricades thinking that they *might* be right, that they are *pretty sure* justice is on their side.

All of us want to achieve and maintain power. But again, we don't like to think that that is all we are doing. Maybe it *is* mostly about power, but we don't want to acknowledge that fact. So we tell ourselves stories to justify our position and create at least a veneer in which we don't look so bad to either ourselves and/or others.

For Niebuhr, every group, no matter how noble its purpose, is thus compromised by hypocrisy.

> The inevitable hypocrisy, which is associated with all of the collective activities of the human race, springs chiefly from this source: that individuals have a moral code which makes the actions of collective man an outrage to their conscience. They therefore invent romantic and moral interpretations of the real facts, preferring to obscure rather than reveal the true character of their collective behavior. [11]

Those in power tell stories that give legitimacy to their position. They come up with rationalizations that make their dominance of others not only legitimate but laudable. Slave owners told themselves these stories. So did Henry Ford. And so do all of us. Power is accompanied by the sincere belief that the way things are corresponds to the way things ought to be, that power is good and right, that it is administered justly and that it therefore should continue. In fact, those in power most often believe that they occupy their position with the full assent of God, and that any challenge to the former is an affront to the latter.

But these stories are also found among those groups that find themselves on the wrong side of the power relationship. Pride does not allow the downtrodden to simply accept the fact that they are oppressed, let alone that their position is justified by some innate inferiority. So they too come up with explanations as to why things are the way they are. "Sometimes they are as anxious to offer moral justifications for the brutalities from which they suffer as for those which they commit." [12] Niebuhr's idea that our beliefs are simply products of power relationships has clear echoes of Marx. But in connecting that process to oppressed classes, there is also a hint of Nietzsche. [13] For if nothing else, stories allow those on the short end of history to claim the moral high ground: "We are not on top because we are more moral than our oppressors, and if and when the situation is reversed, you can be sure that we would not behave like our masters." Of course, Niebuhr believes that these claims are fallacious. And indeed, no one with much knowledge of human history would attach much confidence to a claim like that. But accuracy is, after all, beside the point. We don't have to convince history; we just have to convince ourselves, and we are a ready audience.

There is much more to say about the science of groups, and what impact groups have on political beliefs, but for now, it is sufficient to sum up: Niebuhr argues that groups are a means by which we humans inevitably strive to connect with others, to achieve power and to find a salve for our anxiety. But by joining ourselves with others, we become less likely to feel or express any kind of innate sympathy for nonmembers, and more likely to act selfishly, irrationally, and even viciously. However, despite this rather significant difference, groups are even more hypocritical than individuals; they are even more likely to find ways to justify—even laud—their behavior, and thereby maintain their pride.

THE CASE FOR DEMOCRACY

Every group thinks this way: those out of power and especially those in power. And since every group is similarly immoral, hypocritical and deluded, how can anyone—any class, race, or group—be trusted with unchecked power? Short answer: they can't. Show Niebuhr any group with unchecked power and he will show you oppression and tyranny.

Democracy is the only viable means for organizing ourselves together peacefully for this very reason: because none of us can be trusted. And because this is the case, the only way to achieve even a modicum of justice is to make sure that all interests, all impaired visions, all alloyed truths, are represented and able to contest freely against each other. "Democratic checks and counterchecks are the best method of neutralizing special interests and of arriving at the truth by allowing various corruptions of the truth to destroy each other."[14] Nobody comes at this game with uncompromised access to the way things really are, though all of us believe that we belong to the one group that does; the truth therefore, or the closest we can come to it, is what is left after we have exposed each other's hypocrisies and half-truths. And that can only happen through democracy.

To be sure, this is not Normal Rockwell's vision. There are no dewy-eyed paeans to the *vox populi* here. Instead, because nobody can be trusted, because we are all corrupted, the best we can do is to construct a politics that makes it very difficult for any single individual or group to rule, where lies combat other lies, and where everyone has enough power to hamstring their enemies. Reflecting on one of Niebuhr's more familiar and enduring quotations, we start with the second half: "Man's capacity for injustice makes democracy necessary." Because of human depravity, there is no way that one group of us would ever responsibly and justly rule over another. Democracy is the only way to deal with this reality, and that is why it is necessary.

But as is always the case with Niebuhr, there is more to it than that. Niebuhr rejects the romanticism that so many associated with democracy. But he also rejects an easy cynicism about human beings and power. We can't escape self-interest, but if that were the whole story, there would be no democracy. It would be a war of all against all. Because we think and because we are free, we can be exquisitely creative in our cruelty to each other, and we can be equally creative in coming up with rationalizations to justify, even celebrate, those cruelties. But we are not all bad. We can also look past our all-consuming self-regard and recall the sympathy that is also part of who we are. The fact is we want to live in a just world (at least a little bit, some of the time, when it doesn't cause us too much trouble) and because we do, democracy is possible. A free society requires that we find some kind of order, that we reach agreements about how to work through our differences, and that we come up with some notion of justice and the good which are common to all. Thus, the first half of the famous quotation: "Man's capacity for justice makes democracy possible." So a proper understanding of democracy requires neither a too optimistic nor a too pessimistic or cynical understanding of human beings. And thus it is that for Niebuhr the Christian view of human nature is more adequate for developing and sustaining a democratic society.

CHILDREN OF LIGHT, CHILDREN OF DARKNESS

These words about capacities and incapacities come from Niebuhr's book *The Children of Light and the Children of Darkness*. Again, for Niebuhr, strategizing about what must be done is pointless unless we have a realistic understanding of ourselves in all our paradoxical glory. Niebuhr believes that democracy grew out of a naïve understanding of human beings, and "a too consistent optimism" of the possibility of a conflict-free world. The long-standing remnants of this belief, Niebuhr believes, continue to undermine and endanger American democracy, leaving us unprepared to deal with very real threats, both external and internal. His task in this book is to lay out a concept of democracy that understands and works within the eternal realities of human behavior: both the capacity for justice that makes democracy possible, and the capacity for injustice which makes democracy necessary. These are the parameters within which human society must operate if it is to sustain some measure of peace and justice. More, they are the eternal parameters within which democracy must operate if it is to succeed, and even to survive.

The naïve idealism associated with the advent of democracy continues to be manifested in what Niebuhr calls Children of Light. Since this notion is central to my purposes, I should be clear as to the derivation. The term is biblical; it appears four times in the New Testament. Paul uses it in Ephesians and Thessalonians, where he tells new converts to live as Children of Light. In this case, the Children of Light compare favorably to those who live in darkness. It also appears in John's Gospel, where Jesus tells his disciples to believe in the light so that they may be Children of Light. Given that backdrop, one certainly would not expect the term to have a negative connotation. But this is not the verse that Niebuhr references. Instead he refers to Jesus' words in Luke's Gospel: "[F]or the children of this world are in their generation wiser than the Children of Light." This verse, Niebuhr says, "fits the modern situation,"[15] for it explains the wobbly foundations of our democratic civilization. The Children of Light, Jesus appears to say, are foolish and naïve. At any rate, that is the verse that Niebuhr chooses to reference his term. Being a Child of Light is not a good thing.

Or at any rate, it is not a completely good thing. It is also true that the goodness that Paul attaches to the term is also present in Niebuhr's definition. There is something admirable and fundamentally decent about the Children of Light. They want the world to be a better place, and they believe that through their work, they can help bring it about. Children of Light are also virtuous. They believe that there is some kind of higher set of ideals against which their actions are judged. And therefore they are inclined to act in support of the common good.

Most fundamentally, however, all Children of Light believe that there is a way for humans to get past the suffering and tragedy that characterizes human existence. Whatever form it may take, all Children of Light have what Niebuhr calls a "touching faith" in the idea that there is a way to transcend our predicament, that humans can move beyond contentious self-interest to a placid and harmonious common interest. Marxists think (or maybe now, thought) that once the Proletarians get power, the class conflict created by capitalism will evaporate. Many liberals believe (or maybe now, believed) that conflict is simply a matter of inadequate or incorrect information. Increase human knowledge, make sure everyone has the right information, and the right decisions will surely follow. Similarly, faithful followers of science thought and some still think that technology is going to create an abundance that will render conflict obsolete.

There is another example of such optimism that is forefront in Niebuhr's mind. The Social Gospel movement was one that initially attracted Niebuhr. Coming to prominence at the turn of the 20th century, Social Gospelers were committed to connecting the moral core of Christianity with the newfound

knowledge of social science, thereby addressing the awful realities of a newly industrial society. Building a more just and more decent life for everyone,
they thought, was both possible and their Christian duty. These words from
Walter Rauschenbusch, one of the central figures in the movement, are representative of the mindset behind the movement: "We have the possibility of so
directing religious energy by scientific knowledge that a comprehensive and
continuous reconstruction of social life in the name of God is within the
bounds of human possibility."[16] I will return to the Social Gospel and its
legacy in American Protestantism in chapter 9, but for now it is enough to
say that while Niebuhr too struggled with the rank injustices of his time and
felt compelled by his faith to confront them, he ultimately came to reject the
movement.

The problem for Niebuhr is that the Social Gospelers, and for that matter
all Children of Light, are naïve. They fail to appreciate that inordinate self-
interest and the will to power are inevitable manifestations of human freedom and anxiety. These are inescapable aspects of this existence; we can
therefore no more transcend them than we can escape mortality. That means
there is no once and for all solution to injustice and human suffering. There is
only muddling through, working very hard to improve things, sometimes
significantly, but more often at the margins. If you do not accept that, if you
act as if this is not true, not only will you fail, but you will endanger the "vast
moral and historical artifact" that is human society. This is the problem with
the followers of the Social Gospel and Marx and a whole host of fellow
travelers throughout history. At least to some degree, their hearts are in the
right place, but their hope is grounded on a "stupid" misunderstanding of
how human beings really think and operate. Children of Light are doomed to
failure, and their actions and beliefs threaten to undermine some hard-won
features that make our social life more decent and just.

But worse, these Children of Light are naïve about themselves; they fail
to appreciate that they themselves are guilty of the very same failings they
attribute to their adversaries. Children of Light are "unconscious of the corruption of self-interest in all ideal achievements and pretensions of human
culture."[17] They think that they are fundamentally different from their adversaries: better, smarter and more moral. Oblivious in their self-righteousness,
the Children of Light have got it all figured out. All that is required is for
them to convince the fools or defeat the fiends who think otherwise. Once
they do that, the problem of conflict will be resolved and all will be well.
There is a pathetic quality to these ideas. So much passion, so much good
intention, so much struggle, all in service of a delusion.

But it gets still worse. Because they are so far from the truth, the noble but
airy ideals that define any Child of Light are open to exploitation by what
Niebuhr calls the Children of Darkness. Their foolish and fruitless hopes for
the future have no prospect of success, but their self-delusion succeeds in

opening the door to tyranny. Marxism leads to Stalin, Romanticism to Hitler, Liberalism to Napoleon, faith in science to nuclear weaponry.

Niebuhr calls these and other Children of Darkness "moral cynics," for they "know no law beyond their own will and interest." Their anxiety and freedom manifest themselves in a will to power, and their actions are simply means for achieving that will. In the international arena, Children of Darkness "declare that a strong nation need acknowledge no law beyond its own strength."[18] Might doesn't make right; might is indifferent to right. Within the domestic sphere, as well, politics is simply another battlefield, another means for securing power. Now of course, Children of Darkness can talk a good game, if that is what the game requires. They will say all the right things about the common good, if doing so improves their chances of getting what they want. But they don't believe that such a thing exists, and therefore certainly have no interest in fomenting it. They will likewise say good things about the outlier, the person who lies beyond their own group's identity, but that person is at best an obstacle if not a combatant in the path toward the group's own safety and security. So a democracy is acceptable to the Child of Darkness, so long as it is the most expeditious and effective way for them to get what they want.

The Children of Darkness are therefore "evil," for "evil is always the assertion of some self-interest without concern for the whole."[19] But make no mistake; the Children of Darkness are also "wise." They understand human beings much better than the Children of Light. Most relevantly, they under-stand the power of self-interest and the degree to which it inevitably orients human behavior. This understanding gives Children of Darkness a distinct advantage. Of course, without even a passing acknowledgement of justice and rights, they are free to play outside the rules. Since their opponent is constrained in ways that they are not (by law, ethics, and a sense of human decency) they have an easier path to victory. (Niebuhr is clearly thinking about Nazis here; as he delivered these lectures, World War II was not over, but the end was in sight.) But their success is not simply because of their ruthlessness. Because Children of Darkness are not naïve about the root of human action, they are therefore better at predicting, responding to and ma-nipulating people to achieve the ends they want.

DEMOCRACY'S PERIL

So there are two kinds of children, neither one apparently very admirable. So what? Well, for one thing, Niebuhr is exhorting the Children of Light to be more realistic about the world and themselves. If they were more attuned to the endemic realities of human existence, they would be more effective, better able to achieve the ends for which they rightly and even valiantly strive. But there is a more fundamental argument going on here. Niebuhr believes that the well-being of democracy lies between these two extremes. In Gary Dorrien's words, "America needed to find a moral balance between the cynical amorality of the fascist and Stalinist 'children of darkness' and the sentimental idealism of the modern liberal 'children of light.'"[20] For Niebuhr, democracy is not a given. It is simply not true that now that it has been established, things will simply continue on without much thought. Rather, the well-being of democratic society requires that we constantly fight against some natural, unavoidable and distinctively human failings. For it is our nature not only to sin, but to sin in ways that make it very hard to sustain a democracy. There are two ways that things can go wrong and they constitute a path through which we must continually pass: we can, as Children of Light, ignore the ugly realities of human sinfulness, embrace an unreal sentimentality about our own goodness and our opponent's depravity, and thereby override the innate capacity for justice that makes democracy possible. Or we can, as Children of Darkness, give ourselves over to those realities, embrace a cynicism that is beneath us, and embrace a war of all against all. We live out our lives, singularly and together, straining to find our way between this never-ending Scylla and Charybdis.

Now because these choices are set before us because of who we are as human beings, there is an eternal character to them. They were just as operative for our grandparents as they will be for our grandchildren. But Niebuhr sees this two-sided peril in terms that are specific to democracy: one external, and one internal. The former, comes from succumbing to Children of Darkness. "Democracy may be challenged from without by the force of barbarism and the creed of cynicism."[21] Niebuhr and his audience knew too well about this possibility. They saw how too much optimism about the future of human cooperation opened the door for Hitler. To be sure, the Nazis were falling, but the fact that they conquered so much of Europe and the world showed just how real the danger was. After the war, naïve optimism about the human condition was hard to muster. More, even at that point, those in the West knew that the end of the current struggle meant the beginning of another. The battle with the Soviets was only beginning.

But there is a danger with Children of Light, as well, no less real and no less dangerous. Democracy's "internal peril lies in the conflict of various schools and classes of idealists, who profess different ideals but exhibit a common conviction that their own ideals are perfect."[22] These children understand themselves to be morally and intellectually superior; they are unable to see their own failures, and unable to understand that the same hypocrisy and duplicity that is rife within their opponents is just as present in their own thinking and actions. Just so, these children are unable to see their opponents as anything but enemies, they cannot see any wisdom or truth in their beliefs, cannot identify a good that is common, cannot compromise with them, cannot even act in good faith toward them. Their battle is permanent and for keeps.

Of course, such a path ignores the pluralistic reality that brought democracy into existence in the first place. The wars of religion showed that there is no "winning" anymore; it is simply no longer possible to construct a society *a la* Medieval Europe in which everyone accepted the notion that a society needed to profess the same beliefs about God and God's will. Worse, this myopia destroys the spirit of commonality and compromise that is required for democracy to function. At its worst, the Children of Light bring us to effective equivalent of war. "Whenever a community faces an issue without any common ground between opposing forces, the resulting social friction may attain the proportions of a civil war."[23] An internal war, yes, but still a war.

Again, there is no transcending these twin dangers. There is no once and for all solution. We are always threatened with cynicism on the one hand and romanticism on the other: a war external or internal. The best we can do is strive to mitigate our innate human proclivities and find a balance appropriate for the times we live in. Niebuhr insists that democracy is the best way politically to do so, but he is just as clear that having a democracy does not make these problems go away. And this is no less true for democracy in its American variety. The continual task is to navigate ourselves between the disasters represented by both the Children of Light and Children of Darkness.

THE PERIL FOR AMERICAN DEMOCRACY

This task is different for every democracy and for that matter, at every time. For every nation has its own culture and history, and its own form of spiritual pride, and it must engage a unique set of circumstances. In fact, "no politically crystalized social group has, therefore, ever existed without entertaining, or succumbing to, the temptation of making idolatrous claims for itself."[24] Nations are really just the biggest group of them all, no less egotistical and irrational, and because of its access to power and panoply, inevitably driven to idolatry. In sum, "the nation pretends to be God."[25] But Americans are particularly susceptible to self-righteousness. And that means, for Niebuhr, the Children of Light was and is the distinctively American peril.

As far as we see it, we are, always and everywhere, the good guys. We embrace the idea that we have a special place in history, and even in God's providence. America is exceptional. While our economic power and military might are unmatched in the world and have been for over a century, and while this position of power makes it even less likely that we are going to do anything that is not focused on preserving that position, we nevertheless remain firmly convinced in our good intentions. From the time of Puritans (in fact, before they even landed), America was the city on the hill, and this myth rolls on unabated by context or counterevidence. (It didn't become a *shining* city until Reagan; but that change simply bespeaks the staying power of the myth.) In Niebuhr's terms, the prevailing power of this myth demonstrates that Americans are Children of Light. And that fact creates for us an equally distinctive danger.

Niebuhr points to two wellsprings for the American myth: New England Calvinism (from the Puritans), and "Jeffersonianism." The power of the myth stems the fact that despite their obvious differences, they both paint the same picture.

> [W]e came into existence with the sense of being a "separated" nation, which God was using to make a new beginning for mankind. We had renounced the evils of European feudalism. We had escaped from the evils of European religious bigotry. We had found broad spaces for the satisfaction of human desires in the place of the crowded Europe. . . . We were God's "American Israel." Our pretensions of innocency therefore heightened the whole concept of a virtuous humanity which characterizes the culture of our era. [26]

This quotation, from his book *The Irony of American History*, buttresses Niebuhr's argument that Americans have a distinctive over-confidence regarding our virtue. In terms outlined in chapter 1, we Americans are distinctively vain. We have too high an opinion of ourselves. We presume our standing as God's favored nation, but we are oblivious to the fact that the pursuit of power drives our actions just as it does those of our enemies. In terms that will occupy the second half of this book, we Americans do not know ourselves as we truly are, we are deluded by contradictory notions of innocence and self-importance, and are therefore unable to muster the humility that a well-ordered democracy requires.

BACK TO SCIENCE

I have noted above where Niebuhr's anthropology is commensurate with the latest scientific research. I showed that there was scientific evidence behind Niebuhr's notion of pride. But those issues were less fundamental to the issue at hand. The question of what a Child of Light is, how she thinks, and what it can mean for a democracy, is a much larger question and for my purposes a central claim. My objective is to appeal to Niebuhr's prescription for preserving the democratic commonwealth. In order to do that, I need to show that his analysis is scientifically defensible and even how science might cause us to modify Niebuhr's concepts. I therefore need to make the scientific case in more detail. That is the task of the next two chapters.

NOTES

1. Paleontologist Stephen Jay Gould said in an interview, "There's been no biological change in humans in 40,000 or 50,000 years. Everything we call culture and civilization we've built with the same body and brain." See Tyson, "Are We Still Evolving?" *Inquiry: An Occasional Column.*

2. MMIS, 2.

3. NDM1, 212

4. Quoted in Haidt, *The Righteous Mind*, 221.

5. NDM1, 213.

6. MMIS, xxv.

7. Years later, Niebuhr half-jokingly suggested a better title: "The Not So Moral Man and His Less Moral Communities." To my mind, that really is a more accurate accounting of his argument.

8. NDM1, 208.

9. Niebuhr, *Does Civilization Need Religion?* 131.

10. Bennett, "Reinhold Niebuhr's Social Ethics," 53.

11. MMIS, 8-9.

12. MMIS, 9.

13. It is worth noting at this point that some scholars have criticized Niebuhr for neglecting the sin of "self-abasement," especially as it relates to the experience of oppressed minorities. See Gamwell, *Democracy on Purpose*, 84-91.

14. Quoted in Fox, *Reinhold Niebuhr*, 219.

15. The verse appears as part of what is known as the parable of the unjust steward. This is not the place to explain or account for that reference, but it is important to note that this is a difficult and morally ambiguous story. This fact only adds to the feeling that the Child of Light is neither a simple nor simply laudatory term.

16. Rauschenbusch, *Christianity and the Social Crisis*, 209.

17. CLCD, 15.

18. CLCD, 10.

19. CLCD, 9.

20. Dorrien, *Social Ethics in the Making,* 261.

21. CLCD, 152.

22. CLCD, 152. Same quotation continued.

23. CLCD, 88.

24. NDM1, 210.

25. NDM1, 212.

26. IAH, 24.

Chapter Three

Neuroscientists for Niebuhr[1]

Go back to that same savannah, 40,000 years ago. Once again, you find yourself walking along, minding your own business, when suddenly you jump. By the time you are even aware that anything has happened, you find yourself a few feet distant from the path, your heart pounding and your palms sweaty. You look where you just were. What is that in the weeds there? Is it a snake? No, you see, it's only a stick. You take a deep breath, try to compose yourself, and go along with your walk.[2]

The story of what happened in your ancestor's brain, and the legacy of that system in your own, explains much about why Niebuhr is right in his anthropology and his analysis of democratic politics. Evidence from psychology and neuroscience—some of it quite recent—shows that in fundamental and inescapable ways, all of us are Children of Light, firmly convinced of our own righteousness, seeing both stupidity and malignancy in our opponents, and all the while unfailingly oblivious to the fact that we are as benighted and guilty as they.

THE AMYGDALA: START HERE

The principle task of any organism is to find what it needs to survive, and to fight, avoid or escape that which threatens its survival. In this regard at least we are no different from chipmunks, sea lions or spider monkeys. The brain of any organism helps it achieve these goals. In Damasio's words, "achieving survival coincides with the ultimate reduction of unpleasant body states and the attaining of homeostatic ones, i.e., functionally balanced biological states."[3] The brain thus evaluates the things we encounter in terms of whether they help us or harm us and then works to get us more of the former and less of the latter. Now getting more of the former—i.e., what we want—can

31

be rather complicated: Is that fruit good to eat or did it make me sick last time? Is it ripe? How do I get to it? All this takes time, reason and memory. And because it does, the process is much harder to track in the brain. But threats, on the other hand, can come in an instant—like the snake on the ground—so it's easier to track how the brain responds.[4]

Since a threat can come instantly, an organism must react instantly as well; survival may well depend on it. Processing detail is therefore less important than sheer speed. Our brain is far and away the most evolved of any animal, but not all of our brain is equally evolved. The part of our brain that responds to threats is much older, and much the same as that in any other animal. It is called the limbic system.[5] In the midst of this lower part of our brain, we share with most of our fellow complex vertebrates two tiny almond-shaped pieces called the amygdalae. What is more, the function of this part of our brain is similar in all animals that have one: "The amygdala seems to do the same thing—take care of fear responses—in all species that have an amygdala."[6] As a matter of fact, scientists understood the amygdala's function in animal brains before they understood it in ours.

So is it a snake or a stick? You may have some past experience with snakes. Likely your parents were afraid of snakes and passed along that fear to you.[7] For all these reasons, your brain already knows that snakes are a threat. So the amygdala does not wait for you—i.e., the conscious part of you—to figure out the right answer to the snake vs. stick conundrum. In fact, it does not wait for you even to become aware of the question. Before you know what you are doing, you jump. Your brain is out to preserve you, and this "hijack" by the amygdala is the best strategy to accomplish that goal.[8] Now the fact that you are here and that you have this ability is evidence that, from an evolutionary point of view, it's a good strategy. The guy who only jumped after he figured out that he was indeed looking at a snake was more likely to get bit and thus not be around to pass along his genes. The hijack works in just the way it's supposed to. And because it worked so well, both for other species and for our ancestors, it continues to work much the same for us.

Now if the amygdala reacts immediately, it must be working constantly, assessing every stimulus that comes our way in terms of their potential threat to ourselves: not just sticks and snakes, but every stimuli that we come in contact with at every moment of our waking day. Every time we see something familiar—a bicycle, or a can of beer, or a picture of Groucho Marx— our brain races through our memory, finding associations with that image, assessing it in terms of our safety and well-being. If the image is unfamiliar to us (say, a letter from the Coptic alphabet), or if the image is largely neutral (a spoon, say) then the brain simply assesses the image and passes it on to our conscious selves so we can say: "That's a spoon." But if the image is familiar, and not neutral, that is, if it has any implication for our well-being, if it means much of anything in terms of what we want and what we want to avoid, then our limbic system will find these associations and issue an emotional response.

Recall that this response is meant to help us react instantly: It's a snake! Jump! That means that this assessment, and therefore these emotions, arise instantly—much more quickly than the reasoning part of our brains, much more quickly in fact, even than our conscience. We know that this initial assessment takes a few milliseconds. And since it must be so quick, and since it assesses every potential threat, the limbic system can only vary in terms of degree. The stimulus of a man threatening us with a knife produces a bigger reaction than a knife or a picture of a knife, but all three cause a reaction. The amygdala works well because it works fast, but it therefore does not have time to be very discriminating. A threat is a threat is a threat.

We all are consciously aware of emotions, of course, so this initial assessment does not always stay unconscious. It often bubbles up to become a conscious feeling—joy, disgust, fear, anger, etc.—but all this happens long after the brain has processed the image (long after in the brain's terms, really a few hundreds of milliseconds). But this initial assessment happens first, before consciousness. More importantly, the resultant reaction sometimes never does rise to the level of our conscious awareness. Here is Damasio's summation:

> [A]lthough many important choices involve feelings, a good number of daily decisions apparently proceed without feelings [i.e., without consciousness]. . . . Quite simply, a signal body state or its surrogate may have been activated but not been made the focus of attention. Without attention, neither will be part of consciousness, although either can be part of a covert action on the mechanisms that govern, without willful control, our appetitive (approach) or aversion (withdrawal) attitudes toward the world. While the hidden machinery underneath has been activated, our consciousness will never know it.[9]

The idea that your brain might process something and react to it without you ever being aware of it might strike you as bizarre. It is your brain after all. But consciousness is only a tiny part of what is going on between our ears. In fact, we take in information at rates that are exponentially greater than our ability to consciously process it. According to Timothy Wilson, the brain can—"generously" speaking—consciously process about 40 pieces of information in a second. During that same second, the senses are taking in around 11,000,000 pieces of information. That leaves, roughly, 10,999,960 pieces of information that are received by the brain and never consciously registered.[10]

Still not convinced? Stop for a moment and just listen. Do you hear any noises? Where are they coming from? Now that you know, were you aware of your cochlea changing vibrations from sound waves into electrical impulses? Did you notice how those electrical impulses were sent to the brain's primary auditory cortex and then compared to the millions and millions of sounds that you recognize? Did you experience the brain assessing the difference in volume between your two ears to estimate the location and distance of the sound? No, it was only after all this astoundingly complex and wholly unconscious work was completed that you had the conscious thought: there is a car coming down the street, or someone walking down the hall, or the dishwasher is running. In fact, not only is there much of the working of your brain that is beyond your conscious awareness, it is also the case that you cannot make yourself aware of these operations no matter how hard you try. More often than not, there is simply no connection between these operations and your conscious self. You just can't get there from here.

Just so with this kind of emotional evaluation. "Although people can report accurately on the contents of their thoughts and deliberations, the psychological processes and the true determinants of their behavior are often inaccessible to introspection." Even when you believe that you are examining your beliefs, those beliefs, and the associations and memories that gave rise to them, are farther down than your examination is able to go. Thus, "the difficulty of avoiding bias is exacerbated precisely because the relevant influence so often occurs outside of conscious awareness."[11] Just like we cannot access how we determine where the sound is coming from, we cannot access how our brain is assessing the emotional dimension of a given stimulus.

MOTIVATED REASONING

Regardless of whether the stimuli-assessing process ultimately produces a conscious thought, the brain is always assessing its emotional content, and if it finds one, producing an emotional reaction. You have perhaps heard Mark Twain's line that a lie can get halfway around the world before the truth can get its shoes on. There is something similar going on here. We think, we assimilate, and we consider information, but long before any of that, the brain has already conducted an emotional assessment. And if that information does indeed have an emotional dimension for us, then we have already produced an emotional reaction to the information before the thinking even begins. Conscious thinking happens only in the context of that reaction. Even when we are trying to be completely rational, our emotions have come in first and set the table. Our brains evaluate data—again, any data—as either with us or against us, as either endangering or enhancing our well-being. This is an inescapable aspect of our innate drive for self-preservation. But as a result, our reasoning is therefore motivated. We want what we want, and the more the information is associated with what we want, the less likely our reasoning will operate in a wholly rational way.

We all have some appreciation of this phenomenon. In her book *On Death and Dying*, Elizabeth Kübler-Ross establishes denial as the first stage of grief. She writes, "among the over two hundred dying patients we have interviewed, most reacted to the awareness of a terminal illness first with the statement, 'No, not me, it cannot be true.'"[12] The human drive to self-preservation meant her terminal patients were strongly motivated to reject the notion that they would, far sooner than expected, fail in that effort. And does anyone believe that if they were to receive similar news about themselves or a loved one that they would behave differently? With some kind of benign equanimity? Indeed, the natural and nearly inevitable reaction to news of some terrible illness is to find reasons to dispute its accuracy—to wonder if someone misread the test, or got my results mixed up with someone else. Now consider the opposite circumstance: someone hears good news about a test. How many times, in the history of our species, has someone reacted to such news by demanding a second opinion? Of course, as Kübler-Ross's model also notes, we humans frequently if not easily move beyond denial to acceptance. But the fundamental point is this: when our lives are on the line, our initial willingness to accept information depends on how much it conforms to what we want it to say.

Again, all this will likely not strike anyone as controversial. But motivated reasoning is manifested in circumstances far less dire than a cancer test. We human beings are out to preserve not just ourselves, but our image of ourselves. As we have seen, we want to see ourselves as lovable, decent, reasonable people. We want to believe that we have made the right choices, that we believe, value and think the right things. And we therefore want information that conforms to that perception. If it does not, then the same mechanisms motivate us to push us away from objectivity and toward the rejection of things we do not want to hear. In Ziva Kunda's words, "the cognition that one has knowingly chosen to engage in a bad or foolish behavior is inconsistent with the self-image as a decent and intelligent person." Such cognition is thus properly understood as "a threat to the self."[13] And the more the information is seen as a threat to our self-image, the greater the inconsistency between the two, the harder our brain works to undermine the legitimacy of the information.

Let me offer a concrete example of how this all works. Say you are convinced that there has never been a better car than the 1967 Ford Mustang. After years of dithering and saving, you finally own such a car. Meticulously restored, it's your pride and joy; you would sell your left arm before you would sell it. Let's say you belong to a local Mustang club. You have made friends and see them regularly at car shows and other events. You have a key chain and a baseball hat and a cool bomber jacket. Every time you hear someone ask you if it's for sale, every time someone yells "nice car," every time you drive it down the street in the 4th of July parade, your soul swells with satisfaction.

Your conviction about Mustangs is thus part of who you are. So it is with beliefs. They make up our identity, both our self-identity and the identity we present to others. If you think gun control is a terrible idea, or that there is no breed of dog like a Golden Retriever, or that all food additives are bad, these beliefs define you, just like the kind of clothes you wear and the kind of home you live in. As the title of Robert Abelson's famous paper from 1986 has it, "Beliefs are Like Possessions."[14]

This connection between beliefs and self-identity also causes us to seek out and connect with people who have the same possessions—beliefs—that we do. We form relationships with these people, often interacting socially. Thus, our beliefs are a part of our social identity, as well. Abelson notes that if we like the people who believe a certain thing, if we want to hang out with them and be part of their group, there is a strong incentive to adopt their beliefs and to attach strong value thereto: "sharedness with valued others is a prime source of belief value."[15] If you find such a claim farfetched, consider the following example (which conveniently continues the car theme):

> Even a trivial human kind [of group], defined by nothing more consequential than what people buy, can call up the intense emotions supposedly reserved for the serious tribes. That's what happened to one owner of a Porsche 911 sports car after he learned that the company had started to make sports utility vehicles. "Every SUV I've seen is driven by some soccer mom on her cellphone," he told a reporter. "I hate these people, and that Porsche would throw me into that category made me speechless. Just speechless."[16]

To give these beliefs up would likely mean giving all this up, as well: our sense of identity and the relationships that come with it. (Abelson calls these "sunk costs.") That is rarely a simple, let alone a desirable thing to accomplish. Thus, once a belief is acquired, it becomes part of us, something that we do indeed own and which we therefore embrace as very valuable. The very word reflects this aspect. "Believe" comes from the old English verb "to hold dear."[17] We are therefore inclined to defend the former in the same way that we do any other possession. What's more, over time that value only increases. "The longer we hold a belief, the more we have invested in it; the more publicly committed we are to it, the more we endow it with value and the less likely we are to give it up."[18] The preservation of these beliefs is therefore an important part of our self-preservation. In fact, as far as our limbic system is concerned, they are one and the same.

So return to yourself as the Mustang aficionado. One day, minding your own business, you hear something very disconcerting. A colleague at work tells you about a great story in a muscle car magazine that celebrates the

1969 Pontiac GTO ("The Judge") as the ideal American car. What happens next?

What happens is that your brain will start to assess the information in terms of its threat potential: "The Pontiac GTO?! What of my club? My smug satisfaction as I drive down the street? My cool jacket?" It will then instantly fire off a very negative response to the new information. Your sweat glands will start to dilate, as will your pupils, and your heart rate and blood pressure will increase. (A lie detector, by the way, seeks to measure these automatic, unconscious responses.) Eventually some of these thoughts will rise to your consciousness, but by the time they do, your brain will have already determined that this proposition is dangerous to your well-being: "The idea that any American car is better than a Mustang is unpleasant. It is a threat to my well-being. It is therefore also obviously wrong. I need to come up with a reason why I can ignore or dismiss this information. When I do that, I will have disposed of the threat, and I will feel better." Because our beliefs are so caught up in our identity, because we are so invested in them, we defend them: we work hard to find evidence that support them, and discount anything that contradicts them. In fact, because this is our self-preservation we are talking about, we are more concerned with protecting our beliefs than we are in the truth. Before we are even consciously aware of the threat, our brain has already decided that for the sake of our well-being, that threat must be eliminated. Thus, before you read a single word of the article about the GTO, your brain has ensured that your assessment of the article will be driven more by your goal of self-preservation than by the pursuit of the truth. Our reasoning is simply the means we use to achieve this pre-established objective.

It is certainly true that we are very smart creatures with formidable reasoning power. Emotions do not cause our rationality to evaporate. In chapter 1, I recalled Crouter's comment that we humans are sinners, we are not evil. A similar distinction is operative here: we humans are biased, we are not irrational. For that matter, we really do want to know the truth. But if our emotions are involved, which is to say, if we perceive that our well-being is threatened, then that perception can quite often and quite effectively over-whelm any such desire, especially in the short term.

In short, when our emotions are involved our reasoning is almost always motivated reasoning. Drew Westen, a psychologist who, as we shall see, has gone on to examine specifically political questions, defines the process this way: "Motivated reasoning can be viewed as a form of implicit affect [affect is a scientific word for emotions] regulation in which the brain converges on solutions that minimize negative and maximize positive affect states."[19] Scientists like Westen argue that when our brains react to a threat, our brains are very likely to use our reasoning abilities not to get at the truth, but to justify our pre-existing beliefs. In short, Westen and his co-authors argue that emotion makes our brains act differently. "Neural information processing related to motivated reasoning appears to be qualitatively different from reasoning in the absence of a strong emotional stake in the conclusions reached."[20] Where such a stake is indeed present, we assess data in order to confirm that we were right all along.

CONFIRMATION BIAS

So how does motivated reasoning work? How does one reason in a motivated way? There are literally dozens of bias and beliefs that our brains employ to get us to the conclusion we desire. I am going to focus on one that is especially germane. One that the *Believing Brain* calls "the mother of all biases"[21]: the confirmation bias. Confirmation bias means that we seek out information that confirms what we already believe, and we ignore or actively disparage evidence that does not.[22]

The term was coined by psychologist Peter Wason in the 1960s. In his experiment, he came up with a mathematical rule for three numbers. The rule was "any ascending sequence." The job of the subject was simply to figure out this rule. Subjects were asked to come up with their own three numbers and the experimenter would then tell them whether their three numbers conformed to the rule or not. Pretty simple, right? Well, maybe too simple. For Wason then told subjects that the numbers 2, 4, and 6 fit the rule.

Once the idea of 2, 4, and 6 was placed in their head, the subjects found it incredibly difficult to figure out the rule. They kept going back to the numbers in the example, and then made up rules that were far more complex. For example, "all the numbers are even and separated by two," or "the middle number is the average of the first and last," or even "all three numbers are multiples of the first number." And once they came up with this answer, once they had the idea that this rule that might possibly be *the* rule, the subjects had a hard time letting it go—even to the point of ignoring answers that proved their rule was incorrect. The subjects became committed to their idea, acting as if it belonged to them. And once that happened, the subjects tended to interpret new evidence in ways that confirmed what they already believed. Their choices showed that the subjects were more intent on proving their own rule than they were on discovering what the rule actually was. Their interest in confirmation overwhelmed their desire to find the actual answer. Thus the term: "confirmation bias."[23]

It doesn't matter that the belief at issue in Wason's experiment is not one that anyone would regard as critical to one's identity, let alone self-preservation. That belief had after all been developed only moments before and after only moments of reflection. But being right is something that all of us want to be. And again, our limbic system reacts instantly and therefore does a bad job of discriminating: a threat is a threat is a threat. And once our brain identifies a threat, the bias for self-preservation automatically kicks in. Our brain knows what conclusion it wants to reach before the reasoning part of our brain is even aware of the question.

Since Wason's original research, there are now many, many experiments that reach the same conclusion: if we hear or read something that conforms to our point of view, we are likely to find it convincing and sound. But if the message is one with which we do not agree, we will find something wrong with the research, or the analysis, or the presentation. Now when we are talking about politics, we are quite likely to find beliefs to which people are strongly committed, and which are very much tied up to their notions of self and self-worth. And therefore, we would also expect to find evidence of motivated reasoning and cognitive bias.

In 1979, in a classic experiment, researchers Lord, Ross, and Lepper selected 48 undergraduates: half of the participants supported capital punishment because they believed it had a deterrent effect on crime, and the other 24 were opposed to the death penalty and doubted that it had much if any deterrent effect. The students were shown index cards that described the results of two made-up scientific studies: one supporting the idea that capital punishment had a deterrent effect, and the other disputing that claim. The students were also shown scientific critiques of both fake studies as well as responses from the "authors." Now the two studies were carefully counter-balanced—neither made a stronger case than the other—nevertheless the students' conclusions about the studies followed naturally from their pre-existing beliefs. The students criticized the study that reached a conclusion contrary to their opinion, while claiming that the study that corresponded to their opinion was significantly more convincing. The authors concluded: "the same study can elicit entirely opposite evaluations from people who hold different initial beliefs about a complex social issue."[24]

So far, all this falls in line with all that has been recounted previously. The students unconsciously assessed the studies in terms of their pre-existing belief. The study that ran counter to that belief was perceived as a threat and as a result the brain found ways to denigrate its conclusions. At the same time, confirming evidence was remembered better, and seen as both more credible and more relevant to the question at hand. It is a classic example of motivated reasoning.

But that isn't the half of it. Again, all students were shown both studies and both sets of critiques and responses. So all were exposed to "research" that conflicted with their beliefs. One might expect, and even hope, that this experience would lead them to consider the question unsettled and therefore reopen the matter in their own minds. The students might therefore think about what other questions to ask, how the studies might be improved, and the like. Just so, it might lead them to engage the other side, and perhaps work toward a compromise. At the least, one would think it would give them cause to develop some respect for the other point of view.

On the contrary. Instead, when the experimenters asked subjects to reflect on how the experience affected their opinion, subjects on each side said that they emerged all the more convinced that they were right: "The net effect of exposing proponents and opponents of capital punishment to identical evidence—studies ostensibly offering equivalent levels of support and disconfirmation—was to increase further the gap between their views."[25] The exposure to a study that contradicted their beliefs was such a threat that not only did the students find reasons for rejecting the study, that very experience caused them to double down on their original belief. The students—again, on both sides of the issue—were *more* convinced that they were right after having heard from experts, half of whom said they were wrong. The threat of counterevidence, and the mental process of coming up with ways to counter, dismiss or reject it ends up hardening and strengthening one's original opinion. Exposure to an alternative point of view can be such a threat that it can lead us to become more polarized than we were when we started.

The authors did not fault their subjects for their bias. The students were simply interpreting "new evidence in the light of past knowledge and experience." Such behavior, they argued, "is essential for any organism to make sense of, and respond adaptively to, its environment."[26] But the students' bias was reinforced and even strengthened by exposure to contradictory evidence. And for the study's authors, this phenomenon was not so benign.

> Rather, their sin lay in their readiness to use evidence already processed in a biased manner to bolster the very theory or belief that initially "justified" the processing bias. In so doing, subjects exposed themselves to the familiar risk of making their hypothesis unfalsifiable . . . and allowing themselves to be encouraged by patterns of data that they ought to have found troubling.[27]

"Feeling encouraged in their belief when they ought to have felt troubled": for any organism, especially one that relies on its rationality and its assessment of reality, this is quite a problem. The positions that the subjects had walking into the experiment become both more hardened and more polarized—not *despite* evidence to the contrary, but *because* of it. Responding to counterevidence by becoming more confident about one's original belief might offer a temporary and inadequate salve to one's self-image, but it is not a good long-term strategy for making sense of the world.

Now in 2006, researchers Taber and Lodge took issue with these and other similar results. They thought that since "Lord and his colleagues asked subjects to report *subjectively* whether their attitudes have become more extreme," their results were not reliable.[28] Therefore, they developed a more sophisticated experiment of their own. First they had the subjects take a test to determine their knowledge of the two contemporary political issues: affirmative action and gun control. They also tested the subject's knowledge about politics generally and the strength with which they held their opinions. They used real (but similarly long and complex) statements from political interest groups on the two issues so that they were more likely to generate a strong emotional reaction. They were then asked to call up arguments on a computer screen by their identified source (the NRA, Citizens Against Handguns, etc.). The subjects were told "to view the information in an evenhanded way so they could explain the issue to other students."[29] Then, without the subject's awareness, the computer recorded the order and viewing time for each argument selected. The researcher's hypothesis was that subjects would be more inclined to view arguments that conformed to—and did not threaten—their pre-established point of view.

This less subjective way of tracking motivated reasoning ended with the same result. Despite the researcher's efforts to promote the subject's evenhanded assessment of the issues, they found "that people are often unable to escape the pull of their prior attitudes and beliefs, which guide the processing of new information in predictable and sometimes insidious ways." Subjects found the arguments that supported their opinions more compelling than those against. And the stronger their views were going in, the more powerful was the effect. Finally, at the end of this process, respondents took a similar post-test. Researchers discovered that subjects held more extreme opinions than they did before they started. And the more extreme their opinions were when they started, the more pronounced this effect. In sum, while they took issue with the methodology of Lord, Ross, and Lepper, their new and improved testing procedures produced almost identical results.

It is worth noting one more point about the Taber and Lodge experiment. Those people least affected by confirmation bias were those who were least knowledgeable about the issues at hand. In other words, by far the best strategy for avoiding confirmation bias was to be without emotional investment. That is, to not care about the question. For individuals who did not care, there could be no potential threat. The amygdala takes a look and, unconcerned, passes it on the conscious brain.

YOU MAYBE, BUT NOT ME

Now most people hear this description and dissent, at least with respect to themselves. Odds are quite good that you are thinking something very similar right now. "This whole motivated reasoning thing might be true of most people, but it is not true for me. I call 'em like I see 'em. And I am certainly not stupid enough to end up more wrong than I was when I started."

For one thing, you might think that only unsophisticated people (e.g., people who don't read books like this one!) are subject to such biases. Sorry. Smart people are *not* more likely to consider the issue in all its complexity. In fact, they are no less likely than anybody else to have their emotions direct their reason. That is to say, their reasoning is no less motivated than anyone else's. The only difference is that they are better at it. The smarter we are, the better we are at coming up with strategies that allow us to dismiss the threatening information and preserve our well-being. *Righteous Mind* recalls an experiment in which people who had strong opinions were asked to write down reasons for and against the given question. People with higher IQs could come up with more arguments that supported their position, but "they are no better than others at finding reasons for the other side."[30] People who have more powerful brains are just better at finding ways to preserve their egos. Even social scientists—i.e., those who have been trained in detecting and combatting the effects of bias—are susceptible. In 1977, Michael. J. Mahoney showed that professional judgments about research quality and subsequent recommendations about publication (coin of the realm in the academic world) varied dramatically based on whether the findings under review were commensurate with their own.[31]

"OK," you say, "but what about people who are distinguished not because of their sheer candle power, but because of how knowledgeable they are about a given issue? What about those people who make it a point to educate themselves about daily events, or some specific issue? These people have accumulated enough knowledge about the subject that they have immunized themselves from the effects of emotion, right?" I will admit that this was my reaction. I had spent too many years in graduate school and too much time in the library for this kind of thing to work with me. Too bad for those poor benighted losers, but I studied enough that I am able to rise above such reactive and emotional thinking. Again, no. Here, too, the difference is not how the brain reacts emotionally, but how good it is at the rationalization task. "The more people know about an issue, the more able they are to develop complex rationalizations for dismissing data they don't want to believe."[32] But here too, the brain's basic need to rationalize is no less operative or powerful.

VAIN ABOUT OUR BRAINS

Though they don't hold up to scrutiny, objections like these are rooted in the fact that all of us believe we are different: we are less susceptible to biases than other people. Even if we are willing to accept that sometimes our thinking may be motivated, we believe that it happens to us much less than it does to others. A 2002 study gave Stanford undergraduates a list of specific biases, along with a brief description. They were asked to rate their own susceptibility to the biases on the list as well as those of the average American. The students "overwhelmingly reported that they personally were less susceptible to each of these biases than the average American."[33] Now lest you think that this is kind of conceit is the product of attending an elite university, the survey was also given to random travelers at San Francisco International Airport. These participants, too, claimed to be less biased than their fellow travelers. All of us find it difficult to recognize bias in ourselves, and even when we allow for the possibility, we insist that we are less biased than most.

But note that there are two sides to this phenomenon. For while it is very difficult for us to recognize or even accept that there is bias in our own actions, thinking, etc., we are quite ready to throw our fellow humans under the bus. That is, it is very easy for us to believe that such bias is present in the actions and thinking of others. So why is that? Why should we be so quick to judge others as biased and so unable to see it in ourselves?

Well, for one thing, it's a matter of perspective. At one time or another you have no doubt examined your opinion, wondering whether it is the product of your biases: "Do I find this person persuasive and intelligent just because she's saying what I want to hear?" Or "Could it be that I am denigrating this argument just because he's coming to conclusion that I don't like?" And therefore it is quite reasonable to remain skeptical: "If I am capable of this kind of introspection, then do I not have reason to believe that my beliefs are honest and not subject—or at minimum, not as subject—to the biases that corrupt the minds of so many others?" You can also probably point to times when you have been so convinced by someone that you changed your mind. So here again: "If I can be so convinced that I am able to jettison a belief that I ostensibly own, and that I have done so despite the fact that it is supposed to have caused me such pain, then I must be more honest and more objective than the average Joe and Jane."

So this introspection helps to account for why we think we are different from others. We are aware of our own thought processes. We know about our own uncertainty, our efforts to be introspective and fair. We also know how long it can be between the question, the decision and the accordant action. But we can only know this about ourselves. With respect to others this knowledge is quite beyond us. All we can do is listen to their words and observe their behavior. In short, no one of us knows what the rest of us are really thinking. We are unable to observe anybody else's internal debate, and therefore it is much easier to consider the possibility that they are subject to biases about which they are not even aware.

But there is another reason that accounts for our belief that we are less biased than others. It's called "naïve realism." Just as we are all intellectually aware of the possibility of bias, we are also aware that there is not complete correspondence between what we perceive and the way things actually are.

We know, for example, that we don't all see colors exactly the same. (Women tend to have more rods and cones in their retina, for example, so they see colors in more detail than men. Next time you get in an argument about paint for the kitchen, you will know why.) We know that even though the moon looks bigger when it's closer to the horizon, it really isn't. We know that even though the stick in the glass of water looks broken, it's not. But as we go about our days, it is very difficult to act in accord with this knowledge. For very practical purposes, we forget this knowledge and act as if there is complete correspondence between what we perceive and what is really there. In fact, the conviction that we see the world the way it really is, is both "inescapable and deep."[34]

Our beliefs and values stem in large measure from our observations of the world. We think about and form opinions based on what we see, hear, observe, read, etc. Therefore, as a result of this naïve realism, we also tend to place a similarly firm confidence in our "social attitudes, beliefs, preferences, priorities, and the like." All of these, we believe, likewise "follow from a relatively dispassionate, unbiased and essentially 'unmediated' apprehension of the information or evidence at hand."[35] If we believe that our perception corresponds to the way things really are, then we can and do believe ourselves to be on firm foundation whenever we use that perception to draw inferences or reason to conclusions. In short, we all believe that we do indeed call 'em like we see 'em. And because we believe we do, we expect that others will come to the same conclusions that we do.

So what of others who do not share our beliefs? What do we make of someone who sees things differently? If we are convinced that we see things as they really are, then there are only so many possible explanations to account for those who think otherwise. Ross and Ward list three: 1. They just missed something (which can happen to anyone), and as long as they are reasonable they will come to our point of view once they see what we see; 2. They are unable or unwilling to see what we see. They might be lazy or stupid or otherwise irrational; or 3. Their view is compromised because self-interest or ideology (as we have seen, this amounts to the same thing) has distorted their ability to move objectively from observation to conclusion.[36] Any of these three possibilities allow us to maintain our perception that we have it all figured out, that we have a hot line to objective reality and any disagreement between us and the other guy is because of some problem with the other guy. Naïve realism accounts for the difference between how we view ourselves and how we view others: why we find it extremely difficult to perceive bias in ourselves, but a fairly simple and straightforward thing to perceive bias and for that matter, stupidity, in others.

BUT WE DO CHANGE OUR MINDS

Now to be sure, we *can* change our minds. As individuals, groups, societies and even beyond, we have come to settled positions that our peers centuries ago would not even have conceived of. Again, we are biased, we are not irrational. As Kunda has it, "people will come to believe what they want to believe only to the extent that reason permits."[37] Consider, as a brief example, public opinion regarding the issues of gay marriage. Within the span of a few years, a policy question that had been settled for centuries has almost completely flipped. So how does something like this happen? And what does it have to do with what we know about the brain?

The first point is that we can ignore only so much counter evidence for only so long. The more often we hear (or see) a counter argument, the more frequently we receive information that does not fit our preconceived notions, the more likely we are to eventually question our position. A few times here or there is fairly easy to discount, but the more often this happens, the less able we are to convince ourselves that such information is without warrant. This is why when people do change their minds, they often cannot point to a specific time or event when it happened. Most often it is a gradual process, so gradual that we don't even know it's happening. We only know that it has happened.

It is also true that these repeated pieces of counter evidence are far more effective, and have more impact on our opinion, when they are presented without anger or confrontation. Since threat is what leads us to motivated reasoning in the first place, it is not just the information that matters, but how it is presented to us. When a counter argument comes along with assaults to our intelligence, sanity, or patriotism, the threat to our well-being is simply too high to allow us to change. In fact, not only are we unlikely to change our mind under such circumstances, we are more likely to become more extreme in our position, and farther away from the one advanced by the person insulting us. Abelson calls this "the boomerang effect of insult."[38]

In the case of gay marriage, the counter evidence conformed precisely to these features: it was both frequent and benign. As more and more gay people came out and moved in together, the more frequently Americans came to interact and associate with gay couples. The frequency of these interactions coupled with their sheer banality constituted a living argument against the notion that gays were immoral or that their behavior or "lifestyle" undermined society.

> There are . . . ways to communicate and enlighten not dependent on mere information that can overcome deeply embedded prejudices better than argument. A life can be an argument; being can be a reason. An idea can be

embodied in a person, and in human form it may break down barriers and
soften hardness of heart that words could not.[39]

Indeed. In fact, in a 2013 survey, 14 percent of all Americans said that they
had changed their minds on the issue. When those who had were asked why
they changed their minds, "roughly a third (32 percent) say it is because they
know someone—a friend, family member or other acquaintance—who is
homosexual."[40]

There will be more to say about how we change our minds in the next
chapter. But the point here is simply to acknowledge that they *can* change. If
we are given enough time and evidence, and especially if the evidence is
presented without confrontation, then our motivated brain will slowly yield.
Thus, while motivated reasoning is a formidable power within our brains, it
is not impermeable. Of course, even when we do change our mind, our vanity
remains. Often, we conveniently forget that we did not always think this way,
or at least dispute the notion that we were quite so ardent in our opposition.
Here, too, others might well remember things differently, but our brains will
frequently come up with an account that presents ourselves to ourselves in
the best light possible.

BACK TO THE BEGINNING

At the end of this trip through psychology and neuroscience, we arrive in a
familiar and very Niebuhrian place. Just as Niebuhr recounted, science affirms that we are inherently self-deceivers.[41] For reasons that go back eons,
the drive to survive has left a legacy that impacts how we experience the
world. We evaluate everything we take in according to whether it is or is not
a threat. As a result, our thinking is a form of defense. We are therefore
inclined to bias in ways that are so deep that they are beyond our awareness.
Even though we are quite able to see others as either stupid or delusional,
immoral or biased, we are convinced that we ourselves are not subject to
such failures.

If anything, scientific evidence out-Niebuhrs Niebuhr. For Niebuhr uses
the term Children of Light to identify a specific subset of the American body
politic. It does not apply to everybody. Even though he says that Americans
are distinctively drawn to this democratic peril, he does not say that its
features are present within all of us. It is rather something that particularly
effects the romantic optimists among us. But science, on the contrary, shows
us that the features that characterize a Child of Light are born of endemic
features of the human brain. We are all vain: that is, naïvely confident that
we know what is going on, that we are morally and intellectually superior to
those with whom we disagree. We are all likewise confident that the bias and
disconnect that we so readily see in others is somehow inoperative in our-

selves. In what follows, I will be using the term Children of Light largely as Niebuhr meant it, but in accord with the scientific research recounted above. That is to say, I will use it as a term that refers to all of us human beings— romantic or not, American or not, democrat or not. It remains then to show what science has to say about how these realities play out in the political realm.

NOTES

1. During the Cold War, there was a famous group of non-believers at Harvard, Arthur Schlesinger and Morton White especially, who were very impressed with Niebuhr's analysis of democracy and foreign policy. They called themselves "Atheists for Niebuhr."

2. The snake vs. stick story comes from LeDoux, *The Emotional Brain*, 166.

3. Damasio, *Descartes' Error*, 179.

4. I will therefore focus on the brain's assessment of threat because the process is better understood. But the basal ganglia, located near the amygdala and also part of the limbic system, appear to play a key role in the assessment of positive stimuli. When we perform a behavior that gets us what we want (like tasty fruit), that behavior and its associative cues get mapped. The basal ganglia are one place where this mapping takes place.

5. The idea of the limbic system as a unified unit, and especially one that does most of the brain's emotional processing, has come under criticism. But most scientists continue to use and accept the term.

6. LeDoux, *The Emotional Brain*, 174.

7. You might wonder if we have an innate fear of snakes. It is true that rats raised in the lab will still freeze when they see a cat for the first time. But lab-raised monkeys will not show the same fear when they see a snake.

8. Goldman is the first to refer to this circuitry as a "hijack." See *Emotional Intelligence*, 13.

9. Damasio, *Descartes Error*, 184-185.

10. Wilson, *Strangers to Ourselves*, 24.

11. Both this quotation and the preceding one in this paragraph are from Pronin, Gilovich, and Ross, "Objectivity in the Eye of the Beholder, 784.

12. Kübler-Ross, *On Death and Dying*, 51.

13. Kunda, "The Case for Motivated Reasoning," 484.

14. Abelson, "Beliefs are Like Possessions."

15. Ibid., 237.

16. Berreby, *Us and Them*, 27.

17. In Schulz, *Being Wrong*, 104.

18. Shermer, *The Believing Brain*, 268.

19. Westen, et al., "Neural bases of motivated reasoning," 1947.

20. Ibid., 1955.

21. Shermer's *The Believing Brain* lists over 30 such biases.

22. Some call the rejection of evidence we don't like a *dis*-confirmation bias, but the point is the same.

23. Wason, "On the Failure to Eliminate Hypotheses in a Conceptual Task," 129-137.

24. Lord, Ross, and Lepper, "Biased Assimilation and Attitude Polarization," 2102.

25. Ibid., 2105.

26. Ibid., 2107. Many researchers similarly contend that emotionally-laden reasoning is a good thing. Emotions help us ignore unimportant questions, reduce our choices to a manageable number, and come to a conclusion. Confirmation bias is thus a prudent strategy: it helps us to function in an absurdly complicated world.

27. Ibid. Recall that in chapter 2, I said that science followed Niebuhr's description "except for the sin part." While I do not expect that these researchers have a Niebuhrian concept of the word in mind, it is telling that they use it to describe this oh so human failing.
28. Taber and Lodge, "Motivated Skepticism in the Evaluation of Political Beliefs," 756.
29. Ibid., 759.
30. Haidt, *Righteous Mind*, 81.
31. Mahoney, "Publication Prejudices," 161-175.
32. Westen, *The Political Brain*, 100.
33. Pronin, Gilovich and Ross, "Objectivity in the Eye of the Beholder," 788.
34. Ibid., 782.
35. Ross and Ward, "Naive Realism in Everyday Life," 110.
36. Ibid., 11.
37. Kunda, "The Case for Motivated Reasoning," 483.
38. Abelson, "Beliefs Are Like Possessions," 228.
39. Boswell, "Logos and Biography," 361.
40. Pew Research Center for the People and the Press, "Growing Support for Gay Marriage."
41. There is an important issue here that I need to at least reference. In Niebuhr's famous formulation, sin is "inevitable but not necessary." That is to say, all of us are sinners, and cannot not be so. Nevertheless, we are also fully responsible for our sins. For Niebuhr and indeed any Christian, this must be the case, for if sin were not necessary, then we would not be guilty of it, and therefore there would be no need of the salvific work of Jesus. But Franklin Gamwell has pointed out to me a problem: if vanity is a product of evolution and thus "hard-wired" in our brains, then does that not put even more strain on Niebuhr's paradox? If much of our operating, emoting brain is beyond our consciousness, then how can our decisions be understood as free? In short, how can sin be understood as anything but fully and completely necessary?

This is a larger question than I can take up here. It is certainly true that data about how the brain works implicate fundamental questions about how we understand human freedom and responsibility (and for that matter, even human identity). But as I recount in chapter 9, brain research also shows that even if we cannot prevent the pre-conscious workings of our brain, we can address and to some degree even override them. That fact would seem to me to preserve some of Niebuhr's tension between inevitability and freedom. But one must also admit that this stance is precarious. The more we learn about the operations of the brain, the more these and similar questions will continue to demand our attention.

Chapter Four

Rattlers and Eagles/Democrats and Republicans

In 1954, 22 11-year-old boys were invited to a two-week summer camp at the Robber's Cave State Park in Oklahoma. (It was called "Robber's Cave" because the area had been a hideout for Jesse James.) Complete with ball fields, swimming holes, and this very cool history, this was a pretty sweet gig for the boys involved. It was also an experiment. Led by Muzafer Sherif and his colleagues, this setting tested how people form groups, how groups come to feel animosity and prejudice toward others, and how that animosity can be abated, if not overcome.

The boys were screened to ensure they were well-adjusted and of average (or slightly above average) intelligence. In addition, all of them came from a similar background: white, Protestant, middle class, and stable, two-parent families. The boys were selected from different schools and neighborhoods, so none of them knew each other. The boys were randomly divided into two groups and then bussed, separately, to the camp.

During the first week of the experiment, the groups were kept separate. For some time, they did not even know the existence of the other group. They spent their time swimming and playing various games. Yet all the while the researchers, who doubled as the camp counselors, focused on group formation. Each group came up with its own group name. One group became the Eagles while the other group called themselves the Rattlers. Both groups made a group flag and stenciled their name on their shirts. As each group developed its own identity, leaders emerged, and they came up with a set of characteristics that defined a Rattler or Eagle. The Rattlers established norms of "cursing," acting tough, and ignoring small injuries. The Eagles swam in the nude and frowned on any expression of homesickness. In sum, "[w]ays of doing things, of meeting problems, of behaving under certain conditions were standardized, permitting variation only within limits. Beyond the limits of group norms, behavior was subject to group sanctions. . . ."[1]

In the second phase of the experiment, the two groups were made aware of the other and the researchers created opportunities for the two groups to compete. Baseball and touch football games, and a tug of war contest were organized, along with cabin cleanliness awards and acting contests. The Eagles, the winning group, received a medal and a pocket knife (very cool stuff for the boys in question); the Rattlers, meanwhile, received nothing.

As you might expect, the groups did not like each other very much. Even before the contests were concluded, the groups refused to eat together. They also taunted each other, holding their noses when the other group was in sight, and calling each other just about any slur that an 11-year-old in 1954 could come up with: cheaters, stinkers, even "Communists." But things didn't stop there: the Eagles burned the Rattlers' flag, then put the tattered remnants back up the flag pole and hummed taps. (See chapter 7.) The next day, the Rattlers raided the Eagles' cabin, overturned beds, and stole whatever pocket knives and medals they could find. The two groups became so aggressive that the researchers had to physically separate them.

The boys were given two days to cool off. During this time, they were asked to list the characteristics of the two groups: theirs and the other. "Our" group conjured up words like "friendly," "tough," and "brave." The other group were described as "sneaks," "cheats," "bums," "cowards," and "stinkers." They were also given a bean collecting task for a bean bag toss game, and were then asked to estimate the numbers of beans collected by boys in their group and by those in the other: the boys consistently overestimated the former and underestimated the latter. "Thus," the researchers concluded, "competition and rivalry between the groups led to attribution of unfavorable characteristics to the out-group, while this same pattern of intergroup relations was accompanied by a marked tendency to see members of one's own group in a highly favorable light."[2]

In the third and final phase, the researchers wanted to determine if they could create cooperation between the two groups. They manufactured a problem in which the camp's water supply had been blocked by "vandals." The groups had to cooperate in order to solve the problem. After a few more similar contrivances that required cooperation between the two groups ("superordinate goals," the researchers called them) the animosity began to wane. By the end of the experiment, the two groups were eating dinner together, dividing things equitably and even asked to go home together in the same bus.[3]

In the last chapter, I showed that beliefs are tied up with our self-image, and that we therefore unconsciously defend those beliefs against any perceived threat—through confirmation bias and other forms of motivated reasoning. That immediate, unconscious defense is a legacy that helped to preserve the species. I also noted that individuals who belonged to groups with high levels of cohesion were also more likely to survive. Thus, a desire to belong, and rewarding chemicals that reinforce that behavior, are likewise part of our species' evolutionary endowment. Just as there are psychic and physical benefits to our self-deception, there are similar benefits to feeling part of a group, and health detriments to feeling stigmatized or otherwise excluded. When we feel connected, part of a group, our bodies produce less stress hormones; we sleep better and are less likely to get sick. On the other hand, if we feel excluded, our blood pressure rises and we feel more stress; if such feelings continue, we are more likely to suffer from depression, and ultimately are more likely to die early. "So," as David Berreby has it, "an innate preference for good human-kind feelings over bad ones, for feeling like Us and not like Them, is no sideshow. It's one of life's main events."[4] In this chapter, I mean to show that the groups we are part of are likewise tied to our identity, and that we therefore defend them in very similar ways. Most to the point, I will show that political parties fit that description very well.

GROUPS ARE PART OF US

Sherif's experiment confirms the idea that joining groups is a human compulsion. For reasons that extend back to that savannah long ago, as soon as human beings come together, for whatever reason and under whatever occasion, we almost immediately start to find reasons to identify ourselves as either the same or different from others. But more importantly, he shows that a group is defined by a set of shared beliefs; that by joining, we become committed to those beliefs, and that we will likewise disparage anybody who does not share them, and defend them against any perceived threat, even at some risk to ourselves.

All of this is consistent with Niebuhr's anthropology. Indeed, for Niebuhr, joining a group is just another manifestation of *the* main event: the battle against anxiety. By joining a group, separating the world into those who are with me and those who are not, an individual receives comfort and security, but he also receives a sense of identity and purpose. To say I am a Rattler is to say that I adhere to a set of beliefs, a code of conduct, an ethos (though of course they never used those words). As I become a Rattler, as that identity becomes united with my own, it becomes a part of me and in that context even overwhelms what is distinctive about me. I become more significant by becoming less unique and more connected to the group.

But if this strategy is to succeed, I need my group to be successful, to have a high status and to be better than other groups. The Rattlers must be good and powerful and important and its members must be "friendly," "tough" and "brave." And, if that is what they must be, then any group that is not mine must be not as good and not as significant. What starts as a way of doing things that identifies us as the Eagles thus inescapably becomes a condemnation of any group that does things differently. If Rattlers do things the right way, then the Eagles—insofar as they do different things and believe different things—do things the wrong way. And therefore, they must be "cheaters," "bums," and "sissies." Of course, this strategy for eliminating anxiety is ultimately no less successful than any other. In fact, for Niebuhr, it forces us into a level of immorality, and thus hypocrisy, that individuals on their own are unlikely to reach. But Sherif's experiment demonstrates both the innateness of the strategy and the inevitability of the results.

POLITICAL BELIEFS, POLITICAL GROUPS

Recall our Mustang aficionado. His passion led him to join a group of Mustang collectors. He sees people he knows at every car show and he enjoys chatting, sharing advice, and gossiping with them. He knows that they would share his unbridled contempt at the article on the GTO. In short, his car club functions in many ways like our tribe on the savannah. The camaraderie, the feeling of mutual support and belonging that he feels is different in degree but not in kind from what our ancestors felt for those in their tribe. Our need to be part of a tribe remains innate and inescapable, and our Mustang club is an example of one of these post-tribal tribes.

Political beliefs work much the same way, although in this case, members are "bound together not by a shared history, and not by proper nouns, but by a set of abstract ideals."[5] The NRA on the one hand and the Coalition to Stop Gun Violence on the other are made up of people who share a number of ardent beliefs about gun control. This belief is important enough to them that they devote resources of time, energy and money toward advancing their point of view. The Mustang enthusiast is more likely to socialize with other aficionados; members of the NRA may do no more than send it their annual dues and display a sticker on their car. Nevertheless, for issue groups as well, membership is an important part of one's identity. (You might have seen the bumper sticker that confirms this idea: "I am the NRA.") In fact, because the beliefs in question are fairly limited and defined, support is likely to be both strong and universal. (Everybody who belongs to the CSGV would support an assault weapons ban. If they didn't, why would they join the group in the first place?) So one's commitment to these kinds of issue groups, one's identity investment if you will, is likewise often deep and passionate.

But no matter how strongly one feels about gun control, or for that matter just about any political position, that belief is not likely to exist in isolation. Someone who is against gun control laws, for example, will probably also have positive beliefs about hunting and habitat preservation, support a strong defense budget, and argue against what they see as government interference in our private lives. Beliefs come in bunches, and if a bunch of beliefs are sufficiently comprehensive and consistent, they are properly called an ideology: libertarian, conservative, liberal, authoritarian, and so forth. Ideologies like these tend to foster their own groups, of course. And as the number of implicated beliefs expand, so too do the number of issues they attend to. The American Civil Liberties Union has a larger pallet of issues than does the Coalition to Stop Gun Violence (though there is clearly overlap between the two). Still, George H. W. Bush's accusation in 1988 that Michael Dukakis was "a card-carrying member of the ACLU" speaks to the fact that even as groups increase in size and scope, they can continue to play an important role in establishing our social identity—of who is with us, and who is not.

Ultimately, the most relevant ideological groups, at least in the United States, are the Democratic and Republican parties. And the same dynamic works here, as well. These two parties are of course very big groups, much bigger than even the biggest advocacy group. And for that matter, the costs of entrance to belong to a party are comparatively small. Though the request for donations is chronic, there are no dues that one *has* to pay, no meetings you *have* to go to. Usually all one has to do to become a Republican is say that you are and, in most states, choose a Republican ballot come primary day. But despite these differences, the same aspects that are operative with any group are operative here: namely, political parties as well provide a way to connect with others with similar beliefs and thereby establish and maintain one's social identity.

A political party claims to offer citizens a more or less coherent set of ideals, goals and policy positions. If those beliefs resonate sufficiently with an individual's beliefs, he or she chooses the party as a form of self-identification. To say I am a Democrat or Republican is to affirm a series of policy positions: from trade with China, to the domestic production of coal, to immigration policy and on and on. There are hundreds of questions like these. (Take a look at either party's platform if you doubt this.) Few people know the party's position on every single issue, and one's support for any such position will waver depending on what is being talked about. But the presumption, the default setting, as it were, is that our individual positions conform to our party's.

Party affiliation also implies agreement with a whole host of broader and deeper beliefs, not just about this or that piece of legislation, but about the proper scope of government; not just about some new weapon system, but the appropriate size and role about the military, and so on. Finally, one's party choice ultimately implicates very fundamental beliefs about what we judge most important, whether we are more concerned with freedom or fairness, law abidingness or creativity, for example. Some research goes even farther and demonstrates that our politics are reflected in our brain architecture. Avi Tuschman claims that Republicans tend to have larger amygdalae, and Democrats have a larger anterior cingular cortex, and that this physiology accords with very deep beliefs about how trusting one should be about other people, how dangerous the world is, and the like.[6] I don't want to pursue this claim further. The data here are quite new, and for many, quite controversial. I would say that if there is indeed a connection between our brain architecture and our political beliefs, then that would be another very good reason to guard against the idea that our partisan beliefs are uniquely in accord with reality. But my point is more general: that one's political party offers an ideological home for people who agree about the most fundamental of beliefs and values. And that means that parties are very good and able post-tribal tribes.

Of course, no matter how opinionated we are, a party's positions extend well beyond our own set of concerns. The world is complex, and we can't know or care about everything in it. And this is especially true about politics. Every day we need to figure out which socks to wear, what to make for dinner, and why our team traded away their right fielder. Few of us have either the time or the inclination to wade through all the intricacies associated with our trade policy with China. Because of this, connecting with a party gives us more than just a place to hang our ideological hat. It gives us a kind of crib sheet for making political judgments. One of the parties appears to match up with my beliefs about the big questions. Having thus identified myself as either a Democrat or Republican, I am inclined to take their word for it on these political questions that are beyond my awareness or interest. If my party says that our trade policy with China is good or bad or needs to change in this specific way, and I don't have a dog in the fight, their opinion is good enough for me. So by helping us thus fill out our beliefs, a political party further helps us cement our sense of identity. It tells us what we would likely think if we were to take the time to think about it ourselves.

Finally, just like any other group we belong to, each party also serves as a kind of social identifier. The party is a group that is strongly connected with our social identity, and all the other groups we belong to. We are therefore inclined to connect to one party over the other. We all know that Americans sort themselves out according in all kinds of ways that strongly connect with party. Southern evangelicals are likely to vote Republican, so too with gun owners, NASCAR fans, and so on. Gays, urban blacks, and social workers, etc., are likely to vote Democratic. One's party affiliation will often correspond and even be driven by those social groups that a citizen feels most connected to. If someone is a Missouri Synod Lutheran, for example, it would be socially awkward, even difficult for them to express support for some Democratic point of view. So too, there are not a lot of folks connected with Green Peace or the local Organic Foods co-op who are likely to stick up for part of the Republican platform. Of course, in either case, such paragons of social courage no doubt exist; but they are the outliers. It is also true that some ethnic or cultural groups have ties to parties that are so long established that social identity can swamp ideology. Black church goers, for example, might differ strongly with the Democratic position on gay marriage, but almost all of them are going to remain Democrats. These exceptions aside, for the most part social identity and ideology reinforce each other. Ideology is social identity and vice versa. In terms of our innate human biases, this unique combination makes for a potent brew.

GROUPISH, NOT SELFISH

If our deep beliefs cause us to identify ourselves as member of a political party, and to some degree tie its well-being and success to our own, how does that affect our behavior, including our innate propensity to bias?

Geoffrey Cohen, then at Yale, selected a group of liberal and conservative students who had strong opinions about welfare reform. He had the students read a simulated news story about a new welfare reform proposal. In some cases, the new proposal was very generous (more generous in fact than the United States has ever had), and in others, the proposal was extremely harsh: only $250 a month with an imposed lifetime limit of 1.5 years. As you might expect, the liberal students liked the plan with greater benefits and conservatives favored the option with less. Cohen then had another group of liberals and conservatives look at the same plans, but this time, the story said that the proposal was authored by either the Democrats or the Republicans. Half of the time, the party affiliation was one you would expect. The other half though, the generous proposal was associated with the Republicans, and the stingy program with the Democrats. Again, the difference between the proposal in question and that held by the party in question was extreme. The liberal version was to the left of the Democrats, the conservative version more extreme than most Republicans. Yet in both cases, partisan identity was more important to the students than the actual content of the proposal. The students' social identity was tied to their partisan identity—so much so that both liberals and conservatives followed their parties wherever the party went. Democrats agreed with the harsh welfare reform proposal if it had been proposed by the Democrats. And if the Republicans were thought to be behind the generous proposal, then the Republican students were all for it. Indeed, "[o]nce the policy was socially defined as liberal or conservative, the persuasive impact of its objective content was reduced to nil."[7] Again: "reduced to nil."

Now despite the rather extraordinary effect that party had on their decisions, the students themselves denied any connection between policy options and their politics. Just like a real crib sheet, the impact of party identification was kept hidden, at least to the students themselves. "Participants . . . asserted that they had based their attitude on an autonomous and rational consideration of the facts."[8] What's more, knowledge about America's welfare system did not alter this effect. Even those students who claimed to be highly knowledgeable were just as likely to choose party over policy as those who made no such claim. And they were just as likely to deny that party support had had any impact on their choice. Just as we saw in the last chapter, knowledge or smarts does not change the inclination to bias nor our obliviousness to what is going on in our own heads.

One more thing: "participants view[ed] their peers as more conformist and less rational than themselves."[9] That is, even as the subjects insisted on the autonomy of their own decisions, they were perfectly willing to believe that their fellow students had been unduly influenced by their connection between policy and party. Because of our high opinion of ourselves, and our inability to see into the minds of others, we are more likely to disparage (or, as you prefer, evaluate realistically) the workings of any brain that is not our own.

The Rattlers and Eagles saw themselves as good and worthy, and they developed very low opinions of those in the other group. Just so, Democrats and Republicans are likely to believe that the positions of their party conform better to objective reality. They are more likely to analyze the situation better, propose better policy solutions, and conform better to authentic American values. And they are also likely to judge their opponents as irrational and more likely to be influenced by bias. In sum, we hold our noses when the other party walks by.

CHEATING TO WIN

It is not enough to be in a group. To combat my anxiety, I must be in the good group, the better group, the winning group. Therefore, my group—my party—needs to prevail. Our need for that is so great that we will even cheat to make it happen, even as we maintain the belief that we are members of the good party and the other party is the bad one, and that this state of affairs is simply an objective accounting of the facts. That is a good trick. Fortunately, our unconscious brain is a ready and quite adept accomplice.

Geoffrey Munro, Terrell Lasane, and Scott Leary created an experiment in which participants with admitted partisan preferences were asked to act as admission counselors, comparing two college applications and deciding which student merited an invitation for an on-campus interview. Both made-up candidates were given very similar characteristics: both were white males from small towns, both had taken the same number of AP classes, and both had letters of recommendation that were largely positive, but each had one

slightly negative comment as well. There were meaningful distinctions between the two, however. One student had slightly higher class ranking, SAT
scores, and GPA. This objective information "rather unambiguously" favored one candidate over the other. The control group made no mention of
politics, but in the other group, the letter of recommendation mentioned that
the slightly stronger candidate "is passionate about his involvement in the
Young [Democrats/Republicans] and has shown a great deal of maturity
assisting in the presidential campaign of [Al Gore/George W. Bush]."[10]

The control group consistently recommended the candidate with the slight
edge in objective scores. And for those evaluators who expressed no or weak
partisan identification, the addition of political information made no difference in that result. But for strong partisans in the preference group, "the same
two applicants were judged differently when one of them supported a presidential candidate of a political party opposing the participants' preferred
party than when he did not."[11] That is, if the student with the higher GPA,
class rank, and SAT scores worked for the party that the evaluator did not
belong to, he or she was more likely to pick the other student.

Of course none of the evaluators, no matter how partisan, would admit
that they voted against the stronger candidate simply because he was a
Democrat/Republican. Indeed, from what we have seen, we would expect
that none of them were even aware of their bias. So how did their unconscious pull this off? How did they reject the candidate who was, by all
objective standards, slightly preferable, and yet still claim that their analysis
was objective? The partisans simply placed more emphasis on the least objective piece of evidence: the letters of recommendation. Whereas the control
group said that the objective evidence was much more important than the
letters of recommendation, partisans placed far greater weight on the letters.
By unconsciously placing so much importance on this most ambiguous piece
of data, the partisans were able to get the result they wanted and support the
success of their own group, even as they maintained the self-imposed illusion
that they are objective, and that they are members of the more objective
party. Finally, lest your own partisan brain is grasping for some way to spin
these results, note that the effects were the same for members of either party:
"Democrats and Republicans did not differ in the degree to which they dis-
played the political partisan prejudice effect."[12]

THE POLITICAL BRAIN

In the last chapter, I argued that our capacity for self-deception is wired deep
within our brains. We are designed to preserve ourselves, to quickly identify
any and all threats, and respond accordingly. In this chapter, I have shown
that we self-select into groups (including parties) which reinforce our beliefs

and which in turn reinforce our sense of who we are and our connection to those groups. I have also shown that because partisan affiliation is so important to our identity, it causes us to follow our party even when, in the abstract, we would be inclined to disagree. Finally, our ties to partisanship lead us to support the success of our own group, and even to discriminate against outsiders—even while we successfully delude ourselves that we have done no such thing, and that we are, in fact, the good guys.

But I have not yet said anything about how all of this operates in the brain. If our amygdala causes us to bias ourselves against any possible threat to our beliefs, what does neuroscience tell us about how our brains react to threats to our partisan identity? Allow me to describe one more experiment.

You have no doubt seen a picture of a brain scan: colors scattered around what appears to show the inside of a human head. Often these pictures are comparative: they show the difference between a healthy brain and an unhealthy one, or they show the difference between one state of action or thinking vs. another. These pictures are most often made by an fMRI machine (functional magnetic resonance imagery). The colors in the scan represent the BOLD: the blood oxygenation-level dependent signal. Changes in the BOLD reflect where the brain is using the most blood, and therefore, where it is doing the most work. To put it simply, blood that is oxygenated is slightly less magnetic than blood that is not. Scanning the brain with very powerful magnets therefore provides a picture, albeit a very crude one, of the brain in operation. The researcher is seeking to find a correlation between the task the brain is performing (recalling a name, doing a math problem, etc.) and what part of the brain appears most active.

During the 2004 presidential campaign, psychologist Drew Westen selected 30 men—half described themselves as "strong" Republicans and the other half "strong" Democrats. The brains of all 30 subjects were scanned in an fMRI machine while they were reading statements—"edited or fictionalized," but very believable—in which both George W. Bush and John Kerry clearly contradicted themselves. Kerry's statements were regarding his support (or not) for the First Iraq War. And for George W. Bush, the two statements concerned his support for wounded veterans. You will not be surprised to learn that the subjects all practiced motivated reasoning. The Republicans seized on Kerry's contradictory statement, but let their guy, George Bush, off the hook. And exactly the opposite happened with the Democrats.

So far, none of this is inconsistent with what we already know. But this experiment showed the brain in action. While the subjects were reading and evaluating the statements of the candidate they liked and the candidate they did not, the fMRIs showed that the reasoning part of the brain was comparatively inactive. Rather, it was the parts of the brain associated with the processing of emotion, especially the anterior cingulate cortex, that lit up the most. What is more, as the brain continued to work, the picture changed. The ventral striatum—a part of the brain associated with reinforcement, that is to say, with chemical reward—suddenly showed significant activity.[13]

Now before we go any farther, it must be said that there are all kinds of reasons to be suspicious about pictures like those Westen is describing. Nothing that we can see from an fMRI image comes close to showing what is happening at the level where the real action is: that is, between the roughly 100 billion neurons and the roughly 1 quadrillion synapses. It's like judging the bacterial count of a water sample by smelling it. You can certainly learn something, but it is degrees removed from what is really going on. Nevertheless, these images are data and they bring us unprecedented (and for that matter astonishing) information about how the brain really works. More to the point, this information is in accord with what we have learned about the brain through psychological experimentation.

When we hear information that goes against our party, that assault to our well-being is accompanied by chemicals that make us feel bad. "When confronted with potentially troubling political information, a network of neurons becomes active that produces distress."[14] Now we do not know whether this distress is conscious, unconscious, or both. We know that much of the workings of the limbic system work outside of our awareness, but we also know that often those workings eventually percolate up to our consciousness. (Westen also identifies an intermediate step between the two that he calls "implicit consciousness."[15] Gut feelings or intuitions might also describe this state hovering between conscious and unconscious feelings.) So determining where one stops and the other begins is not always clear, especially from an fMRI image. But whether we consciously feel it or not, it is distress, and our brains want to make that distress stop. We thus have physical evidence that conforms to what we know about the connection between our beliefs and our well-being, and how we react to information that threatens those beliefs.

As we have seen, motivated reasoning is how we make the distress stop. We discount the source or find other ways to convince ourselves that the argument being presented need not be taken seriously. Our brain already knows what conclusion we want to reach, and we use our reasoning power to get us there. But once we have done this, once we have indeed convinced ourselves that this threat has been rationalized away, our brain makes sure that this pattern is reinforced. In Westen's experiment, once the subjects let their candidate off the hook,

> not only did neural circuits involved in negative emotions turn off, but circuits involved in positive emotions turned on. The partisan brain didn't seem satisfied in just feeling better. It worked overtime to feel good, activating reward circuits that give partisans a jolt of positive reinforcement for their biased reasoning. These reward circuits overlap substantially with those activated

when drug addicts get their "fix," giving new meaning to the term political junkie.[16]

Our brain is well equipped to get us to do what it wants. (It is worth letting that sentence sink in for a moment.) Once we have reasoned away any information that threatens our partisan identity, not only do we cease feeling distress, we get rewarded with feel good chemicals. Again, we do not know how conscious this operation is, but we do know that—as with the amygdala hijack—the process of rewarding a successful escape with chemicals is one that has been shown in animals. Westen again: "[S]everal researchers have found avoidance and escape conditioning to be associated with dopamine release . . . in other animals."[17] Here too, similar operation in a less conscious animal would imply that consciousness is not necessary when this same process takes place in our brains. But whether we are consciously aware of it, there is little doubt that our brains are. Indeed, if Westen is right, finding reasons to disregard conflicting information produces the very same feel good chemical involved in drugs, food and sex. Our brain, it would appear, has quite an effective arsenal.

GROUPS AND CHANGING MINDS

In the last chapter, I used the change associated with the issue of gay marriage to show how repeated and comparatively benign exposure to information that counters our opinion can cause us to change our beliefs. It is also true that the very same group identity that makes us reject competing information can, under the right circumstances, cause us to be more open to it.

When we hear an argument that our brain sees as a threat, it immediately finds ways to discount that argument. But when that argument is presented in a way that conforms to our group's values, we are more likely to listen to it. In 1989, Andrew Sullivan made a conservative argument for gay marriage in *The New Republic*. Legalizing gay marriage, Sullivan argued, would offer homosexuals the same deal society now offers heterosexuals: general social approval and specific legal advantages in exchange for a deeper and harder-to-extract-yourself-from commitment to another human being. Like straight marriage, it would foster social cohesion, emotional security, and economic prudence.[18] Before Sullivan's article, homosexuals more frequently saw themselves as outsiders, unwelcome and uninterested in bourgeois culture. Sullivan's article was an early effort to argue against that characterization. It deliberately strove to argue for marriage in terms that resonated with traditional, even conservative American values. Reaction to this piece was strong in both communities, and it did not lead to anything like an overnight change. (And regardless, I am not making any causal argument about the relative historical impact of this piece. Here again, my point is simply illustrative.)

But if nothing else, it forced conservatives to change the terms by which they argued against the idea. And that, in and of itself, was an important milestone in the debate.

More recent evidence shows that the same effect occurs when threatening information is presented by someone who we take to be in our group. In 2013, Republican Senator Rob Portman of Ohio became the first GOP senator to announce support for same-sex marriage after his son came out to him as gay. Portman supports gun rights, wants to restrict access to abortion, and hates Obamacare. When someone like that comes out in favor of gay marriage, it is harder for Republicans to dismiss it. Of course, many Republicans decry Portman's position, and continue to reject the idea, but many others see it as reason to reconsider the question. At minimum, such a statement takes the wind out of one's sails. Opponents see it as evidence that the shift has taken on an air of inevitability.

Thus, the power of group identity works both ways. The presentation of counter arguments by people who are part of the in group and in ways that conform to the group's values, are far more likely to impact on our hearing and we are far more likely to respond favorably to those arguments. Thus, we can change our mind, and any such change becomes most possible when it operates within the terms of our biased brain.

POLITICS WITH THE BRAINS WE HAVE

Groups are irresistible. We humans cannot not form them. When we are in one, we feel connected to others and we absorb the group's identity to our own. We develop a set of common beliefs, attributes and behaviors, and all of which makes us feel good. Political parties are just big groups, with identifying beliefs that go way down, and which correspond to a whole host of often quite coordinated social identities. Once we tie the group's identity to our own, we are constrained to see our group as better, superior, as more successful and more worthy of it. We are inclined to follow such a group even when its beliefs and actions contradict our own. And we are inclined to view other groups as both threatening and inferior, and to treat them accordingly. Yet as Niebuhr noted, however we treat them, however immorally we are inclined to act, we find ways to justify our actions, and affirm our own superiority. In Niebuhrian terms, science again confirms that as groups and as individuals, we are all indeed Children of Light.

These features are endemic. They are the hard wired into our brains, products of evolution that extend beyond the history of even our own species. My claim, of course, is that all of this has extremely important implications for democracy, but it is not obvious that this is so. For if all this is indeed hardwired, then would that not imply that our democracy has had to deal with this reality since its inception? We may be only muddling through. It may even be true that the condition of our democracy might even be a bit worse than it has been in times past. But other generations surely had their own muddling. And if that is true, then why fret about it? Is there really anything that different about our contemporary politics, or is the concern of mine and others just another manifestation of our self-importance? I think there is reason for fretting. And I want to argue that changes over the past generation have made these realities more important and more dangerous. As a result, our democracy is more imperiled now than it has been in the recent memory. That is the subject of the next two chapters.

NOTES

1. Sherif, et al., *Intergroup Conflict and Cooperation*, 206.
2. Ibid., 139.
3. Ibid.
4. Berreby, *Us and Them*, 223.
5. Green, *Moral Tribes*, 334.
6. See Tuschman, *Our Political Nature*, 31-32. See also e.g., Mooney, *The Republican Brain*.
7. Cohen, "Party Over Policy," 811.
8. Ibid., 819.
9. Ibid.
10. Munro, Lasane, and Leary, "Political Partisan Prejudice," 2442.
11. Ibid., 2444.
12. Ibid., 2443.
13. Westen, et al., "Neural bases of motivated reasoning," 1954.
14. Westen, *The Political Brain*, xiii.
15. Ibid., 59.
16. Ibid., xiv.
17. Westen, et al., "Neural bases of motivated reasoning," 1956.
18. Sullivan, "Here Comes the Groom."

Chapter Five

Partisan Infotainment: A New Business Model for the New Media

Shortly after President Obama was reelected in 2012, military expert Tom Ricks appeared on Fox News to discuss the recent attack on the American consulate in Benghazi. Here is the entire transcript of that interview. [1]

> JON SCOTT (co-host): Pressure mounting on the Obama administration over its response to the deadly attack on our consulate in Benghazi, as [Fox News correspondent] Catherine Herridge reported just minutes ago. Several top GOP lawmakers are backing off their criticism of U.N. Ambassador Susan Rice, instead focusing on the White House. Two senators even expressing concerns about a possible White House cover-up. Let's talk about it with Tom Ricks. He is author of *The Generals*. He has spent decades covering our military. He joins us now.
> Senator John McCain said in the past he would block any attempt to nominate Susan Rice to become U.N.—I'm sorry, Secretary of State. She's currently the U.N. ambassador. He seems to be backing away from that. What do you make of it?
> RICKS: I think that Benghazi generally was hyped, by this network especially, and that now that the campaign is over, I think he's backing off a little bit. They're not going to stop Susan Rice from being secretary of state.
> SCOTT: When you have four people dead, including the first dead U.N. ambassador—U.S. ambassador in more than 30 years, how do you call that hype?
> RICKS: How many security contractors died in Iraq, do you know?
> SCOTT: I don't.
> RICKS: No. Nobody does, because nobody cared. We know that several hundred died, but there was never an official count done of security contractors dead in Iraq. So when I see this focus on what was essentially a small firefight, I think, number one, I've covered a lot of firefights. It's impossible to figure out what happens in them sometimes. And second, I think that the emphasis on

Benghazi has been extremely political, partly because Fox was operating as a
wing of Republican Party.
SCOTT: All right. Tom Ricks, thanks very much for joining us today.
RICKS: You're welcome.

This "interview" consisted of two questions (unless you count the question
that Ricks asked Scott). No doubt both parties expected things to go longer,
(Ricks said that he was told that it would likely last about three minutes) but
once Mr. Ricks's opinion about the partisan dimension of Fox News became
clear, the interview was abruptly ended.

Lest you dismiss Ricks's assessment as merely the product of his own
partisanship, note that shortly after this exchange, Washington Post media
critic Melinda Henneberfer reported that Ricks had also received an invitation to appear on MSNBC. Ricks recounted: "MSNBC invited me, but I said,
'You're just like Fox, but not as good at it.' They wrote back and said,
'Thank you for your candor.'"[2]

Ricks explained himself this way: "Fox really seems to sell outrage as its
product, and MSNBC doesn't as much. But they both seem to me to be
running political campaigns almost more than they are running news networks. So I don't particularly like either."[3] For Ricks, both networks are
similar—if not similarly effective—in that they operate in service of partisan
politics. What's more, he believes that this service overrides any commitment to an objective accounting of what happened and why it matters. That is
a fairly damning claim, to be sure, but it is relevant to note that neither
network chose to challenge Ricks's contention. Fox yanked him off the air
rather than contest his assertion. (They later claimed that Ricks had "ignored
the question" and "that his goal had been to draw attention to himself.")[4]
MSNBC chose simply to withdraw their invitation and send him on his way.

OBJECTIVITY: THE OLD BUSINESS MODEL

In 1980, the combined viewership for the evening newscasts of the "big
three" broadcast networks was about 52 million. That is certainly a large
number, but consider that in 1980 the total U.S. population was 226 million.
That means on any given weekday, almost one fourth of all Americans (23
percent), were watching one of the big three nightly newscasts. With an
audience so vast, and with two other networks the only competition, captur-
ing that market required that all three offer news programming that could
appeal to everybody. The network news shows therefore strove to present an
image that was classy yet bland, professional yet friendly, and, ostensibly at
least, unbiased, objective, and nonpartisan.

Of course, this model fit with more than just market realities. From 1949
until 1987, the Federal Communications Commission enforced "the fairness

doctrine," holding that all stations broadcasting on public airwaves—including the three television networks and their affiliates—present both sides on matters of public import. This period of almost four decades corresponds very well to what was perhaps the high water mark for objectivity in American news. In the words of Michael Schudson and Susan E. Tifft, "As the country entered the postwar era, objectively was universally acknowledged to be the spine of the journalist's moral code."[5] A few questioned their ability to achieve such a high standard, but all three networks professed a desire to live up to it and most Americans trusted that they were doing so.

Walter Cronkite, anchor for CBS news for almost two decades, regularly polled as the most trusted man in America. And he took that title very seriously. In a fairly typical display of his scrupulousness, when he would end the broadcast with commentary, he would not use his standard sign off: "And that's the way it is." Reporting the news both could and should claim such a level of objectivity, but opinion—Cronkite's or anybody else's—should not. David Brinkley, on NBC, was known for his restrained wit, but he saw the Huntley and Brinkley Report as even more committed to balanced, rigorous journalism. Brinkley said, "I suspect we cover more of the important dull news than Cronkite does."[6]

This conscientiousness no doubt appears quaint to some, an outright lie to others. But by anybody's account, contemporary journalism is certainly different. With the rise of cable and later satellite television, the options for television news and entertainment suddenly expanded exponentially. The 1984 Cable Act changed the regulatory climate, leading to enormous investments in infrastructure and an explosion in new programming. Direct Broadcast Satellite (DBS) to home consumers began in the early 1990s, further expanding both options and availability. As a result of these new delivery systems, the average number of channels per home went from 7.1 in 1970 to 71.2 in 2001.[7] Only a handful of these new channels were solely devoted to news, but all of them were seeking some sliver of the same audience.

About this same time, during the late 1970s and into the '80s, AM radio stations began to lose market share as music listeners migrated to the FM band and its better sound quality. Over time, this migration became extreme, and station owners were desperate for new programming. Rush Limbaugh began his talk radio show in Sacramento, California in 1984. His show cost very little to produce and the absence of high fidelity was not an issue. More importantly, his bombastic, derisive attack of liberal politicians and policies got great ratings. Three years later, in 1987, the Federal Communications Commission withdrew the Fairness Doctrine, which meant anyone with a broadcast license was no longer required to present both sides on matters of public import. This allowed Limbaugh (and anyone else) to say whatever they wanted without fear of constraint or demands for equal time. Only four years after that withdrawal, Rush Limbaugh was the most syndicated radio program in the country. By 1995, there were over 1,000 talk-radio programs, most of which were eager to cash in with a very similar market model. [8]

The expansion of the internet is a similar, if more recent story. As late as 1997, the rate of internet use in the developed world was about 11 percent (Google was not even founded until 1998). Fifteen years later, that rate was estimated at 74 percent. In that same time period, the number of websites has gone from roughly 100,000 to well over 200,000,000. As a result, people can now choose from countless outlets for news, video and commentary. They also have a heretofore unimaginable opportunity to create and present their own. The number of blogs in the United States is over 30 million, and tens of thousands of new ones are created every day. On YouTube, which only began operation in 2005, videos are downloaded at the rate of well over one hour of video every second of every day. In fact, more video is uploaded to YouTube in one month than the three major U.S. networks created in sixty years. [9] Twitter, which is now routinely used by most politicians, campaigns and pundits, has only been in operation since 2007; in 2012—five years later—Twitter accounts moved past the 1 billion mark.

All these changes are obvious to anyone old enough to have lived through them, as is their impact. In the span of little more than a generation, technology has completely transformed the marketplace for news and information.

Of course, not everything has changed. Network news shows still have comparatively massive audiences—on average 25 million—though most watchers are older (actually, a lot older). The Associated Press (another stalwart member of the old media) continues to insist that employees refrain from political contributions. And while news on the web is a recent phenomenon, many of the most visited news websites represent more traditional venues (e.g., New York Times, Reuters, ABC News). Most importantly, though, journalism was and remains a business. Now, no less than in 1980, news shows are driven to make a profit, and there remains a direct relationship between numbers of viewers, readers or listeners and the rates programs can charge for advertising. TV and radio shows want ratings. Websites want clicks. And tweeters want followers.

But because of all this technological change, the prospects for making money have changed, as well. Journalism is different because the market is different. Indeed, changes in the former are driven by the latter: "Since market forces have played the most decisive role in transforming the delivery of the news, the history of the American press from the 1970s to the present is economic history." [10] Whereas the former market was vast and constrained all competitors to at least strive for objectivity, the current market is so fragmented that no one can hope to capture even a significant portion of it. News outlets now have to be content to find a small fraction of the aggregate number of viewers. In the words of communications scholar Matthew Baum,

The so-called new media, by which I refer primarily to cable news channels and the Internet but also to political talk radio, differ in important ways from their traditional media cousins. Most notably, nearly all such outlets self-consciously seek to appeal to relatively narrow, and hence more loyal, niches of the public. Rather than seek to be all things to all people—as the major networks did during their heyday—new media outlets try to provide a product that more closely fits the preferences of a particular subset of the public. [11]

In previous chapters, I have described some features of human behavior that Reinhold Niebuhr presented as sin and science understands to be the product of neurological evolution. Those inclinations can be quickly summarized: We human beings are innately disposed to see ourselves and the groups we belong to as superior. Anybody who doesn't agree with us is wrong, biased, stupid, and/or immoral. However, to a degree that we cannot possibly comprehend, none of us is immune to vanity, error or bias. Finally, all of us fight anxiety by lying to ourselves and by ignoring or discrediting anything that conflicts with our beliefs. My purpose in this chapter is to consider how these innate inclinations, sin or motivated reasoning as you wish, are impacted by the new media and the accompanying marketing realities.

PARTISAN INFOTAINMENT

Now to say these features are innate is to say that there is nothing dramatically new about them. Therefore it need not delay us to note that the history of journalism in America is filled with virulent partisanship and that any commitment to objectivity was a relatively recent development—say the last 75 years or so. [12] It is also true that for all the talk about "the Big Sort," people in the past manifested much the same desire (if not the same ability) to develop and maintain connections with those who are like them: including with those who think and believe the same things they do. [13] After a famous paper regarding the 1940 election, one of the first empirical studies of its kind, the authors concluded that "a person thinks, politically, as he is socially. Social characteristics determine political preference." [14] Seen in this light, much that characterizes the new media—chat groups, websites and talk radio, for example—are just new opportunities to manifest these same inclinations. What *is* different about the contemporary media climate is that new technologies and the vast expanse of options facilitate these natural inclinations in ways that were heretofore unavailable, even unimaginable. In this new media market, producers must find a way to create and maintain a loyal niche audience. For those concerned with politics, that most frequently means presenting news and commentary in a way that confirms our opinions and our beliefs and thus our high opinions of ourselves, and which helps us simultaneously avoid, dismiss, denounce, or ridicule any information or point of view that might contradict with those beliefs and opinions.[15]

Consider a day in the life of a partisan media consumer. A conservative wakes up in the morning and turns on *Fox and Friends*. During the day, he checks out tweets from his favorite Republican commentators and listens to Rush Limbaugh over the lunch hour. At home, he goes to websites like *Redstate* and *Townhall*, vents his spleen at blogs like *Hotair*, and again checks in with Fox to watch The O'Reilly Factor and Sean Hannity. The pattern is similar for Liberals, though perhaps less intense. While liberals have a strong aversion to Fox, they have only moderate loyalty to CNN or MSNBC. (So they are at least sure about what they will *not* watch.)[16] It is also true that Air America, the liberal effort to get in on the talk radio game, died out in 2010.[17] A few liberal voices remain on the radio, but their audience is a fraction of those on the right. But liberals are just as likely to visit liberal websites, follow liberal tweeters, and many end the day watching either MSNBC pundits like Lawrence O'Donnell and Rachel Maddow, or, alternatively, *The Daily Show* and *The Colbert Report*, both of which were (at least until recently) very funny and likewise offer viewers comforting confirmation of the Left's superiority.

Partisan news outlets may or may not profess objectivity (with brass that would make Orwell blush, the motto of Fox News is "fair and balanced"), but the reality is that the selection and presentation of news on the part of Fox News, MSNBC and other outlets manifests a clear partisan bias. Partisan news outlets are far more likely to select and emphasize stories that support their ideological slant, or that make their party look good and the other one look bad. Content analyses of Fox News demonstrate that they are far more supportive of conservative and Republican interests in their coverage of issues and events.[18] Likewise, during the 2008 presidential campaign, MSNBC was more likely to run negative stories about Republican candidate John McCain and less likely to run negative stories about Democratic nominee Barack Obama.[19] A similar bi-partisan effect can be found among websites as well. "Daily Kos on the left and Free Republic and Fox News on the right demonstrate clear and strong preferences for news stories that benefit the part most closely associated with their own ideological orientation."[20]

In the new media marketplace, throughout the day and regardless of the venue they choose, partisans now have the opportunity to hear news and commentary that conform to what they already think. And in most cases that is precisely the option they choose. Republicans are far more likely to watch Fox News and Democrats, MSNBC. Talk radio listeners tend to choose radio programs that correspond to their politics. And "those accessing liberal Web sites nearly universally identified as liberal democrats and those accessing conservative Web sites nearly universally identified as conservative Republicans."[21] What's more, these sources support and echo each other. The Wall

Street Journal rounds up editors for the weekly "Journal Edition Report" on Fox News. Ed Schultz has a talk radio show as well as an evening talk show on MSNBC. And everyone has their own website, all of which are far more likely to link to other sites that present a similar point of view. It is true that many partisans also avail themselves of more mainstream media options,[22] but all day every day, Republicans and Democrats are now able to surround themselves comfortably in a cocoon of partisan unanimity. And for many that is the choice they make. In her study, *Niche News*, Natalie Jomini Stroud concludes, "It doesn't matter whether I analyze the use of newspapers, radio, cable television, or the Internet; political leanings are related to media selections."[23]

Unanimity is also reflected in what these consumers hear and what they do not hear. These same partisan choices allow consumers to avoid the discomfort that comes from hearing opinions that conflict with their own. Partisans turn on Fox News secure in the knowledge that they will not hear a substantive accounting of the overwhelming science behind climate change. MSNBC regulars would be equally surprised to hear a report documenting increased health care costs associated with the Affordable Care Act. Reports like these would run counter to the beliefs and expectations of most viewers, causing them discomfort (and no doubt some confusion). Network executives are fully aware of this, and they know that such an experience risks consumer loyalty.

Of course, this does not mean that the alternative position is not presented; it most certainly is. In some cases, the entertainment value stems directly from contention between competing views. Bill O'Reilly, host of *The O'Reilly Factor* on Fox News: "If a radio producer can find someone who eggs on conservative listeners to spout off and prods liberals into shouting back, he's got a hit show. The best host is the guy or gal who can get the most listeners extremely annoyed—over and over and over again." But sometimes loyal consumers listen to competing views secure in the knowledge that there is no threat of discomfort. On the contrary, such presentations offer the consumer yet another chance to confirm that they are on the right side. The other side is presented along with counter arguments and talking points which confirm to the consumer that the other side is indeed wrong and not to be taken seriously. Alternatively, the new media paints the other side as worthy of derision. Rush Limbaugh is of course the master at this form of argument: "Those who differ with Limbaugh are not portrayed as offering reasoned alternatives. They are instead operating from a playbook with not many pages. At worst they are deranged, suffering from mental illness, nuts or wacko."[24] Because this pattern conforms very well to our conscious and unconscious desires, it is therefore also extremely effective at attracting and sustaining a niche audience.

This model of conflict as confirmation is not confined to the AM radio dial; it has become dominant throughout the new media. When his *Countdown* was the highest rated show on MSNBC, Keith Olbermann used to regularly present the "Worst Person in the World." Rarely was that epithet a fair accounting of the person in question (the *worst* person in the world covers a lot of ground), and almost as rarely was the person associated with the left side of American politics. Jon Scott, who conducted the world's shortest interview with Tom Ricks, hosts the Fox Network's show *News Watch*. This show identifies and laments evidence of "mainstream media bias." His year-end show in December of 2012 presented year-end awards for media bias including such categories of "Obamagasm" and "The Audacity of Dopes." (Not incidentally, in both cases the "winners" were from MSNBC. MSNBC and Fox News frequently use the other to demonstrate the irrationality and stridence of the other side. Theirs is a symbiotic relationship.)

As for bloggers, Cass Sunstein notes that "many bloggers are linking to like-minded others—and that when they link to opinions that diverge from their own, it is often to cast ridicule and scorn on them."[25] Comments on these partisan websites are encouraged, but only if they conform to a strong set of shared presuppositions. Anyone whose opinions run counter to the prevailing tide is referred to as a "troll." The term conveys the idea that such views undermine the fellow feeling that such forums produce.

Sarah Sobeiraj and Jeffrey M. Berry tried to quantify these features of strident attacks of the other side. They designate all varieties of these attacks as "outrage." Their definition:

> a particular form of political discourse involving efforts to provoke visceral responses (e.g., anger, righteousness, fear, moral indignation) from the audience through the use of overgeneralizations, sensationalism, misleading or patently inaccurate information, ad hominen attacks, and partial truths about opponents.[26]

In sum, outrage is "incivility writ large." For a ten-week period in 2009, the researchers reviewed the content of selected examples from both ends of the spectrum, as well as more mainstream media. They found that in the partisan media 100 percent of TV shows, 98.8 percent of talk radio programs, and "only" 82.8 percent of blog posts "contained at least one outrage incident."[27] These numbers are dramatic, to be sure. But I suspect for most, they only confirm what we already know: that regardless of the venue or the partisan point of view, outrage—the idea that the other side is not only wrong, but stupid, irrational, and evil—is now both ubiquitous, chronic, and lucrative.

Less apparent, perhaps, but just as effective, the new media seeks to give consumers the comfort that comes from knowing that they are members in the "in" group. People choose media outlets based on the expectation that they will hear confirmation that they are on the same side as the presenters, members in good standing, just like the Rattlers and Eagles.[28] On the right, listeners are regularly reminded that they are the real American patriots or the real Christians. On the left, people expect to hear confirmation that they are the ones who understand and respect science and who really care about others. Likewise, just as with the boys in Oklahoma, to attach superiority to my group's beliefs and ways of doing things is necessarily to denigrate any group that thinks or behaves differently. Members of a group naturally exaggerate their differences with out-groups, and use language that identifies members of out-groups to be less human than those in the in-group.[29] Therefore, listeners also expect to hear that those who think and believe differently are outsiders, with all the moral opprobrium that attaches thereto. Their beliefs are not merely different; they are inferior. Their actions and desires are not merely incorrect, they are beyond the pale. They threaten to destroy all that is good and true in our society and they must be stopped.

Again, Limbaugh is the master. *Us and Them*, a book I referenced in chapter 4, addresses the natural human inclination to distinguish between those who are in my group and those who are not, and, accordingly, to laud the former and loathe the latter. David Berreby includes an analysis of Rush Limbaugh not so much to criticize the host, but to demonstrate how stigmatizing language creates a clear moral distinction between those inside the group, and those outside:

> Here, for example, is Rush Limbaugh, the talk-radio star, stigmatizing Iraqis who were abused by U.S. troops. I've marked the appearances, in this transcript from 2004, of the coded cues: "They're the ones who are sick. [Diseased] They're the ones who are perverted. [Don't know how to behave] They are the ones who are dangerous. [Help Enemies] They are the ones who are subhuman. [Not Human] They are the ones who are human debris [Filth], not the United States of America, and not our soldiers and not our prison guards."[30]

Limbaugh's audience, who he regularly refers to as "my friends," is repeatedly reminded that they are the hardworking, upstanding moral core of our country, the normal, decent, and intelligent human beings. Those who think otherwise are not, and they therefore deserve all the derision that he gives them.

Partisan news shows appeal to insider language to make sure regulars feel connected to the moderator and part of the in crowd. Ed Schultz begins each show with the tag line: "Let's get to work." Rush Limbaugh followers call themselves "dittoheads." They buy ties and t-shirts from Limbaugh's website not simply to further line his pockets, but to identify themselves to other devotees. Limbaugh's "friends" language is also copied by other outlets.

Fox's morning news show even includes the word in its title: *Fox and Friends*. (If this does not strike you as unusual, compare it to the name of any other morning talk show that you know.) Of course all of us want to be liked, and all of us want to be part of the in group. So we derive pleasure every time we hear these kinds of associations. Fostering this pleasure, making sure that listeners know that they are part of us, part of the in group, is another effective way to maintain a loyal and profitable following in the world of the new media.

Talk Radio and partisan news and commentary are often referred to as examples of infotainment—a broad and usually derogatory term that refers to the blending of news and entertainment, with the emphasis on the latter. There are any number of examples that do not concern me here, including so-called soft news shows or segments. But considering the new partisan media, psychology, neuroscience and group theory makes clear that the entertainment value of this kind of presentation—call it partisan infotainment—is found precisely here: in the pleasure that comes from confirmation. For those on the right, Rush Limbaugh and lesser lights are extremely good at giving them confirmation of their superiority. That confirmation feels good, even in ways that are beyond our conscious awareness. That is why we seek it out, and why, once we find it, we remain loyal viewers and listeners.

GIVING PEOPLE WHAT THEY WANT

In the contemporary media market, where options are virtually endless, this model of finding a niche audience and confirming their innate dispositions has become dominant if not ubiquitous. While some may point to some elaborate left-wing or right-wing conspiracy, the more plausible explanation is that journalism is and remains a business, and the fact is that infotainment can make the owners a lot of money. In 2002, Fox News Channel had total revenue of 281 million, while CNN's was 814 million. By 2009, Fox News became the revenue leader. In 2011, CNN total revenue was 1.294 billion, an increase from 2002 of almost 59 percent. In the same year, Fox news made 1.6 billion, increasing its revenue over the same period by 569 percent. (It should be said that since 2011 Fox has seen a slight decline in viewership.)

And MSNBC? The network began as joint venture between NBC and Microsoft in 1996. The network struggled for viewers for many years, with ratings well below Fox and CNN. However, by 2006, the network had begun to turn things around.

> While MSNBC isn't anywhere near the level of the other two channels, its estimates continue to be optimistic. Kagan [a media research firm] expected profits at MSNBC to rise to $64 million in 2006—a leap of almost 400% from the $13 million it made the previous year, and a sign that the news channel

will, at long last, become a contributor of some value to NBC television's bottom line.[31]

Not coincidentally, that same report noted that "MSNBC put new personnel in charge of the news channel, which seems to have hit upon a new style and brand—politics and opinion." The network had hired Keith Olbermann to go up directly against Fox News Channel's Bill O'Reilly in 2003. By 2007, the direction of MSNBC as a liberal alternative to Fox was well established. And this direction has proved to be very profitable. By 2010 MSNBC and its new model surpassed CNN with the second highest viewership and total revenues were close to 400 million. In sum, the Fox News model is extremely lucrative; that is why MSNBC adopted it, and that is why MSNBC is now making a lot of money as well.[32]

Talk Radio is equally profitable, especially when you are on top. Limbaugh's weekly audience has been estimated at between 14 and 20 million, and whatever it is, no one else comes close.[33] In 2008, Limbaugh signed a contract extension with Clear Communications through 2016 that is worth over $400 million. When you have Limbaugh's audience, you are worth this kind of money. But that is the point. Limbaugh's model is successful precisely because he is able to create and sustain a very large audience despite a cacophony of other options. And he is able to do that because he is such a good entertainer. Here are Limbaugh's own words on the matter:

> "Do you know what bought me all this?" he asked, waving his hand in the general direction of his prosperity. "Not my political ideas. Conservatism didn't buy this house. First and foremost I'm a businessman. My first goal is to attract the largest possible audience so I can charge confiscatory ad rates. I happen to have great entertainment skills, but that enables me to sell airtime."[34]

Limbaugh is successful because he is so adept at giving conservatives exactly what they want to hear: that their opinions are correct, that they are part of the right crowd, that they are better and smarter and more moral than those who think otherwise, that their opponents are either evil or fools, and that their actions and beliefs threaten to destroy the country. That confirmation is what makes Limbaugh and others entertaining. In the new media, that is the best way to find and secure an audience and make money, and the incredible success of Fox News and Limbaugh accounts for the model's ubiquity.[35]

SO WHAT?

I have tried to show that people now receive news and information in ways that confirm their high opinion of themselves, their groups and their beliefs.

But it is fair to ask why these changes are important. It is no doubt true that the web has dramatically altered the journalism landscape. No doubt people fretted about the impact of technological changes like the telegraph, as well. Why isn't this just more of the same? Too, anybody who knows anything about the brain knows that we are all constantly on the lookout for feel-good chemicals. A large subset of the American population happens to choose partisan infotainment as their supplier. Others like roller coasters or dark chocolate or whatever. What difference, really, does this make? I want to argue that these changes *are* important. In fact, they risk undermining, and in Niebuhr's words *imperiling*, our democracy. The next chapter will seek to make that case.

NOTES

1. Rudman, "On Fox, Journalist Tom Ricks Accuses The Network Of Operating As A Wing Of The Republican Party."
2. Henneberfer, "Tom Ricks to MSNBC: You're just like Fox, only not as good at it."
3. Shapiro, "Tom-Ricks: Fox News Statement About My Apology Is 'Horseshit.'"
4. Ibid.
5. Schudson and Tifft, "American Journalism in Historical Perspective," 27.
6. Whitworth, "Chet Huntley and David Brinkley," 59.
7. Hamilton, "The Market and the Media," 352.
8. Streitmatter, *Mightier than the Sword,* 234.
9. Bullas, "35 Mind Numbing YouTube Facts."
10. Hamilton, "The Market and the Media," 351
11. Baum, "Red State, Blue State, Flu State," 1024.
12. See, e.g., Schudson, *Discovering the News.*
13. Bishop with Cushing, *The Big Sort.* To be sure, it is likely the case that for a variety of reasons, people are both more mobile and more able to identify towns and neighborhoods that suit themselves socially and politically. As we have seen, partisanship and social identity are highly associated. My point here is simply that people's desire to associate with others like themselves was as operative then as it is now.
14. Lazarfeld, Berelson, and Gaudet, *The People's Choice,* 27.
15. There are other ways of creating a niche news market, of course. Univision for example largely avoids partisan bias, but it is explicitly pro-Latino in its coverage. The Christian Broadcasting Network, on the other hand, appeals to Evangelical Christians, most of whom are politically conservative.
16. Stroud, *Niche News,* 54: "Strong Republicans are far more likely to watch Fox News. Strong liberal Democrats are far more likely to watch CNN or MSNBC."
17. Of course, conservatives frequently assert that National Public Radio is the functional equivalent, the partisan doppelganger as it were, to talk radio, but this claim simply does not bear scrutiny.
18. Pew Research Center's Journalism Project Staff, "The Invisible Primary—Invisible No Longer."
19. Ibid.
20. Baum and Groeling, "New Media and the Polarization of American Political Discourse," 359.
21. Stroud, *Niche News,* 59.
22. See Jamieson and Cappella, *Echo Chamber,* 240: "We are not arguing, however, that conservatives have barricaded themselves within the conservative media establishment, they

demonstrably have not. Consumption of mainstream print remains high, for example, among Limbaugh listeners."

23. Stroud, *Niche News*, 21.

24. Jamieson and Joseph Cappella, *Echo Chamber*, 186.

25. Sunstein, *Republic.com 2.0*, 148.

26. Sobeiraj and Berry, "From Incivility to Outrage," 20.

27. Ibid., 27. Recall at the beginning of this chapter, Tom Ricks's comment: "Fox really seems to sell outrage as its product."

28. See chapter 4.

29. See Berreby, *Us and Them.*

30. Ibid., 239. David Livingstone Smith references the same quote for the same illustrative purpose in his book *Less Than Human: Why We Demean, Enslave, and Exterminate Others* (New York: St. Martin's Press, 2011), 22.

31. The Project for Excellence in Journalism, *State of the News Media, 2007: An Annual Report on American Journalism.*

32. The financial story of MSNBC thus confirms the analysis of Mann and Ornstein: "The Fox business model is based on securing and maintaining a loyal audience of conservatives eager to hear the same message presented in different ways by different hosts over and over again. MSNBC has adopted the Fox model on the left, in a milder form (especially in the daytime)." Mann and Ornstein, *Even worse than it looks,* 61.

33. Chafets, "Late-Period Limbaugh."

34. Ibid.

35. Of course, compared to talk radio, websites are comparatively new, and many continue to struggle to find a sustainable business stream. But it was lost on no one that in 2011, the left-leaning website *Huffington Post* sold for 400 million dollars.

Chapter Six

Partisan Infotainment and Democracy: Not All Bad, Not Half Good

Defenders of partisan infotainment claim that the former commitment to objectivity and fairness was really a make-no-waves model, bland pabulum that made boring a virtue. It only flourished because there were no alternatives. Once people had options, the old model simply could not compete. The market has spoken. What's more, whatever you might remember about Walter Cronkite and his ilk, their objectivity was never more than skin deep. In fact, the former media model betrayed a distinct liberal bias that was as pernicious as it was clandestine. (For that matter, they would say much the same about the so-called mainstream media today.) The new model simply evens the playing field, plus it is honest enough to put its ideology out front. Most relevantly, they say, concerns about the new media are just so much elitist hand-wringing. Partisan infotainment is not undermining democracy. On the contrary, it is creating a stronger, more engaged democracy.

All the other claims aside, the case regarding the new media and democracy is fairly straightforward. The extension of journalistic and editorial tools like YouTube videos and tweets into the hands of ordinary citizens has surely democratized the media and opened access to forms of political power. Cynics would argue that the end result of this democratization has been lots of cat videos. But it has also led to profound and heretofore unimaginable events like the Arab Spring. Ordinary citizens in America of all persuasions have likewise taken advantage of these tools. Political speeches routinely end up on YouTube, even when the politician would rather they had not. And political commentary requires nothing more than a new web address.

The rise of entertaining news shows also correlates with an increased interest in politics and news as well as increased political activity.

Americans today are more interested in politics, better informed about public
affairs, and more politically active than at any time during the past half century. On every one of these measures, including interviewers' assessments of the
respondents; level of political information, Americans during the first decade
of the twenty-first century scored higher than their counterparts in the 1960s,
1970s, 1980s and 1990s.[1]

Whatever other variables might be involved, there can be no doubt that this
development is directly related to the rise of the new media. Indeed, Natalie
Stroud concludes that consumers of partisan infotainment are more likely to
participate in a campaign by attending a political rally, arguing politics, and
the like.[2]

From what has come before, this ought not to sound terribly surprising. If
you regularly consume programming that tells you that the actions of the
other side are a mortal threat to the nation, it is fairly predictable that you will
strive to ensure that they are unsuccessful. In fact, even if one stipulates that
partisan infotainment has led to a more engaged body politic, there is a good
deal more to the story. Many of the features most closely associated with
partisan infotainment—limited and contrived exposure to counter arguments,
a strong group identity (who is in and who is out), and an affirmation of the
consumer's innate biases—are conducive to a whole host of behaviors and
beliefs that are not at all good for democracy. In this chapter, I want to
account for how the new media's business model of partisan infotainment
directly leads to these damaging outcomes.

RED AND BLUE COLORADO

If you know the state of Colorado at all, you know that Colorado Springs and
Boulder are about as different as two cities can get. Colorado Springs is
home to the United States Air Force Academy, the U.S. Olympic Training
Center, and Focus on the Family (a nonprofit Christian organization advocat-
ing "traditional family values"). It is also a very conservative place. Here is a
description from the Colorado Gazette, a local and very partisan newspaper.

> Conservatives and libertarians, welcome to Colorado Springs. This is your
> home away from home. The local culture is overwhelmingly pro-military, pro-
> gun, pro-religion, pro-family, pro-business and pro-life. We elected the most
> conservative mayor in the country. City and state laws prevent unrestrained
> government spending and force politicians to ask taxpayers for new taxes.
> Yes, it is nirvana.[3]

Boulder, on the other hand, is *not* conservative nirvana. Home to the University of Colorado, it is one of the most educated and affluent communities in
America. It is also a town known for environmental consciousness, tie-dye,

vegan restaurants, and dispensaries of marijuana. The strong partisan leanings of both communities are part of the reason that Colorado, in the aggregate, is understood to be a "purple" state.

In what was perhaps the easiest selection process ever, David Schkade, Reid Hastie, and Cass Sunstein identified 60 individuals from both communities with partisan leanings commensurate with type: liberals from Boulder and conservatives from Colorado Springs. The individuals were given surveys about their personal beliefs and then set up in five "red state" groups and five "blue state" groups. Each group was asked to "explore three of the most controversial issues of the day: affirmative action, an international treaty to control global warming, and civil unions for same-sex couples." In the brief discussion time allotted—only about 15 minutes—each group was asked to consider the facts and discuss their opinions. After the conversations were completed, each individual was again asked to complete a survey about their personal beliefs.

So what happened? Sunstein recounts that "In almost every group, members ended up with more extreme positions after they spoke with one another."[4] Regarding each of the three issues—civil unions, global warming, and affirmative action—discussion left both liberals and conservatives with stronger opinions than they had when they started. In other words, results from the second set of surveys demonstrated that the group discussion (the only intervening variable) resulted in individual opinions on both sides becoming more extreme, more polarized than they were before the conversation took place. And that's not all: "Aside from increasing extremism, the experiment also had an independent effect: it made both liberal groups and conservative groups significantly more homogeneous—and thus squelched diversity."[5] Again, the groups were put together based on their common partisan identities. There wasn't a lot of diversity to begin with. But whatever diversity was present in the initial surveys was greatly diminished. And again, that diminishment was solely a result of the conversation.

For researchers in group theory, the Colorado results are to be expected. Indeed, Sunstein argues that if the group in question is fairly unified in its opinions, and there is little to no input from those with contradictory opinions, "group polarization will be the inevitable consequence."[6] The reason for this result has nothing to do with which partisan group is represented, or what issue they are discussing, or even the background of those taking part in the discussion. (Sunstein recounts research that shows that three judge panels who share the same partisan identity are subject to the same effect.)[7] Nor for that matter does the conversation in question have to be face to face. A number of studies have shown evidence of polarization when the meeting in question was in Internet chat rooms, or via Twitter.[8] None of these variables affect the result. That is, none of them make polarization less likely. Why? Because none of them alter the principal condition that drives the group toward polarization. Namely, our natural inclination to be liked, to be counted among the in group, and to have our beliefs affirmed.

When we are in a group, however it began and whatever the context, we want the members of the group to like us. Membership is a kind of possession, just like our beliefs. And as with our beliefs, the success of our group is part of our fight against anxiety. Therefore, we are looking for every piece of evidence both that ours is the better group, and that we are members in good standing. When we take part in a discussion, we come to learn about the views of the members of the group. Because we want to be liked, we tend to be quiet about views that appear outside the prevailing view, and we modify our own views based on what we come to learn about the views of others. As Sunstein has it, "once we hear what others believe, some of us will adjust our positions at least slightly in the direction of the dominant position, to hold onto our preserved self-presentation."[9] We may do this consciously; we may not; we might believe that this was our opinion all along. But regardless, the combination of all these individual inclinations brings everyone to a very homogenous, very polarized position. The evaporation of diversity and the movement of the group to the extreme is the result of our very human desire for group affirmation.

But why does this process push the group to extremes? What is the connection between our desire to be liked, and the polarization of the group as a whole? Two reasons: First, if we are in a group of like-minded people, most if not all of the evidence and arguments that the group hears will support that position. In the face of this preponderance of evidence, it is natural for people to feel more confident and more extreme in their original position. Second, once we find out where others are on a given issue, we often pursue our desire to be liked by getting out ahead of the pack. And this impetus on the part of many in the group drives the group as a whole to a consensus that is farther from the center, closer to the extreme, than many of the individuals who make up the group would otherwise have been. Of course, neither phenomenon is inevitable. Not all of us are willing to push the envelope. Some of us are wall flowers. On the opposite side of the fence, some of us are so strong willed that we will push our point of view regardless of what the group thinks (think of the movie *Twelve Angry Men*). To be sure, it is not easy to be the outlier. One must be willing to risk one's identity and self-esteem. That is a very strong current, one that most of us are unable or unwilling to swim against. But when your group contains such an outlier, or when you have a group with a lot of wall flowers, polarization will be less pronounced, and may not happen at all. Most of the time, however, this combination of forces makes it likely that a given group will end up more in agreement and closer to the extreme than the individual members were when the conversation started.

Again, this inclination toward polarization has been found in every variety of group and circumstance. Most relevantly, and in contrast to what any partisan would like to believe, Republicans and Democrats are just as likely to manifest this behavior. Still, it is noteworthy that some groups *are* more likely to go farther toward the extreme than others. That is to say, there is one variable, at least, that *does* matter. In chapter 4, I showed that the groups we belong to become part of our identity; by degrees we grow committed to the group and its members. Its beliefs and values become ever more inseparable from our own. This, too, is an innate human drive. And in this case, it is a drive that can enhance the group polarization effect. When, for whatever reason, the group develops a strong group identity, or when the individual members of the group possess a strong and common identity before the group comes into existence, polarization is more likely to be extreme. Sunstein again: "Group polarization will significantly increase if people think of themselves, antecedently or otherwise, as part of a group having a shared identity and a degree of solidarity."[10] This point is intuitive, as well. Imagine our Mustang owner is with a group of fellow aficionados and the topic of the Pontiac GTO comes up. Or imagine a group of NRA or PETA members. In sum, the more a person connects their identity to membership in a given group, the more passionately they claim that membership, and the more that group is associated with the group doing the discussing, the more value that person is likely to attach to being liked by the group, and the more likely that person will be inclined to, so to speak, up the rhetorical ante.

GROUP POLARIZATION THROUGH INFOTAINMENT

It might be objected that this experiment is not at all relevant to the business model outlined in the last chapter. The Colorado experiment involved short, face to face, small group conversation, whereas many examples from partisan infotainment don't involve conversation at all. Rush Limbaugh most often goes it alone, as do, for example, Jon Stewart and Sean Hannity. And even panel discussions on Fox News and MSNBC do not involve the viewer directly. There are precious few examples from the new media that directly conform to what took place in Colorado. On the other hand, all forms of the new media are far more interactive than previous iterations. Rush Limbaugh's show is a call-in show, after all. Bill O'Reilly will often read and respond to texts and emails on the air. And virtually every partisan news show has its own website where responses and conversation are highly encouraged. Conversation might differ from the controlled experiment in Colorado, but conversation is certainly taking place.

More to the point, that conversation is similarly unperturbed by an alternative point of view or problematic information. In the Colorado discussion there was no one to ask about documented impacts of civil unions in the states that allow them or about current federal policy regarding affirmative action. Just so, the conversation in partisan infotainment that takes place both with and without the consumer is most often conducted without any significant input from someone with a different opinion, or, for that matter, anyone with a desire to lay out an objective accounting of the associated facts. Finally, those who watch Fox News or MSNBC, those who listen to talk radio, and those who frequent partisan Internet blogs and chat rooms do indeed come to the group with a strong partisan identity. In fact, the more loyal consumers they are, the more likely they are to engage online, and the more likely they are to identify themselves as strong partisans. And the new media works hard to foster and enhance this feeling of solidarity.

In the last chapter, I showed that the common features of partisan infotainment constitute a business model for the new media. And I showed that that model is extremely successful and therefore diligently duplicated. The central point here is that these same features also account for the model's powerful political effects. That is, the same features that make network producers lots of money are the same features which have created a more engaged electorate. And these same features also account for the fact that we inhabit such an extreme and polarized politics.

MORE THAN HALF BAD

I have noted that while motivated reasoning is a formidable power within our brains, it is not impermeable. Repeated exposure to counterinformation makes it increasingly harder for the brain to discount it. As well, if counter arguments are made by people in our group, and in terms that resonate with our core beliefs, then we are more likely to hear, and less likely to discount the information.

But if none of this happens, we are likely to become more steadfast in our beliefs, and less susceptible to even the possibility of change. If we do not hear information that conflicts with what we believe, we are less likely to feel the discomfort that comes with that conflict—again, that is part of the reason that we chose the media outlets we do. But such limited exposure also means we are less likely to have even the occasion to think critically about our own beliefs. As we become invested in our own epistemological cocoon and find ourselves pushed farther away from the center, we have less occasion to doubt ourselves, to consider the possibility of our own biases, and to suspect that there is important information that we do not know. In fact, regular consumption of partisan infotainment makes us more likely to appeal to bias as a way of dismissing opinions that run counter to our belief structure. It also makes us less likely to see, or rather, more inclined to ignore, any possibility of bias associated with our own group.

Ultimately, this inability to consider the alternative can become so extreme that it extends to not just opinion, but information, that is to say, facts. The more well-protected our partisan identity, the more likely we are to assume that any contradictory information must be wrong. During the 2004 campaign "Limbaugh listeners, more than other Republicans, regard[ed] facts that advantage the Democratic candidate as suspect, while embracing those advanced by the Republican incumbent's campaign."[11] A 2003 survey found that Fox News viewers were more likely than average to have misperceptions about the Iraq War. And the more they watched, the more likely they were to be wrong. More recently, a 2012 survey conducted by Fairleigh Dickinson University's PublicMind Poll found that Fox News viewers were not better informed for their watching. In fact, given a set about questions about domestic politics, someone who watched only Fox News would be expected to answer fewer questions correctly than someone "who didn't watch any news at all." (MSNBC viewers were second worst, only .04 better than the non-viewer.)[12] Now it is true that in 2011, Politifact surveyed the research and concluded that while Fox viewers did not come off particularly well, viewers of "particular Fox shows—such as *The O'Reilly Factor* and Sean Hannity's show—actually score consistently well." This result, however, does not jettison the problem. It stands to reason that any news program that is designed to affirm a pre-established set of beliefs would present something less than the whole story, and much more about the facts that reflect positively on that established point of view. And that means that even when viewers and listeners of that program score well on a test, they would nevertheless have at best an incomplete picture of the political landscape.

In any event, my point is more general. I have argued that the new media is entertaining because it confirms everything we want to be true about ourselves, including the idea that the other side is not just wrong, they are benighted fools, detached from reality. These examples point to the possibility that with respect to partisan infotainment, the latter half of that hybrid frequently overwhelms the former: the drive to entertain is more important than the conveyance of correct, reliable information. Untroubled by alternative information, and pushed sufficiently to the extreme, partisan viewers find it increasingly difficult to evaluate reality outside the context of their own partisan worldview. Channeling Steven Colbert, for such loyal consumers, reality does indeed come to possess a partisan bias. And if that is true, it would certainly account for why compromise has become so hard to achieve. In the end, this partisan-hued reality gives us reason to question our ability to sustain a democracy. For underneath this effect is the pernicious notion that there is no such thing as objectivity, that even the goal is illusory and a sham. It undermines the idea that there are such things as facts—

common to all of us, accessible to all of us, and which must transcend any partisan point of view.

Consider too what polarization does to our views of those who hold these other opinions, that is, those who disagree with us. Again, our group is part of our identity; it is a strategy to combat anxiety. Therefore, our natural inclination is to disrespect anyone who is not in our group. This is almost the inevitable concomitant of our belief that our group is the good, right and successful one. But if we are constantly reminded that we are members of the right side, then we have even less reason to respect anyone who thinks otherwise. Thus confirmation gives us less reason to practice tolerance. Indeed, it makes us more likely to see our opponent as less of a human being and more of an enemy.

Finally, the expression of this kind of vitriol only produces responses in kind. As we have seen, the pull of group identity is strong. If you think of yourself as a Christian, and someone tells you that you are not, or not a good one, the counter-reaction will be extreme. If you are proud to be an American, and someone tells you that you are harming the country, it is hard not to react emotionally. If you consider yourself an intelligent person (and all of us do), and someone implies that your opinions only confirm your ignorance, then it is hard not to take offense at such words. I have noted in chapter 3 that such insults make it virtually impossible to listen to, let alone evaluate the argument you are hearing. But here it is worth considering why this is the case. In each instance, the claim is a direct and serious threat. It communicates that while you might think you are in the group, you are actually an outsider. You have been stigmatized. It is natural to react viscerally to such a claim because stigma is bad for you.

> It shortens their lives, lessens their abilities, and increases the allure of false consolations, like drugs and drink, that do harm. . . . Stigma drives up blood pressure, scrambles sleep, and increases your chances of dying young. . . . the emotions of Us are good for you, and their opposite, the emotions of not-belonging, are literally toxic. A victim experiences that effect as stress, strain, and grief. [13]

Confronted with such a dire set of consequences, it is not surprising that people will react angrily to such an experience. As it was, it will ever be: "Them's fightin' words." The experience of polarization thus almost invites an equally emotional counter-reaction that both confirms and further reinforces the breakdown of society into groups of partisan enmity.

REPUBLICANS ARE BETTER AT IT

In the last chapter, I recounted what Tom Ricks said to MSNBC: "You're just like Fox News. You're just not as good at it." Indeed. Fox News' domination of the cable news audience makes it clear just how good they are at what they do. Just so, his 400 million dollar contract is sufficient reason to believe that no one is as good at partisan talk radio as Rush Limbaugh. But part of what that means is that conservatives are better at creating outrage. In their systematic survey of TV, talk radio, and websites, Sarah Sobeieraj and Jeffrey M. Berry conclude that "the right uses decidedly more outrage speech than the left. Taken as a whole, liberal content is quite nasty in character . . . Conservatives, however, are even nastier."[14] On TV, radio, and on the web, Ricks's judgment is confirmed: both parties do indeed behave in the same way, and use the new media in the same way, but conservatives are better at it.

But because they are, it is fair to at least speculate that they are therefore better at creating polarization, and therefore, also more to blame for the contemporary condition of American politics. At any rate, this speculation certainly appears consistent with the conclusion that Mann and Ornstein come to. Indeed, much within their description will sound familiar:

> the Republican Party, has become an insurgent outlier—ideologically extreme; contemptuous of the inherited social and economic policy regime; scornful of compromise; unpersuaded by conventional understanding of facts, evidence, and science; and dismissive of the legitimacy of its political opposition. When one party moves this far from the center of American politics, it is extremely difficult to enact policies responsive to the country's most pressing challenges.[15]

I have argued that the business model associated with the new media, what I am calling partisan infotainment, has been extremely successful at creating a loyal niche market. I have also argued that in addition to increasing political engagement, this model also increases political polarization. Here, I am claiming that because one side of the partisan divide is so much better at utilizing and expanding this model, they are also better at creating group polarization, and that means they are also more responsible for the many deleterious effects of polarization on our polity. While there is plenty of blame to throw around, any argument for equivalency would not be in keeping with the facts.

PARTISAN INFOTAINMENT AND THE CHILDREN OF LIGHT

I do not want to claim that partisan infotainment is the only variable that accounts for our polarized politics. Alan Abramowitz, author of *The Disappearing Center* believes that political polarization stems from "an ideological realignment" that began with the passage of civil rights legislation and the subsequent decline of the Dixiecrat. The result, Abramowitz says, "has been a growing consistency between issue positions and party identification."[16] Similarly, Bill Bishop argues that polarization stems from the fact that we have sorted ourselves culturally and socially into separate and politically homogeneous communities: one red and the other blue. In chapter 8, I will argue that the contemporary practice of Christianity manifests and exacerbates our culture's extreme polarization. There are surely others worth mentioning. But whatever the import of these and other explanations, I do not see much use in endeavoring to tease out their relative weight. We are in a climate of extreme polarization. We are also live in a new and far more ideological climate for news media, one that shares many salient features with those environments that are known to produce group polarization. It would be extremely unlikely if the former bore an insignificant relationship to the latter.

Regardless, for my purposes, the more salient point is that the changes recounted in the last two chapters explain why aspects of human behavior that are perilous for democratic society can be both endemic and eternal on the one hand, and especially perilous at this particular historical moment. All of us humans are sinful: enamored of ourselves and our righteousness, and all but unable to recognize our own bias. Without constraint, this sinfulness leads us to become Children of Light: zealots convinced of their own superiority and goodness, and inclined to demonize anyone who thinks differently. Whether or not the old media's ostensible commitment to fairness and objectivity served as one of those constraints, it is self-evident that the new media does not. On the contrary, partisan infotainment makes it just that much easier for us to foster and give vent to these tendencies. And the results of that new found opportunity are very much in keeping with Niebuhr's warnings. To repeat: "Democracy's internal peril" "lies in the conflict of various schools and classes of idealists, who profess different ideals but exhibit a common conviction that their own ideals are perfect."[17] The new media has brought us closer to this condition. Partisan infotainment entertains us by allowing us to see ourselves as morally and intellectually superior, and by helping us ignore our own failures and hypocrisy. It makes it very easy for us to see ourselves, our groups and our ideas as, if not perfect, infinitely preferable to those who think otherwise. Just so, we are encouraged to see our opponents as enemies, as less than human, and to ignore and dispute the idea of a good that is common.

Again, note that for Niebuhr, the peril that stemmed from this internal condition was no less dangerous than the external one posed by Nazis and Communists. In a description that has an uneasy ring of familiarity, Niebuhr warns that "Whenever a community faces an issue without any common ground between opposing forces, the resulting social friction may attain the proportions of a civil war."[18]

There is another dimension to this analysis. For Niebuhr, Nazis and Communists were external threats to democracy. They are the Children of Darkness. Ruthless and manipulative, they may act as if they are committed to a vision of the good, but they are really motivated by the quest for power alone. But while this unyielding commitment to their own self-interest makes them evil, they are also wise. They understand how human beings operate, and are therefore better at manipulating people to achieve the ends they want.

I am certain that different figures come to mind, depending on which side of the partisan divide you find yourself. But is there anyone who does not feel a flicker of recognition here when considering the new media? If I am right that partisan infotainment is a business model designed to produce profits in a new era of competition, and if this method is most profitable when it drives consumers toward extremism and polarization—then there is indeed something here reminiscent of Children of Darkness. Media moguls are not Nazis, but it is hard to believe that their pursuit of profit does not sometimes override other considerations. At minimum, the purveyors of that business model clearly understand human nature very well. And it is in their economic interest to make every effort to exploit that knowledge as best as they can. It would be surprising if they did not strive to do so.

It is worth recalling Niebuhr's musing about Henry Ford so many pages ago. After making his case against the company's actions toward its workers, Niebuhr concluded: "It is difficult to determine whether Mr. Ford is simply a shrewd exploiter of a gullible public in his humanitarian pretensions, or whether he suffers from self-deception."[19] Now clearly Niebuhr had his suspicions, but he knew that he could not know the truth and that it was wrong to presume. I have my suspicions as well. But for every shrewd exploiter, I am also sure that there are many purveyors of partisan infotainment who believe every word they say. And it is at least possible that all of them do. None of us can look into the soul of another. And, based on what we know about the brain, we know that even the individuals themselves can't fully know the answer to the question. Too much of what is going on between our ears is beneath our consciousness. But the fact is that this ignorance does not let them or any of us off the hook. Niebuhr says that either Ford is either consciously lying and thus a Child of Darkness, or he is self-deceived, that is, a Child of Light. There is no third option. The same alternatives apply to those associated with partisan infotainment recounted in this chapter and the previous: either they are moral cynics who exploit true believers for every dollar they can get, and who, despite all their protestations, possess not the slightest concern about the effects their actions have on our democracy, or they are as deluded as their loyal consumers about their own virtue, their own intelligence, and their own superiority. Take your pick. Either way, the model is very bad for democracy.

WHAT TO DO

At this point, I have shown that Niebuhr's analysis, buttressed by science, offers a compelling explanation of the democracy's internal peril. And the last two chapters have sought to demonstrate why our current condition is uniquely perilous.

Before moving on, it is incumbent to reflect on the relationship between this peril and partisan infotainment. Fine says that "recognizing and acknowledging our vulnerability to the many common machinations of the brain provides modest scope to guard against them. Some sources of mental contamination, as it has been called, can be sidestepped by simple avoidance."[20] Given that the examples recounted above foster our natural tendencies to self-delusion and self-righteousness, that they help foster within us the inescapable tendency to become Children of Light, it is legitimate to consider partisan infotainment in precisely these terms: as mental contamination. It would therefore be better if Americans on both sides of the partisan aisle were to acknowledge that as with any such contamination, too much partisan infotainment is not a good thing. It makes it harder to be democrat, and thus harder to sustain a democracy. Likewise, it would be better if those who count themselves as democrats first and partisans second would try to avail themselves of news and information resources that genuinely strive for objectivity and a fair-minded presentation of all competing views. Given that some kind of dictatorial fiat is not in the cards, I have little reason to expect that such a thing might actually happen. But without such a change, it is hard to see hope for improvement in our democracy.

As a start, it might help if those consumers who find partisan infotainment so entertaining simply recognize that, in fact, they are being entertained. And that Rush Limbaugh, Bill O'Reilly, Ed Schulz, and a host of others are, no less than Jon Stewart and Steven Colbert, entertainers. They present information in ways that fills our unconscious need for confirmation, and that feels good. If Fine is right, it might help simply to recognize that fact. Recognize, that is, that partisan infotainment is designed to appeal to features within each of our brains. Such a recognition might indeed provide "modest scope to guard against" its worst effects on ourselves and our democracy.

This, too, is probably a vain hope. At any rate, for those of us who claim to be democrats, it would be comforting if there were more on which we could hang our hats. Since Niebuhr's analysis serves as a very plausible account for our current condition, it is therefore worth attending to what he says we need to do about it. That is the task of the second half of this book.

NOTES

1. Abramowitz, *The Disappearing Center*, 19.
2. Stroud, *Niche News*, 124.
3. Laugesen, "Town Hall: Conservatives converge on Springs (poll)."
4. Sunstein, *Republic.com 2.0*, 61.
5. Ibid., 62.
6. Ibid., 66.
7. Main and Walker examined the decisions of federal district court judges. Judges sitting in groups of three were more than twice as likely to take an extreme course of action as the same judges acting alone. See, "Choice shifts and extreme behavior," 215-221.
8. See, e.g., Sarita Yardi and danah boyd, "Dynamic Debates: An analysis of group polarization over time on Twitter," *Bulletin of Science, Technology and Society* 30, 5: (2010), 16-27.
9. Sunstein, *Going to Extremes*, 26-27. See also Abelson, "Beliefs are Like Possessions," 238: "After exposure to a group discussion by like-minded individuals on a controversial issue, most subjects tend to position themselves a notch more extreme than the perceived consensus. It is as though they are saying, 'I agree, and I'm even a little out front of the others.'"
10. Sunstein, *Republic.Com 2.0*, 67.
11. Jamieson and Cappell, *"Echo Chamber,"* 241.
12. It is worth noting that Fox News's response was almost a textbook example of how we dismiss information we do not like. Rather than question the survey's methodology or offer contrasting data, Fox News simply pointed out that Fairleigh Dickenson University had received a low rating by *US News and World Report*. "Considering FDU's undergraduate school is ranked as one of the worst in the country," said the FNC spokesperson, "we suggest the school invest in improving its weak academic program instead of spending money on frivolous polling—their student body does not deserve to be so ill-informed." Only someone predisposed to reject the findings could find that response even remotely persuasive. Paul Bond, "Fox News Slams Professors Who Claimed Its Viewers Were Ill-Informed," *The Hollywood Reporter*, 5/23/2012. http://www.hollywoodreporter.com/news/fox-news-slams-professors-ill-informed-viewers-fairleigh-dickinson-328771.
13. Berreby, *Us and Them*, 257.
14. Sobeiraj and Berry, "From Incivility to Outrage," 30.
15. Mann and Ornstein, *It's Even Worse than it Looks*, xiv.
16. Abramowitz, *The Disappearing Center*, 9, 37. Abramowitz's argument is not far from Lyndon Johnson's prediction with the signing of the Civil Rights Act: "We just delivered the South to the Republican Party for a long time to come."
17. CLCD, 151.
18. CLCD, 88.
19. Niebuhr, "How Philanthropic is Henry Ford?" 102.
20. Fine, *A Mind of its Own*, 207.

II

Democracy's Bulwarks

So here we are: We are all inclined to sinfulness, to pride, to bias and motivated reasoning—call it what you want. These features are hard-wired. They may make us arrogant and intolerant, self-righteous and delusional, but they are the product of millions of years of evolution and they are not going anywhere. They cannot be eliminated or transcended or anything of the sort. Democratic politics must therefore accommodate and work within these realities. The United States has a more or less successful record in this regard. However, in the current context, we have a media climate that fosters those sins to heretofore unseen and dangerous degrees. This accounts, at least in large measure, for why our contemporary politics is so bad, why it is, in fact, imperiled.

Since this argument follows Niebuhr so directly, then it is certainly appropriate to ask what Niebuhr thinks democratic society can do to mitigate these effects and thereby preserve our democracy. In *Moral Man, Immoral Society*, Niebuhr says that "the problem which society faces is clearly one of . . . bringing forces of moral self-restraint to bear upon types of power which can never be brought completely under social control." This means democratic society needs forces that push against and mitigate our innate tendencies to become Children of Light. We need to foster a specifically democratic form of moral self-restraint. I am calling this democratic humility.

Regarding *Christian* humility, St. Bernard of Clairvoux said that it is the virtue by which we come to a "very true knowledge of ourselves." That is, as we come to understand ourselves as sinful and utterly dependent on God's grace for our salvation, humility about who we are and what we have accomplished comes fairly naturally. Humility in this sense is not self-loathing. It is not manifested in hair shirts or self-degradation. Rather, it means simply a less inordinate regard for ourselves, a more generous regard for our neighbors, and generally a more appropriate response to the way things are.

The same ought to be true for a *democratic* version of humility. We have solid scientific evidence that demonstrates how we human beings think and behave. Unchecked, those behaviors imperil democracy. The objective then, is to make ourselves aware of the truth about ourselves and then to constrain those behaviors accordingly. We need, that is, to find ways to cultivate democratic humility. Niebuhr says there are three institutions that serve this role in democratic society: government, religion, and education. Each of these institutions, Niebuhr says, has the power and standing to serve as a social counter-force, and help us develop moral self-restraint. The second half of this book will address all three institutions in the contemporary context.

Chapter Seven

Weapons and Instruments: Using Government to Fix Government

In chapter 4, I noted that the high water mark for objectivity in American news was between the end of World War II and about 1980. That would just happen to coincide with the Federal Communications Commission's so-called Fairness Doctrine (in fact, 1949–1987). Again, this policy (it was never a law and was never enforced) required that licensed broadcasters present controversial issues in a manner that the FCC judged to be balanced and equitable. That is clearly a long way from what we have now, so should we not consider returning to it? If partisan infotainment is even marginally responsible for us becoming so polarized, self-deluded, intolerant, and un-willing to compromise, then should we not try to restore this former media environment?

To those on the Right, even asking the question is giving up the real game. Any talk about the Fairness Doctrine is nothing more than a veiled effort to restack the deck against conservative voices: the Left cannot win in a free market, so instead they demand that the rules be changed. On top of that, any restrictions imposed by the doctrine amount to an unconstitutional attack on free speech and free enterprise.

Leaving the first claim alone for the moment, with regards to the second, it is worth noting that the Fairness Doctrine did pass constitutional muster. In Red Lion Broadcasting Co., Inc. v. FCC (1969), Justice Byron White wrote,

> There is nothing in the First Amendment which prevents the Government from requiring a licensee to share his frequency with others and to conduct himself as a proxy or fiduciary with obligations to present those views and voices which are representative of his community and which would otherwise, by

necessity, be barred from the airwaves. . . . It is the right of the viewers and listeners, not the right of the broadcasters, which is paramount. [1]

In this ruling and elsewhere, license holders for broadcasting on public airways are understood to be "trustees" of a scarce and precious public resource. That makes what they do a matter of public concern. The Court's affirmation of restrictions on monopolizing speech, and its ringing endorsement of the airwaves as a public good, lends support to those asking for a reconsideration of the issue.

However, it is also true that this ruling was very quickly subject to some second thoughts, both from commentators and the Court itself. In 1974, the Supreme Court ruled that newspapers do not have to provide equal space for opposing views. Of course, because there are no licensing requirements or bandwidth scarcity, newspapers have always had more freedom than broadcasters. However, in this ruling the Court also referenced broadcast news, noting that any policy like the Fairness Doctrine "inescapably dampens the vigor and limits the variety of public debate."[2] Ten years later, in 1984, the Court again stood its ground about the Constitutionality of the regulation of public airwaves, but admitted that in the eyes of many critics, "technological developments have advanced so far that some revision of the system of broadcast regulation may be required."[3] Almost immediately then, First Amendment concerns as well as a burgeoning media market increasingly called the Fairness Doctrine into question.

Just one year later, the FCC issued a report that argued against continuing the doctrine. It noted that

> growth in the number of broadcast outlets reduced any need for the doctrine, that the doctrine often worked to dissuade broadcasters from presenting any treatment of controversial viewpoints, that it put the government in the doubtful position of evaluating program content, and that it created an opportunity for incumbents to abuse it for partisan purposes. [4]

In August 1987, by a 4-0 vote, the FCC abolished the doctrine. Finally, in 2000, the Fairness Doctrine was removed from FCC regulations altogether. In so doing, FCC Chair Genachowski (a Democrat, incidentally) wrote, "striking this from our books ensures there can be no mistake that what has long been a dead letter remains dead. . . . The Fairness Doctrine holds the potential to chill free speech and the free flow of ideas and was properly abandoned over two decades ago."[5]

The death of the Fairness Doctrine results primarily from the fact that the circumstances in which it operated had also died. With the advent of cable and the internet, the scarcity argument became ever harder to sustain and ultimately wholly obsolete. In other words, technology expanded the airwaves to such a degree that they became more and more like newspapers.

The subsequent rise of the internet only further reinforces the point. That reality, along with second thoughts from the Courts regarding First Amendment concerns, has tipped the balance against any revival of the Fairness Doctrine. If there is a strategy for improving our political climate, it will not be found in some FCC regulation.

But while the Fairness Doctrine is a dead end, the issue of its revival raises a broader question about the regulatory role of government. It is one thing to state that any such revival is driven by partisan objectives—there are certainly reasons for those on the Right to be suspicious—but it is quite another to say it was initially adopted for those reasons. In 1949, in its Report on Editorializing, the FCC wrote, "[T]he public interest requires ample play for the free and fair competition of opposing views, and the commission believes that the principle applies . . . to all discussion of issues of importance to the public."[6] For all its handwringing, the Court never disputed the idea that the public airwaves are a public good and should therefore serve public ends. If the Fairness Doctrine is no longer a legitimate way to support those public ends, is there not something else that government could do, through regulation or legislation or otherwise, that could change the incentives, and improve the political climate? This question brings us back to Reinhold Niebuhr.

GOVERNMENT AS WEAPON

Government by definition has the power to place limits on what we are inclined to do, and thus, to place limits on freedom. Government is therefore appropriately understood as a form of coercion. Most democrats acknowledge this fact, but they don't particularly like it and they want to make sure that such power does not extend any farther than absolutely necessary. But Niebuhr does not run away from the term; he maintains that coercion is "an inevitable part of the process of social cohesion."[7] No coercion, no society. What's more, for Niebuhr, government's coercive role is particularly important in a democratic society. But if Niebuhr insists that government is coercive, he is equally adamant that it is not *merely* so.

> Though it is true that government must have the power to subdue recalcitrance, it also has a more positive function. It must guide, direct, deflect and rechannel conflicting and competing forces in a community in the interest of a higher order. It must provide instruments for the expression of the individual's sense of obligation to the community as well as weapons against the individual's anti-social lusts and ambitions.[8]

Government has "weapons" that constrain our selfish behavior, but it also can and should develop "instruments" that help build social cohesion. Both of these roles, stick and carrot as it were, are thus means by which government moves us beyond our inclinations to self-righteousness and intolerance. Let me start with the idea that the law is a weapon.

Like most people, I suspect, I would prefer to drive faster than the posted speed limit. I would also prefer to pay less taxes than I owe. However, if I were to choose to act in accordance with these preferences, the government has the power to take away my money and my freedom. The law therefore changes my evaluation of my self-interest, and thereby constrains me to do things I do not want to do.

All of this is true of any laws, anywhere. But in a democracy the law is self-imposed. Because we are sovereign, the law is not merely a weapon of constraint; it has a different and just as important social function. First, in a democracy, we *place ourselves* under the law. It is one of the central means by which we place restraints on ourselves. Second, because we all ultimately have a say in the laws that we are subject to, the laws (ostensibly and ideally) apply to all, irrespective of class, race, gender, etc. Of course equality before the law is an ideal. History is and will always be the story of how we failed fully to achieve it (though we are getting better). But as an ideal, it is something that gauges our efforts as we strive, fail and strive again. Statues of Justice are allegorical, but they are blind for a reason. All of this pushes against our self-importance. When everyone has to obey the speed limit, or serve on a jury, when everyone's vote counts no more and no less than anyone else's, and when everybody has to stand in line at the DMV, it becomes harder for us to sustain the fiction that we are better than everyone else. In this limited sense, law in a democracy pushes back against the very roots of our sinfulness and fosters at least a modicum of humility. The law doesn't make us less sinful, but it does more than simply constrain our actions, ideally it ought to act as an internal commentary on those actions and desires in the first place. That function, too, is part of "subduing recalcitrance."

Now of course, government is not always a good thing. Governments can be more than just coercive; they can be tyrannical. Indeed, every government will inevitably act in ways that are contrary to justice. "There is no historical reality, whether it be church or government . . . which is not involved in the flux and relativity of human existence; which is not subject to error and sin, and which is not tempted to exaggerate its errors and sins when they are made immune to criticism."[9] Again, that is why—and really, for Niebuhr, it is the only persuasive reason why—democracy is the best form of government. If we are all sovereign, then laws are constraints that we put on ourselves, and by contesting with each other politically, we are best able to ensure that the laws are fair and applied equally. Democratic governments are thus less likely to become tyrannical, and more likely to sustain some measure of justice than any other form. And again, there is no meaningful alternative. The opposite of governmental coercion is not freedom; it is an-archy. It is no society at all.

So Niebuhr thinks laws are weapons—an especially important force for fostering moral self-restraint which can help us mitigate some of our anti-social desires and ambitions. And in a democracy, laws also help remind us that we are all equal. Now if all this is so, and since we find ourselves in a condition in which we need more of that kind of mitigation, then perhaps there are changes in laws that we ought to consider. Maybe there are laws and regulations that could do for our democracy what the Fairness Doctrine cannot.

CHOOSE YOUR WEAPON

It is not hard to find candidates for consideration. A short and by no means complete list will make the point. In his book *Republic, Lost*, Lawrence Lessing argues that money has corrupted Congress, and he lays out an exten-sive plan for campaign finance reform.[10] Similarly, the League of Women Voters says that campaign finance reform is needed in order to "ensure the public's right to know, combat corruption and undue influence, enable candi-dates to compete more equitably for public office and allow maximum citi-zen participation in the political process."[11] Common Cause wants to get the decennial redistricting process out of the hands of state legislatures.[12] Many (including Mann and Ornstein and the bi-partisan group *No Labels*) call for reform of the Senate filibuster and silent holds.[13] The former also want to put term limits on Supreme Court justices, so that the stakes for any opening on the bench are driven down to manageable levels. Others want to tinker with elections by making primaries open to anyone, so that there is more of an incentive for candidates to move toward the center.[14] Polls continually show majority support for a balanced budget amendment as the only way to force fiscal discipline upon an out of control Congress. As well, especially on the Right, term limits are touted as a way to destroy the power and constraint of incumbency, and restore the idea of the citizen legislator. Gutmann and Thompson want to attack the problem of "the permanent campaign."[15] Some want to abolish political parties altogether. Others want to replace our politi-cal system with a parliamentary one.

Of course, not everyone is going to like all of these proposals. I certainly don't. And it is by no means certain that enactment of any one of them would bring about the kind of changes we would all like to see.[16] Still less is there any indication that any of these changes would diminish the effects in our politics of the Children of Light. But all of these examples and many others operate under the assumption that we can use government to create legislation that can positively affect the condition of politics, and thereby make our democratic society work better.

But whether they would work or not, the more salient point is that for the foreseeable future, enactment of any one of these proposals is exceedingly unlikely. As I noted in the introduction, Congress has fallen to levels of distrust, gridlock, and ineffectiveness that are truly historic. The 112th and 113th Congress set a new low for the number of laws passed. This condition would appear to rule out any such attempt before it begins. Even for those policy questions that focus primarily on the process itself, the rules of the game, if you will, prospects are dim.

In a now famous *New Yorker* article from 2010, author George Packer recounts former Senator Chris Dodd's (Dem-CT) description of the Senate: "'There's no trust,' Dodd, whose father was a Senator went on, 'That's really all there is—this place really operates on that. I don't think anyone would argue with that conclusion. And if that's missing. . . .'"[17] For my purposes, the meaning of Dodd's trailing comment is clear enough. Trust requires some assurance that the person you are fighting is nevertheless someone who shares your commitment to the nation and to service, who says what she means and keeps her promises. The Senate, and Washington as a whole, require these features in order to function, in order to bring bills through the messy and complicated process whereby they become law. And if that trust is indeed missing, then there can be no benign idea, no proposal devoid of partisan implications, and what's more, hardly any reason to want to try to find one.

Chris Christie, Republican Governor of New Jersey, offers the same assessment of life inside the beltway.

> It's a vacuum in relationships. The fact of the matter is nobody in this city talks to each other anymore, or if they do, they don't speak to each other civilly. They don't develop relationships. They don't develop any sense of trust between each other and then they expect when . . . problems come up—big, difficult, contentious problems—that they're going to be able to get into a room and fix it.[18]

Governor Christie is no doubt feathering his own presidential bed with this assessment. But that fact does not undermine the relevance of his statement, it confirms it. The lack of trust, and its accompanying infighting and gamesmanship is apparent to even the most casual viewer. And Christie thinks that Americans therefore are looking for potential presidential candidates who might be able to change this condition. But for my purposes, the point is that there is no benign trans-partisan political question, and no good reason to hope that Congress might address it in good faith, and thereby come to any kind of viable policy answer.

BUT WHY IS CONGRESS LIKE THIS?

The home page for the *No Labels* website says "Stop Fighting. Start Fixing," and urges visitors to "Tell Congress: Stop bickering and work together to solve America's big problems."[19] In fact, most of us are inclined to see Congress as the problem. But this view, like Christie's, implies that Congress is somehow driving our condition, operating according to some perverse interest that is contrary to what all Americans really want. This is a satisfying point of view, to be sure, but it is also, at best, an inadequate accounting of the problem. Telling the whole story also better explains why changes in the rules of the game are so unlikely.

Congress is indeed sclerotic, childish, and unproductive. But that does not mean it has somehow ceased to be either rational or representative. First, members of Congress want to keep their seat, and they respond as necessary to any threat thereto. But for most members of Congress, that threat is not from the other party; it comes from insurgents within their own. Political statistician Nate Silver estimates that "in 1992, there were 103 members of the House of Representatives elected from what might be called swing districts: those in which the margin in the presidential race was within five percentage points of the national result . . . in 2012 . . . there are only 35 such Congressional districts."[20] This means that most districts are so hyper-partisan that the other party has virtually no chance to defeat the incumbent. The most serious threat comes from more extreme members of one's own party.

This risk is especially operative for Republicans. Indeed, the best way for a Republican politician to ensure a primary challenge from the right is to work cooperatively with a Democrat As I write, the group Club for Growth (which calls itself a fiscally conservative group) has a website called PrimaryMyCongressman.com which lists Republican members of the U.S. House who they think merit a challenge within the Republic primary.[21] Here, with minor edits, I quote their rationale for launching the site:

Why PrimaryMyCongressman.com?

"Moderate" Republicans often join with liberal Democrats to grow government and increase taxes.

For years moderate Republicans have joined with Democrats to pass liberal policies that harm economic growth. They have passed spending bills that add trillions to our debt, without ever addressing the structural reforms that are needed to balance the budget and create an environment for economic growth and job creation.

These Republicans In Name Only (R.I.N.O.'s) often are elected from conservative districts—districts where winning a Republican primary is tantamount to

*election. This means that in districts that are heavily Republican, there are
literally dozens of missed opportunities to elect real fiscal conservatives to
Congress—not more "moderates" who will compromise with Democrats to
just increase spending and grow government a little bit slower than usual.*

*There's no reason a heavily Republican district should have a R.I.N.O. repre-
senting them in Congress . . . which means PrimaryMyCongressman.com!*

*PrimaryMyCongressman.com will aim to inform Republican voters that the
Members of Congress highlighted here are not voting to limit government or
expand economic freedom in Washington. This website will provide an avenue
for the general public to recommend primary challenges to those members and
any other member they choose.*

In our hyper-polarized political world, "moderate" is a word that belongs in
quotes. In this world, compromise is just a slower trek toward the loss of the
America we love. We are all combatants in a partisan war. And for politicians who might think differently, this website is a gun pointed at their
political career. No Republican politician who wants to get re-elected wants
to be on this site. It is thus yet another strong disincentive toward any behavior that even bears the appearance of respect for the other side, let alone
compromise or moderation.

Of course, PrimaryMyCongressman.com only seeks to exploit the condition of American politics for its own ends. That is how politics and politicians work. In that regard the site is merely reflective of the state of contemporary politics, and, more importantly, the union as a whole. Thus, the more
important reason why Congress is unlikely to stop fighting, to work together
or even to consider a good beyond partisanship is because the majority of the
people who elect them do not want them to. In the words of Alan Abramowitz,

> There is no disconnect between elected officials and the voters who put them
> in office, there is, in fact, a close connection between them. Polarization is not
> a result of a failure of representation; it is a result of successful representa-
> tion. . . . If concerned citizens want to understand the root cause of polarization
> and government gridlock, they should heed the words of Pogo and look in the
> mirror.[22]

Abramowitz shows that since the early '70s members of both parties have
become ever more extreme in their views. And the more engaged a party
member is, the more extreme. Republican voters have become more conservative; liberal Republicans have all but disappeared, and even moderates
have become a tiny minority (from 32 to only 17 percent). Democrats have
grown more extreme as well, although as is so often the case, the phenomenon on their side of the aisle is less dramatic. "Among Democratic voters, the

percentage of liberals increased from 38 to 55 percent while the percentage of moderates declined from 38 to 32 percent, and the percentage of conservatives declined from 24 to 13 percent."[23] This change within the two parties has, accordingly, increased the political gap between the two parties. "Between 1972 and 2008, the gap between the average Democratic voter and average Republican voter on the seven-point liberal-conservative scale increased by 127 percent."[24] As is ever the case, the makeup of Congress simply reflects the condition of the electorate. As the body politic is currently polarized and extreme, politicians simply mirror that condition.[25]

Finally, the new media both manifests and exacerbates this polarization. As I have shown, partisan infotainment—like any business—finds ways to exploit the market as it exists in order to create a profitable niche for itself. So if the population is more polarized, and is already feeling increasingly less connection to those in the other party, then one successful strategy in this market is to confirm these feelings—to tell consumers that they are members of the superior group, and that the other side is wrong, stupid, and immoral. This makes the news product more likely to develop an audience, and thereby make money.

The effects of this model on the body politic are fairly self-evident. For if partisan infotainment confirms and even abets our negative beliefs regarding the decency and intelligence of our partisan rival, then how can working together, bipartisanship, or compromise be seen as a good thing? Instead, for the most avid consumers of the new partisan media, even the most fleeting gesture toward bipartisanship is a clear indication that the perpetrator is not really a member of the in group. The epithet "RINO" is clear enough, but the effects are manifest on the left side of the divide as well. David Brownstein recalls that at the 2008 YearlyKos, the convention for those who follow and contribute to the Democratic website, the Daily Kos, "the names that provoked the loudest catcalls from the YearlyKos audience were not Bush or any of his Republican allies, but Democrats the crowd thought cooperated too much with the GOP."[26] Thus, for both parties, the new media not only exacerbates polarization, it incentivizes the very behavior in Congress that so many Americans claim to reject.

In sum: members of Congress distrust the other side, Congressional seats are only threatened by the radical fringe, the populace is polarized, and the new media reinforces partisan group identity so that it feeds our worst instincts of self-importance and moral superiority. As long as all this remains the case, any legal challenge to our toxic status quo, any weapons that might help us constrain our own worst inclinations, are dead on arrival. Prospects for meaningful change will have to begin elsewhere.

GOVERNMENT AS INSTRUMENT

Recall the quotation from page 93. Niebuhr's government's arsenal includes not just weapons but also "instruments" that can "rechannel" society's "conflicting and competing forces" and allow for the expression of the individual's sense of obligation to the community. The importance of government is thus not limited to the making and enforcement of law, and accordingly, the constraint of individual behavior. Government is also an essential means for building a sense of common purpose, common identity and common duties. How does government do this? In short, if laws are weapons, then symbols and rituals are instruments.

Examples are replete throughout the world of politics—the signing ceremony by which a bill becomes a law, the announcement that begins a campaign, the restraint against applause in a campaign debate, and perhaps most clearly in the events that take place after an election. We all know about the conciliatory phone call where the loser congratulates the winner and pledges his or her support. No matter our age, we have heard the clip from John F. Kennedy's inauguration speech, "Ask not what your country can do for you. . . ." We know that the inaugural ceremony marks the transition from the end of the campaign and its inevitable bitterness to one in which there is one President for all Americans. On the way to this ceremony, the White House's current occupant accompanies the future one. This is true even when, as sometimes happens, this ritual requires that the loser escort the winner. After the election, and once a year thereafter, the Speaker of the House always deems it a great honor to introduce the President for the State of the Union address. And so on.

Of course, sometimes these rituals are conducted without an ounce of sincerity, indeed, with barely concealed bile. But that only reinforces their power. Even in the midst of our opposition and distaste for each other, the fact that we continue to insist on these symbols and rituals reminds us that, after all, there is one—an "us" that transcends all the different groups by which we distinguish ourselves from others. And with that reminder comes all the features that we know to be associated with being part of an "us": both the feeling of belonging, and the notion that we bear responsibilities to those with whom we belong.

This is, after all, one of the core functions of any ritual that is practiced together. A basketball player who without fail bounces the ball three times before shooting a free throw is not doing so to build community, but when she joins her teammates to hop around in a pregame huddle, that is precisely what she is doing. So too with the boys in Oklahoma. When the Eagles found the Rattlers' flag unguarded, they created a series of impromptu rituals: they burned the flag, then put the charred remains back in place and sang taps. In the words of Oxford anthropologist Harvey Whitehouse, these rituals are more similar than different. For any ritual serves as "the glue that holds social groups together." While the features of rituals can vary enormously, "from the recitation of prayers in church, to the sometimes violent and humiliating initiations of U.S. college fraternity pledges, to the bleeding of a young man's penis with bamboo razors and pig incisors in purity rituals among the Ilahita Arapesh of New Guinea . . . rituals are always about building community."[27] By engaging in any ritual, each participant says to the other, "I am a part of this group and I am committed to what it stands for. I attach its identity to my own."

THE RELIGIOUS/RITUALISTIC PART OF POLITICS

Among those concerned about our politics, there is a general sense that partisanship is now overwhelming our common identity as Americans. Therefore, just as there is interest in coming up with new laws and policies, there is likewise interest in coming up with new symbols and ritual. The latter, it is hoped, might help to reinvigorate this feeling of common purpose and identity, both among politicians and those who elect them. For example, in their list of Congressional reforms, the group *No Labels* calls for monthly bipartisan meetings and bipartisan seating at most congressional meetings and events. "The *No Labels* Solution" to the problem of partisan disconnect is, thus, "to get members talking to one another." To that end, first, "both the House and Senate should institute monthly bipartisan gatherings. The gatherings would be off the record and not be televised." And second, "at all joint meetings or sessions of Congress, each member should be seated next to at least one member of the other party. On committees and subcommittees, seating also would be arranged in an alternating bipartisan way (one member would be seated next to at least one member of the other party) by agreement between the chair and ranking member."[28] In the first instance, the group hopes to create a new ritual. In the second, they want to change the ritual to reinforce rather than undermine a sense of common identity and purpose.

These ideas explicitly recall the 2011 State of the Union address. That night, in response to the mass shooting in Tucson that severely injured then-Congresswoman Gabby Giffords (13 others were injured and six people killed in that shooting), dozens of lawmakers crossed the aisle and sat with their colleagues from the other side. There certainly was a ritualistic element to this event. Senators and Representatives talked about calling each other for "dates," and escorting each other to their seats. The idea, then and now, is that this mixed seating arrangement would symbolize to the nation and to themselves that members of Congress saw each other as opponents, not enemies, and that they had a purpose and identity in common that, to some degree anyway, transcended partisan animosity.

This new and (truthfully) flash-in-the-pan ritual recalls one much more significant gesture. In 1997, with much fanfare and hopefulness, 200 members of the House of Representatives (as well as 165 spouses and 100 children) attended a bipartisan retreat in Hershey, Pennsylvania. The objective of the weekend was "to seek a greater degree of civility, mutual respect and, when possible, bipartisanship among Members of the House of Representatives in order to foster an environment in which vigorous debate and mutual respect can coexist."[29] By creating an opportunity for less formal engagement, as well as the opportunity to engage in those most basic of rituals, sharing a meal or a libation, members hoped to improve on what was even then a contentious and unproductive status quo. Initial reports were positive. One year later, Kathleen Hall Jamieson reported that the level of civility had increased as had legislative productivity.[30] This data gave hope to the organizers, within Congress and without, that things could be changed for the better. But this achievement was not to last. 1998 saw the impeachment of President Clinton. Organizers held a second civility retreat in 1999, but by that time, whatever green shoots might have arisen were long vanished.

The intervening years have not caused anyone to reevaluate this significant and sincere effort. Just so, any good feelings that might have come from 60 members of Congress deciding to sit together and support a seriously injured colleague are a distant memory. As a result, it is hard not to view with a jaundiced eye any similar effort to create a new ritual. But while such instrumental efforts might not represent much of a chance, they might be the best chance we have. Referencing the Cold War, Niebuhr wrote that "[i]f we escape disaster it will only be by the slow growth of mutual trust and tissues of community over the awful chasm of the present international tension."[31] Take out the word "international" and you have a fairly good rationale for the little gestures that *No Labels* and others are calling for. They are indeed little gestures, and past history allows no one to be sanguine about their likely impact. Moreover, if the condition of Congress does indeed stem from the hyper-partisan condition of the electorate, it is unlikely that focusing solely on the former will have much of an effect. But given the polarized condition of both government and the populace, for the time being, it may be the only way whereby government can improve the condition of government, let alone foster a renewed sense of mutual obligation, toleration and humility within our national community. Regarding the weapons and instruments of government, the slow growth of the tissues of community is likely the best we can hope for.

Performing a certain act in a specific way and on specific occasions attaches a symbolic meaning and weight to it. In this way, it is through rituals that politics and government, as much as any other social institution, most closely resembles religion. Rituals like those associated with Inauguration Day are the most religious part of politics. As such, this talk about seating arrangements and shared meals is an appropriate transition to the next chapter. For, not surprisingly, Niebuhr also considers religion to be an institution that democratic society needs to push back against our perilous preconditions and moderate our delusions. It is also an arena in which to more directly consider how we might cultivate humility.

NOTES

1. 395 U.S. 367 (1969).
2. 418 U.S. 241 (1974).
3. FCC v. League of Women Voters—468 U.S. 364 (1984).
4. See 867 F. 2d 654—Syracuse Peace Council v. Federal Communications Commission.
5. Federal Communications Commission, "Genachowski Continues Regulatory Reform to Ease Burden on Businesses: Genachowski Announces Elimination of 83 Outdated Media Rules," August 22, 2011.
6. Federal Communications Commission, "Report of the Commission: Docket No, 8516: In the Matter of Editorializing by Broadcast Licenses, Report Appendix."
7. MMIS, 6.
8. CLCD, 44.
9. CLCD, 70-71.
10. Lessig, *Republic, Lost.*
11. League of Women Voters Website, "Our Work."
12. See Dan Vicuña, "Common Cause New York Comments on Redistricting Report," October 9, 2014.
13. In 2013, the Senate approved limited changes to the filibuster. Not incidentally, the change was passed on a strict party line vote, and Republicans warned Democrats that the change would exacerbate distrust and enmity.
14. Brownstein, *The Second Civil War*, 378.
15. Gutmann and Thompson, *The Spirit of Compromise,* 160-167.
16. Alan Abramowitz, for example, says that gerrymandering does not explain the polarized condition of American politics. And if that is true, then redistricting won't make much of an appreciable difference even if it were to be enacted. See *The Disappearing Center,* 143.
17. Packer, "The Empty Chamber: Just how broken is the Senate?"
18. Matthews, "What Would Gov. Chris Christie Change in DC?"
19. www.nolabels.com.
20. Nate Silver, "As Swing Districts Dwindle, Can a Divided House Stand?" FiveThirtyEight, *New York Times,* December 27, 2012. http://fivethirtyeight.com/features/as-swing-districts-dwindle-can-a-divided-house-stand/.
21. I know of no equivalent site for Democrats. Indeed, an entry on the progressive political blog FireDogLake noted the PrimaryMyCongressman site and lamented that there was no liberal equivalent. "Don't Vent, Organize—And "Primary" a Democrat Near You By: Norman Solomon Wednesday May 1, 2013. http://my.firedoglake.com/nsolomon/2013/05/01/dont-vent-organize-and-primary-a-democrat-near-you/. When I checked this site in January, 2015, it was not operating. However, it did say to "check back soon" and noted the site's affiliation with the Club for Growth. It will be interesting to see if it returns as things ratchet up for the 2016 primary election season.
22. Abramowitz, *The Polarized Public,* xiii.
23. Ibid., 43.
24. Ibid., 49.
25. Fiorina and Abrams (among others) argue precisely to the contrary that there is a "disconnect" between politicians and the people they claim to represent. While their representatives have become far more extreme, Americans themselves remain moderate in their opinions. I think Abramowitz has the stronger case here. But it is worth noting that Fiorina and Abrams

fully agree that polarization has made constructive legislative work virtually impossible. See *Disconnect*.

26. Brownstein, *The Second Civil War*, 7.
27. Quoted Jones, "Social evolution: The ritual animal."
28. All quotations from www.nolabels.com.
29. Jamieson and Falk, "Civility in the House of Representatives: The 105th Congress," 3.
30. Ibid.
31. CLCD, x.

Chapter Eight

Religion: "A Constant Fount of Humility"

In December of 1954, William Nichols, editor of *This Week* magazine, put the following question to Reinhold Niebuhr: "If as a result of some cataclysm, it were possible to retain just one passage from the Bible—what would your choice be?" Niebuhr chose a verse from the fourth chapter of Paul's letter to the Ephesians, verse 32: "And be ye kind one to another, tender-hearted, forgiving one another, even as God for Christ's sake hath forgiven you."

Niebuhr explained his choice this way:

> I have chosen this particular passage because it combines the high point of the Christian ethic, which is forgiving love, with a reference to the whole basis of the ethic, which is the historical revelation in Christ. We are asked to forgive one another. The charity of forgiveness is, however, not possible as a duty. It is only possible in terms of the knowledge that we are ourselves sinners, and that we have been forgiven. It therefore combines the Christian Gospel with the Christian ethic in succinct form. [1]

This choice and explanation goes a long way toward explaining the role that Niebuhr believes Christianity, and religion more generally, ought to play in a democratic society. My task in this chapter will be to give a fuller accounting of what that role is, and why, in the present context, Christianity is not fulfilling it.

PROFOUND RELIGION

Just about all religions include worship of some kind of deity (some forms of Buddhism might serve as counter examples). And therefore all religions stand contrary to our innate inclination to think of ourselves as something special. For let's face it: it is harder to sustain the illusion that you are more important than everybody else when you are surrounded by other people who are all acting the same way you are—kneeling, singing, chanting, etc.—and it is harder to feel godlike when everyone around you is worshiping (ostensibly, at least) the real thing. When a religion is "profound," this distinction is not only apparent, it is the fundamental to the enterprise. Profound religion, in Niebuhr's understanding, "recognize[s] the difference between divine majesty and human creatureliness; between the unconditioned character of the divine and the conditioned character of all human enterprise."[2] Religion that functions in this way is thus the paramount example of a force of "moral self-restraint" that Niebuhr thinks democratic society requires.

Niebuhr does not believe that Christianity is the only religion that can function this way. At a minimum, he sees both Christianity and Judaism as drawing directly from the prophetic tradition and thus grounded in this distinction. More, though it is mere speculation on my part, I think Niebuhr would accept the idea that all religion is "profound," if it insists on the idea that God is God and we are not. Nevertheless, he uses the terms religion and Christianity almost interchangeably. Christianity, and Protestant Christianity at that, is the religion that Niebuhr is operating within. It is also the religion that was—and which even now remains—most dominant within American history and culture. In both regards, this religion is most relevant to his concerns. So when Niebuhr speaks about religion, this is what he has in mind.

In part I, I showed that Niebuhr's worth as a democratic thinker extends well beyond the parochial concerns of the Christian community. Niebuhr maintains that he appeals to Christian categories because those categories offer the best account of how we human beings actually behave. Again, Niebuhr says, Christianity makes the most sense of the most facts. I tried to show that as far as his anthropology is concerned, and his notion of politics that derives therefrom, there is scientific evidence that supports his claim.

The same is true here. His appeal to Christianity (at least the one that I will make use of) is grounded in its social utility. As I have shown, Niebuhr believes that democracy only survives if it is able to keep both the Child of Darkness and the Child of Light at bay, counterbalancing our innate inclinations, and keeping our most destructive tendencies under control. Christianity is useful, indeed essential for performing this role, and thereby maintaining a well-ordered democratic society.

According to the Christian faith pride, which seeks to hide the conditioned and finite character of all human endeavor, is the very quintessence of sin. Religious faith ought therefore to be a constant fount of humility; for it ought to encourage men to moderate their natural pride and to achieve some decent consciousness of the relativity of their own statement of even the most ultimate truth. It ought to teach them that their religion is most certainly true if it recognizes the element of error and sin, of finiteness and contingency which creeps into the statement of even the sublimest truth. [3]

Christianity is essential to democracy not only because it reminds us that our innate human pride is inordinate and fundamentally out of synch with reality, but because it also offers us the opportunity and the grounds for cultivating the counterweights of humility and forgiveness.

In order to understand how Christianity does this, it is necessary to say slightly more than has been said already, and recount the most basic outlines of the faith. [4] Christians profess that all humans are guilty of this pride, and moreover, with regards to our moral failure, all are equally guilty: "All have sinned and fallen short of the glory of God" (Romans 3:23). Nobody, not the most saintly priest nor the most humble parishioner is any different in this regard: We are all sinners, condemned by God's righteous judgment. In one of his first interviews, Pope Francis was asked who he was. His answer: "I am a sinner. This is the most accurate definition. It is not a figure of speech, a literary genre. I am a sinner." [5] Second, all of us are equal in our inability to do anything—anything—about our condemnation. We cannot save ourselves. Christians thus possess the inescapable reminder that all human beings are, in a very fundamental and unalterable sense, the same. And because we are the same, and all equally beholden to God's grace for our salvation, we should feel some measure of humility about who we are and what we have or can accomplish. Ephesians 2:8-9: "For by grace are ye saved through faith; and that not of yourselves: it is the gift of God: Not of works, lest any man should boast." Within the Christian understanding, boasting reflects a scandalous disconnect with reality. To repeat the words of St. Bernard of Clairvoux, humility is what happens when we come to a "very true knowledge of ourselves." Humility is simply the most appropriate response to the way things truly are.

On the significantly more positive side, Christians believe that all human beings are God's children and all are equally loved. The ubiquitous John 3:16 makes the point: "For God so loved the world that he gave his only begotten Son, that whosoever believes in him should not perish, but have everlasting life." God loves the *whole* world; nobody is loved less by God than anyone else. Christians differ on how God regards those who do not believe that Jesus is the son of God, but that saving power is available to all. God gave up his son to die, therefore all humans have the possibility of forgiveness, of reunion with God, and of everlasting life. This belief ought to likewise make it difficult for Christians to feel in any way superior to others, including non-Christians and non-believers.

Finally, in the very act of God becoming human, we find the ideal example of humility. Christ is (in the words of the Nicene Creed) "very God," therefore he alone can claim the pride that all of us illegitimately feel. And yet this Christ was willing to take on the mantle of humanity, humble to the point of washing the feet of his disciples, humble enough even to suffer death at the hands of humans for the sins of all humanity. The definitive statement is in Paul's letter to the Philippians (2:8):

> Let this mind be in you, which was also in Christ Jesus: Who, being in the form of God, thought it not robbery to be equal with God: But made himself of no reputation, and took upon him the form of a servant, and was made in the likeness of men: And being found in fashion as a man, he humbled himself, and became obedient unto death, even the death of the cross.

Thus, what Niebuhr calls the Christian Ethic follows from the actions of the Christ and the most elemental features of the faith. Christians reject pride because they know they are sinners who are lost without Christ. More, they are humble because their Christ was humble, even unto death. They treat others equally because God loves us all equally, all of us possess a spark of the divine and the sacrifice of the cross was for humanity, not some subsection thereof. Finally, "the crown" of this Christian Ethics is the doctrine of forgiveness." Niebuhr is fully aware that forgiveness is "the most difficult and impossible of moral achievements." But as Niebuhr explained of his choice, "we forgive because we know that we are all sinners and that we have ourselves been forgiven."

PROFOUND RELIGION'S ROLE IN A DEMOCRACY

Now as we have seen, all of us are power-hungry hypocrites, vainly running away from our inescapable anxiety. For Niebuhr, a democracy is the best means for organizing ourselves because power is spread out between competing interests and therefore no group has enough freely to exploit another. But this competition can sustain itself only if it only goes so far—if the competitors, for all their animosity, can accept each other as full and equal members of society. Democracy is necessary because of our capacity for injustice, but democracy is possible—it is something more than a Hobbesian war—because of our capacity for justice. That is to say, practically speaking, democratic society requires that we tolerate each other.

Now it is true that toleration is a word that often doesn't get a lot of respect. Some dismiss it as empty and vapid. Tolerance is simply making a virtue out of the fact that our society really doesn't believe in, let alone fight for, anything at all. G. K. Chesterton's quip is representative: "Tolerance is the virtue of the man without convictions." Alternatively, it is regarded as a sign more of condescension than true equity. We tolerate the behavior of a two-year-old because we have no reason to expect more. In Goethe's words, "to tolerate means to insult."[6] Neither of these views is Niebuhr's. On the contrary, Niebuhr says that toleration is "an important rational and moral achievement,"[7] one that both requires and reflects "a very high form of religious commitment."[8] Indeed, for Niebuhr, outside of this religious insight, and a firm commitment thereto, toleration, and therefore democracy itself, is nearly unachievable.

Of course, Niebuhr knows that toleration was also championed by central figures in the Enlightenment and was rendered necessary by the reality of religious pluralism in Western Europe; by the 17th century it was clear to most everyone that wars and massive resettlements were never going to solve the problem. Nevertheless, both historically and conceptually, he insists that toleration is possible because religion first demanded it. For Niebuhr, toleration is possible only if we understand and accept "the limited character of each one's vision of the truth."[9] And religion, if it is profound, forces us to admit this limit: that we are mere creatures, and fallen ones at that, and that all of us see through a glass, darkly.[10] "Historically the highest form of democratic toleration is based on these very religious insights."[11] In short, democracy needs toleration, and toleration requires a certain amount of humility, and religion is, or ought to be, a constant fount of that humility. For Niebuhr, "humility . . . springs only from the depth of a religion which confronts the individual with a more ultimate majesty and purity than all human majesties and values. . . . there is none good but one, that is, God."[12] The call to reject pride, including religious pride, and to practice humility and forgiveness toward those with whom we disagree comes first and most importantly from within religion. For those of us who live in a democracy, all of this makes religion very useful, indeed.

PROFANE RELIGION

The social role of religion in a democracy is critically important, but that does not mean we should expect religion and religious people to act accordingly. Take another look at Niebuhr's words from earlier:

> Religious faith *ought* therefore to be a constant fount of humility; for it *ought* to encourage men to moderate their natural pride and to achieve some decent consciousness of the relativity of their own statement of even the most ultimate truth. It *ought* to teach them that their religion is most certainly true if it recognizes the element of error and sin, of finiteness and contingency which creeps into the statement of even the sublimest truth. (Italics added.)

Niebuhr (of all people!) is not deluded. He knows that humility is no less difficult and no less rare for Christians than it is for anyone else. Of course, Christians know and are constantly reminded of the truth; therefore they stand the more condemned by their failure to recognize it and live their lives accordingly. But it is a rare thing indeed for this knowledge to change or even diminish this all too human inclination. "It must be admitted, therefore, that historic Christianity, in common with other religious, usually succumbs to the parochialism of the human heart and lends itself to the sinful inclination of human groups to make themselves God."[13] Given what we know about human sinfulness/self-delusion, this is hardly surprising. By joining a group, individuals receive a sense of identity and purpose, even as they give up some of their distinctiveness. With that transfer, I convince myself that my group is good and powerful and important and that any other group is, at best, significantly less so. Religion is in this sense just like any other human group. But when this pride infects religion, it takes on the antithesis of its appropriate function. Instead of reminding us that we are not God, religion becomes "the sanctifier of whatever we most fervently desire."[14] This use of religion, this sanctification of what we want and who we want to believe we are, is what makes a profound religion profane.

Failing to maintain the distinction that we are not God and that God's will is not ours, replacing the transcendent, unknowable God with one that conveniently does and thinks what we want God to, is a sin. It is a form of idolatry. Just so, profane religion is a disservice to religion. When religion serves our ends, we cannot help but twist, abuse and even ignore its most essential truths. Most to my point, a profane religion is unable to play a salutary role in democratic society. Religion should remind us that we are all sinners, and that none of us have cornered the market on the truth—in short, it should remind us that humility is the most appropriate, most accurate way to go through life. Arthur Schlesinger summarizes Niebuhr's point this way: the proper role of religion "should be not to endorse but to question; to inculcate, not a sense of infallibility, but a sense of humility."[15] Profound religion sets the tone for a well-ordered democratic society; it makes it more possible for believers and ultimately for all members of society to keep self-righteousness in check. By failing to maintain the distinction between God and us, profane religion turns this benefit into another impairment, and therefore a well-ordered democratic society becomes much less likely.

Recall what Niebuhr said about Children of Light. Such people mean well, they want to make the world a better place, but they are hopelessly naïve, especially so about their own virtue, the rightness of their beliefs and opinions, and the righteousness of their cause. For such people, religion is especially dangerous because it gives a very powerful stained glass veneer to their beliefs and actions. Children of Light augment their self-righteousness and self-importance with the ardent yet comfortable belief that God is on their side and pleased with their behavior. Religion becomes both a resource and a sanctifier of the believer's pride, thereby abetting the underlying pathology. Again, this amalgam of pride and religion is all too common, but when it happens, religion ceases to serve society and becomes a menace to it. Niebuhr does not mince words: "When the sanctification of the Church is extended to the sanctification of political programs, movements, or systems, the baneful effects are compounded. One need not be a secularist to believe that politics in the name of God is of the devil." [16]

It is further evidence of the polarized and hyper-partisanized condition of contemporary American society that there are currently two forms of profane Christianity: one on the Left and one on the Right. In neither case does it function as an antidote for pride. Indeed, far from being a way of sustaining democracy, profane Christianity has become, along with partisan infotainment, one of the chief means by which our democracy is undermined.

LEFT-LEANING PROFANITY

You might recall that many pages ago, I mentioned the Social Gospel movement, and its theological lynchpin, an American named Walter Rauschenbusch. Again, this movement began in the early 20th century, in response to the worst excesses of newly industrial society: child labor; cruel, dangerous and mind-numbing working conditions; exploitative wages; and wanton pollution. Rauschenbusch and his fellow travelers recoiled from these features, insisting that God was not indifferent to such suffering and injustice. On the contrary, they argued, it was the job of Christians to fight against such inhumanity, and take on the hard work of building the Kingdom of God.

Now because Rauschenbusch and the followers of the Social Gospel saw the Kingdom of God as a call for Christians to create a more just social world, they naturally looked to politics as a way to build it. And that meant developing a distinctively Christian political agenda. In 1908, Walter Rauschenbusch joined in authoring a statement of principles called the *Social Creed of the Churches* that became the marching orders for what was first known as the Federal Council of Churches. Noting in the preamble it was "the duty of all Christian people to concern themselves directly with certain practical industrial problems," the creed called for ending child labor, shorter work days, provisions for those too old or injured to work, and "the most equitable division of the products of industry that can ultimately be devised." [17] The statement ended by making clear that enacting this agenda into law was "a cause which belongs to all who follow Christ."

The Federal Council of Churches, which later became the National Council of Churches, thus began life as an organizing mechanism of the Social Gospelers. By uniting and mobilizing Christians around this progressive—

and fair to say, socialistic—political agenda, they hoped to develop the political power that could make these things actually happen, and thereby help build the Kingdom of God. The Council therefore vaunted Christian unity. And just as importantly, deliberately minimized doctrinal differences between denominations. Indeed, according to Gary Dorrien, while the Council functioned as "a kind of laboratory for social ideas," divisive elements within Christian doctrine were placed "off limits."[18]

As I have noted, Niebuhr was sympathetic to the Social Gospel School. He understood the dark exploitation of the assembly line, and for a time was even attracted to the idea of building a socialist America. Nevertheless, Niebuhr came to reject the naïveté that he saw at the movement's core. For Niebuhr, this intimate association between God's will and partisan politics was a grave mistake. Equating a partisan agenda with the will of God was to pretend that something transcendent and ultimately unknowable was understandable, even subsumable within our own imminently suspect human objectives. By eliding the Kingdom of God and partisan politics, the Social Gospel was guilty of "sentimentality . . . in which God and the world, the ideal and the real are identified." In *Moral Man and Immoral Society,* Niebuhr sneered with unveiled bile:

> In spite of the disillusionment of the World War, the average liberal Protestant Christian is still convinced that the kingdom of God is gradually approaching, that the League of Nations is its partial fulfillment and the Kellogg Pact its covenant. . . .[19]

The League of Nations and the Kellogg-Briand Pact might well have offered a path to greater justice, even world peace. If so, working for it would have been a good thing for Christians to pursue. But that did not mean that League of Nations was God's will. Still less could one presume that such an institution was part of God's plan. That was something that no human could claim to know.

For Niebuhr this identification of the absolute and the contingent made religion into something else. It caused believers to lose touch with the most fundamental tenets of, in this case, the Christian faith. In *An Interpretation of Christian Ethics*, also written in the '30s, Niebuhr outlines what the sentimentality of liberal Protestantism had done to Christianity. "Liberal Christianity, in adjusting itself to the ethos of this age, therefore sacrificed its most characteristic religious and Christian heritage by destroying the sense of depth and the experience of tension, typical of profound religion."[20] For the followers of the Social Gospel, creating a more just world meant creating a winning political coalition, and that required downplaying the unique and indeed transcendent elements of Christianity.

Finally, Niebuhr saw that this profane religion had turned adherents of the Social Gospel into Children of Light. The fact that so many liberal Protestants were "convinced" that their partisan actions were in tune with God's will was proof that they had lost humility and embraced self-righteous pride. And that meant that their actions undermined democracy as well. Later in his career, Niebuhr would spell out the point: "Nothing is quite so difficult, yet so genuinely Christian, as to remember that in all political struggles there are no saints but only sinners fighting each other. . . . It is well to know that God judges all men and that in His sight no man living is justified."[21] Religion should indeed remind us of these things, but when your religion has become profane, then it is fairly inevitable that you will come to understand yourself to be a saint and your opponent to be God's enemy. In such a circumstance, toleration is illegitimate and humility is impossible. At best, such a religion is of no help to democratic society. At worst, followers of the Social Gospel opened the door to charlatans who could exploit their passion and naïveté to aggrandize their own power and even foster fascism. When Niebuhr was writing in the 1930s, this was no idle fear.

The legacy of this movement continued through the decades, and so did its effects. Even as the National Council of Churches (NCC) emerged in the '50s and '60s as a leader in the civil rights movement and a vigorous opponent of the Vietnam War, it became a lightning rod for criticism. To those who disputed its politics and theology, the Council was a group of naïve bleeding hearts who had allowed themselves to be duped by leftist elements. The latter had used the former to destroy simultaneously the Christian faith and American freedom. One screed published in 1973, argued that "The National Council is a socialistic autocratic organization, deeply infiltrated with pro-Communists, humanists and relativists; and is doing the work of the Communists for world government."[22]

What is more, for these critics this kind of political foolishness was exactly what one could expect when Christians flirted with modernist heresies and jettisoned settled doctrine. The NCC's behavior thus manifested that it was in grave risk of losing its distinctively Christian core. The NCC had changed the Christian understanding of the church: "The church, according to the liberal, is an organization for human betterment."[23] Indeed, they had scandalously diminished the role of Christ himself: "Concerning Jesus, the liberal does not want to have a religious relationship. He does not accept Jesus as one to be worshipped."[24] Finally, these descendants of the Social Gospel tradition had lost touch with the Evangelical idea that the task of the Christian is not to improve society but to bring souls to salvation: "The National Council is promoting the religion of humanism—the glorification of man rather than the glorification of God. The Council is teaching the reconciliation of man with man rather than the reconciliation of man with God.[25] Of course, these quotations are hardly dispositive. As a matter of fact, at minimum they unfairly overstate what the NCC was about. At worst they are unhinged. But regardless, they demonstrate that Niebuhr's concerns did not go away after the Second World War.

The NCC soldiers on, and truth be told, it continues to raise the same criticisms. According to the Institute on Religion and Democracy, another conservative group, an internal NCC strategic planning document discussed at a closed meeting in 2006 makes clear that the very questions that Niebuhr raised remain operative today:

> Some member communions, and some individual leaders, think that the NCC is in danger of losing its basic vision. Instead of serving as embodied within to God's reconciling love, as a place where churches come together even in the midst of theological and political disagreement, the Council, as they see it, is acting increasingly like a political action coalition. [26]

The IRD document notes that the funding sources and their policy positions are routinely and even "overwhelmingly," left of center. Indeed, as far as they are concerned, "the council still stands well to the left of the U.S. political spectrum. If the NCC has shifted at all, it is towards a more open and harsh partisanship." The document makes it clear that in contrast to this partisan objective, "Christian unity and common witness to the Gospel of Jesus Christ do not appear to be among their principal aims."[27] There are reasons to be suspicious of the biases lurking within the IRD. But the NCC's response to this document does not dispute the quotation above. Given that, and given that the issues IRD raises are consistent with those Niebuhr raised over eighty years ago, it is reasonable to take them seriously.

What's more, like the NCC, contemporary liberal religious congregations also remain committed to building the Kingdom, i.e., creating a more just society through politics. For all the press accorded to the Religious Right, Putnam and Campbell found that liberal congregations are more likely to report political activity at church than conservatives.[28] To be sure, religious liberals are not as numerous as their conservative brethren. (Putnam and Campbell say that they represent only 2 percent of all Americans.) But while the apex of mainline liberal Protestantism may be long past, their partisan actions are very similar to those of past generations. More importantly, this political activity continues to exact a very familiar price. With respect to Christian identity, consider this *cri de coeur* from Jim Wallis, an evangelical liberal. His words and sentiment are almost unmistakable from Niebuhr's.

> Many mainline Protestant churches have, since the last century, preached a "social gospel," which often highlights the teachings of Jesus and tries to apply them to issues of poverty, race, war, and peace. And some have shown great courage in doing so. But the real problem comes down to Easter Sunday and what these churches really believe about it. . . . Do we really believe that Jesus

is alive and among us? I am not sure that all of our liberal churches really do. If you don't believe that Jesus is really alive today, all you have is a list of teachings without the Living Teacher.[29]

In Niebuhrian terms, religious progressives continue to render the absolute concrete, to identify God's will with a partisan political agenda, and in the process, diminish some of the most essential features of the faith. It is remarkable to note that the behavior of the religious Left has really not changed much in the 80 years that have passed since Niebuhr offered his critique.

RIGHT-LEANING PROFANITY

Throughout these pages, I have often noted that the status quo can be quickly summarized as follows: the Left is bad, but the Right is worse. Just so with Protestant Christianity in contemporary America. The Religious Right[30] has likewise come to embrace a politicized and profane Christianity. They took much longer to get there, but the right too drains God of transcendence, and assumes full and complete accord between the will of God and their partisan objectives. The difference is that on the right, this form of profanity has come to occupy positions of power within the government. That is, Children of Light are now elected officials, and thus represent a much more operative danger to American democracy.

When the first Fundamentalists arose in the early years of the 20th century, they were fearful and angry about the fate of Christianity. Theological modernism—including of course, the modernism of Rauschenbusch and the Social Gospel—as well as Darwin, Liberalism and Bolshevism, were all endangering the "fundamental" truths of the faith. These original fundamentalists were concerned primarily with theological issues like the unique status of Christ, the inerrancy of the Bible, and the like. Political questions, on the other hand, were understood by most fundamentalists to be utterly beside the point. The world was awash in sin; beyond redemption, it could not be saved. The Christian task was not to save the world but to save souls. The famous words of Evangelist Dwight L. Moody are representative: "I look upon the world as a wrecked vessel. God has given me a life boat and said to me, Moody, save all you can."

Political questions did arise, of course. The American way of life was understood by Fundamentalists to be distinctively Christian, so a threat against one was almost automatically a threat to the other. To note the most significant example, Prohibition was presented as a way to protect both. But while these political efforts amidst pleas about lifeboats revealed a modicum of inconsistency, they were not associated with one political party. William Jennings Bryan, for example, was a staunch Evangelical, but also an ardent progressive, seeing himself as the defender of the farmer and the working man. But after his disastrous experience at the Scopes Trial (and his death just five days later), the Fundamentalists had just that much more reason to withdraw from the broader culture, ignore politics, and concentrate on saving souls.

In the '50s, the fear and anger focused almost exclusively on Communism. Again, Christianity and the American way of life were seen as united, and equally under attack from Communist infiltrators. Anti-Communists were not hard to find in the '50s, so here again, partisan politics could not be assumed. But insofar as the Republican Party was seen as more virulently anti-Communist, and more ardent defenders of the American way of life, they were seen by some Fundamentalists as the only acceptable option for Christians. In 1962, Fundamentalist Billy James Hargis said, "Christ is the heart of the Conservative cause."[31] Nevertheless, most theological conservatives continued to spurn politics. In 1965, fifteen years before he would found the Moral Majority, Jerry Falwell reflected the same political quietism that Dwight L. Moody had articulated decades earlier: "Believing the Bible as I do, I would find it impossible to stop preaching the pure saving gospel of Jesus Christ, and begin doing anything else—including fighting Communism, or participating in civil-rights reforms."[32]

In the '60s and '70s history continued apace, and so too did the fear and anger. Drastic cultural changes, especially regarding the status of women and minorities, drug use, and the rejection of assorted manifestations of '50s cultural conformity were regarded by many Christians as rankly immoral, and an affront to God's law. Evangelicals also expressed anger about a series of Supreme Court rulings that appeared to limit the dominance of Christianity within the culture: including the outlawing of prayer in public schools, free access to birth control, the rescission of tax-exempt status for segregated schools (at the time, Bob Jones University forbade interracial dating), and of course the abortion decision of Roe vs. Wade.[33] Finally, the Watergate scandal proved to many the sorry moral condition of our nation.

All of these changes led these Christians to reconsider the arena of politics. "Now that morality and politics were being discussed in the same breath, evangelicals found it only natural to condone political activities that appeared to uphold standards of morality. The two were so closely linked, in fact, that many evangelicals probably failed to see that for the first time in many years, there were becoming politically involved."[34] Jimmy Carter was an Evangelical born-again Christian, and his candidacy and election in 1976 brought many Evangelicals into politics, many for the first time. But after it became clear that he would not move on legislation they considered essential (including restoring tax-exempt status to Bob Jones University), they began to look for other ways to participate in the political arena.

MAKING GOD A REPUBLICAN

The Moral Majority was founded in 1979 by the Reverend Jerry Falwell and five other prominent religious conservatives.[35] This group affirmed many of the same cultural issues and cultural enemies that Fundamentalists had had for decades. America was a Christian nation with a unique role to play in God's plan; America, Christianity, and therefore God's plan, were again (or still) under siege, and the new enemy, secular humanists, were not that different from the Communist sympathizers of the 1950s, and the liberals and Bolsheviks of the 1920s. But this group has its sights fixed on using politics to address these issues; they were therefore one of the first national efforts to organize conservative Christians to bring power to bear in the political realm. The Moral Majority argued that their platform was not simply affirmed by conservative Protestants, but by the majority of Americans, including Catholics, Jews, and Mormons. All were united in their fear and anger about the moral condition of the nation, and they needed to put their differences aside and focus on their common objectives in order to create a powerful political force. The number is disputed, but at their height, the Moral Majority claimed over four million members.

The Republican Party saw opportunity in this anger and worked hard to mobilize and organize this emerging coalition. In a now famous speech to the National Association of Evangelicals in the 1980 Presidential Campaign, candidate Ronald Reagan said: "Now I know this is a nonpartisan gathering, and so I know that you cannot endorse me. But . . . I want you to know that I endorse you and what you are doing." This declaration is seen by many as the watershed moment, both for the campaign and for the growth of the Religious Right. It was at this point that a preponderance of religious conservatives began to accept politics as a legitimate, even essential place for Christian witness, and to see the Republican Party as the means by which that work might restore a more moral and Godly America. Just like Rauschenbusch and his comrades, the Christian Right unified around a specific partisan agenda in order to do God's will, and to that end, created a coalition around political common ground and ignored points of theological difference.

To be sure, the Moral Majority claimed to be nonpartisan, but it was more closely allied with the Republican Party than any previous Christian Right organization had been. And as this happened, these Christians, just like their brethren on the Left, began to push for partisan issues that had an ever more tenuous connection to Christianity. Abortion and homosexuality are contentious issues within the broad Christian community; believers ardently dispute both sides of the questions. But certainly the argument that these positions follow from Scripture is there to be made. But there are plenty of examples where the connection to scripture is either tenuous or non-existent. Falwell was against the Strategic Arms Limitation Talks and for the MX missile. He called for the elimination of the Occupational Health and Safety Administration. He created a legal defense fund on behalf of Lt. Col. Oliver North, a Reagan aide who was facing charges in the Iran Contra affair. He defended the white apartheid South African government of P. W. Botha (and called Bishop Desmond Tutu a phony) and he defended Ferdinand Marcos, the abjectly corrupt dictator of the Philippines. I believe that every one of these judgments were wrong, but that is not my point. Rather I simply want to insist that whether or not they were prudentially correct, all were partisan positions that do not follow directly from anything specific to Christianity. Thus, just like the religious liberals of Niebuhr's day, Falwell and his followers elided (one is tempted to say demolished) any distinction between God's will and partisan politics, between what God wants and what the Republican Party wants.

In ways that uncannily echo the trail of the Social Gospel, Jerry Falwell pushed Evangelical Christianity from profundity into profanity, and by so doing, he likewise undermined both Christianity and Democracy. In his biography of Falwell, Michael Sean Winters reflects that

> Falwell was completely unalert to the danger of reducing religion to ethics, thereby casting religion in a utilitarian role, as a prop for Americanism. . . . A moralism that is not rooted in doctrine risks that the faithful will lose the forest for the trees and that what is distinctive about Christianity, how and whom it worships, will cease to be of central concern. Religion becomes about us, and not about God.[36]

More importantly to my point, Falwell and his followers also became Children of Light. Profound religion must manifest itself in humility with regard to our own ability to understand God's will, our inevitable failure to overcome sin, and a genuine toleration toward those who disagree with us. But when religion becomes profane, the inevitable result is self-righteousness and intolerance. Falwell was certain that working for the Republican Party was doing the Lord's own work, that he was right and that his enemies were not merely mistaken, not merely sinners like himself, but evil. In a sermon Falwell referred to the Metropolitan Church of Christ, a predominantly Gay church, with these words: "Thank God, this vile and satanic system will one day be utterly annihilated and there will be a celebration in heaven."[37]

Falwell was an adept political actor, and he knew that this kind of over-the-top rhetoric was very effective. He also understood and exploited the newly emerging media market recounted in chapter 6. In the 1970s, the FCC changed its rules regarding religious programming. Thereafter, stations could fulfill their public service requirements with paid religious programming, rather than just local churches that relied on free air time. Audiences for religious programming grew dramatically as a result. And as with partisan infotainment, the most successful new programs were those that appealed to their sense of getting their beliefs confirmed, of being in the superior group, and of seeing their opponents as enemies. Falwell moved into a new church building in 1970 that was designed for television audiences. By 1981 election, the "Old Time Gospel Hour" was carried by over 400 stations nationwide, with millions of loyal viewers. Falwell's comment about this growth reflects his awareness of his status in the broader culture: "And that's 200 more than Johnny Carson."[38]

Such rhetoric also mobilized dollars. Falwell's regular fundraising letters routinely described a world in which God's enemies were bent on destroying America, and that it was up to the Moral Majority to save it. Falwell acknowledged this pattern, but he nevertheless defended it, saying, "[P]eople respond far better when the facts are laid before them in a very emotional appeal. I wish that wasn't true. But I realize everyone is doing it."[39] The growth in the '80s of televangelism, like that of partisan infotainment, confirms that people do indeed respond to very emotional appeals. For a Christian, this prudentialism hardly justifies the choice. But because Falwell was unable to separate his partisan objectives from his understanding of what God wanted, he believed his actions were not only defensible, they were sanctified.

By 1989, the Moral Majority had about run its course, and Falwell shut it down. We are therefore now almost a generation removed from his high water mark of the political power. Things are now both quite similar and yet quite different. In contemporary America, conservative religious leaders continue to connect God's will to partisan politics. Indeed, one is hard pressed to disagree with Randall Balmer, an Evangelical who published a "lament" about the Religious Right. "I'm aware of no way to disentangle the agenda of the Republican Party from the goals of the Religious Right."[40] Just as damning, this state of affairs continues to cause Christians to spurn humility towards those with whom they disagree. Consider Balmer's own experience: "Despite their putative claims to the faith, the leaders of the Religious Right are vicious toward anyone who refuses to kowtow to their version of orthodoxy, and their machinery of vilification strikes with ruthless, dispassionate efficiency."[41] It is hard to imagine a better description of a religion that has become profane.

In both these respects, then, the Religious Right has not changed very much since the halcyon days of the Moral Majority. But in one respect, it has. In the '80s, the leaders of the moral majority were clergy and lay people, but they were not elected officials. (One important counter-example: North Carolina Senator Jesse Helms was a founding member of the Moral Majority.)[42] Today, however, many more Republican leaders are eager to make a direct and explicit connection between God's will and some specific policy question. And that has made things worse. Consider these examples:

- "I think the President will ultimately be forced to repudiate his own signature piece of legislation because the American people will demand it. . . . And I think before his second term is over, we're going to see a miracle before our eyes, I believe God is going to answer our prayers and we'll be freed from the yoke of Obamacare. . . . I believe that's going to happen and we saw step one last week with the repeal of Obamacare in the House. We have two more steps. We serve a mighty God and I believe it can happen." —Former U.S. Rep. and Presidential candidate Michelle Bachman[43]

- "We shall never surrender. We will carry on this struggle until, in God's good time, with all His power and might, He steps forth to the rescue and liberation of our God-given American liberty. That's what will happen in this Congress." —U.S. Rep. Steven King, on Obamacare[44]

- "God's will has to be done, in unifying people and companies to get that gas line built, so pray for that." —Former Governor and Vice Presidential candidate Sarah Palin[45]

- "Well actually the Genesis 8:22 that I use in there is that 'as long as the earth remains there will be springtime and harvest, cold and heat, winter and summer, day and night.' My point is, God's still up there. The arrogance of people to think that we, human beings, would be able to change what He is doing in the climate is to me outrageous." —U.S. Senator James Inhofe[46]

- (Referencing both Genesis 8:22 and Matthew 24:31): "I believe that is the infallible word of God, and that's the way it is going to be for his creation . . . The earth will end only when God declares it's time to be over. Man will not destroy this earth. This earth will not be destroyed by a flood." —U.S. Rep. John Shimkus[47]

- "Some of us believe that the Bible is accurate. Certainly, so many prophesies have been fulfilled. And if that is true, this administration, unless they can find a verse that accurately says that those who betray Israel will be blessed, then this country is being dug in a deeper hole by this administration and its betrayals of Israel's trust and Israel's friendship." —U.S. Rep. Louie Gohmert[48]

There are surely leaders within the Republican Party who would not share such sentiments (though they may well be unwilling to admit so publicly.) But it will not do to reject these comments as representing no more than some rump group within the party. On the contrary, for all their theological bombast, there is no gainsaying the fact that all these quotations come from powerful figures within the party and that their words continue to reflect those of a sizeable percentage of Republicans.

But what exactly is being reflected? In each of these quotations, God's will is both patently obvious and neatly in accord with partisan objectives. God wants to stop Obamacare. God wants a natural gas pipeline to go through. God does not want Israel to declare its Nuclear Weapons. God is in control of the earth's climate and the very idea that human activity could have an effect thereupon is an affront to his sovereignty. Profound religion's adamant distinction between God and the sinful creature is lost, replaced by what Niebuhr calls "a morass of self-esteem." That is bad enough, but for my purposes, it is more relevant to note that these quotations reveal the speakers as Children of Light, manifesting the "fanaticism of moral idealists who are not conscious of the corruption of self-interest in their professed ideals." And in this case, these Children of Light are or were elected representatives, part of, to say the least, a powerful minority within one of two American political parties.

The impact of this profanity is all too apparent. In chapter 7, I recounted how the current Congress manifests broken down comity, unbridled partisanship, and unrelenting gridlock. There can be little dispute that the rise of profane religion has, at minimum, contributed to this state of affairs. Under the spell of profane religion, mere toleration, let alone constructive engagement and honest compromise, becomes impossible. When your religion helps to assure you that God is on your side, that you are in an epic battle that God sanctions and applauds, then it is all too easy, indeed, it is incumbent, to see the other side as demonic, and compromise as a moral and spiritual failure.

THE CONGREGATION AS ECHO CHAMBER

I also argued in chapter 7 that politicians act like they do because their constituents want them to: Politicians behave in ways that help ensure their re-election. Therefore, polarization is the product of a polarized electorate. Here too, profane religion has only made things worse.

Sunday has long been called the most segregated day of the week. With rare and intermittent exceptions, American churches have historically been separated into enclaves of ethnicity, race, class, and education level. This fact is so self-evident that it doesn't require support. But it is also true that some of this segregation might now be diminishing. The 2006 National Congregations Study found that there are fewer all white congregations than there were in the previous study in 1998 (black churches showed no such change).[49] But even if segregation between races may be diminishing, another form has risen in its place. Segregation between political parties is stronger than it has ever been. That is, people in America are more likely to go to church with others who are members of the same political party. In the words of political scientist Diana Mutz, congregations exhibit a "strong, extreme homogeneity" regarding partisan identity. "Overwhelmingly, people said the people they met in church were extremely homogeneous with them politically."[50]

This self-segregation is something that makes many Christians cringe (or ought to anyway): Jesus himself prayed that all who believe in Him may be one (John 17:21). But given what we know about group behavior, it is also not surprising. Again, people feel better, and are more comfortable and more secure in their identity, when they are around people who think, look, act, and believe the way they do. And given that both conservative and liberal Christians have come to embrace a profane version of their faith, it is not surprising that congregations likewise have become more unified in their partisan objectives. Putnam and Campbell reference this same phenomenon:

> People sort themselves—whether consciously or not—into congregations with politically simpatico members, through a self-reinforcing process. The more one kind of person predominates within a given congregation, the more that others who perceive themselves as similar will feel comfortable there (and those who see themselves as different will feel uncomfortable, to the point of leaving).[51]

We have also seen that groups naturally tend to push their shared identity farther toward the extreme. They are more likely to view their group as good and powerful and important, and, accordingly, to view other groups negatively. Indeed, recall Sunstein's conclusion that the more important the group is to each individual's identity, the more group polarization increases.[52] Faith in God, connection to a denomination and a congregation—all of these are extremely important parts of many American's identity, and they are almost universally so for those who regularly attend church. Therefore it is not surprising that as partisan homogeneity increased, partisan views become more monolithic, more inflexible, and more extreme. In words that directly connect to Sunstein, Putnam and Campbell summarize the point this way:

> Religious social networks matter as much as they do, we posit, because they serve as *echo chambers*. Social interaction among like-minded co-religionists *reinforces and even hardens one's beliefs*, even if the process is subtle. . . . in some cases events . . . it will make those beliefs politically salient . . . From

there, it is a short step to identifying with the party that takes the same position on those issues that you do." (Italics added.)[53]

And indeed, for white Protestants at least, that short step has been taken: In 1972, less than half of white evangelical Protestants self-identified as conservative (48 percent); in 2008, that number was close to two-thirds (65 percent). "Religiosity is now a powerful predictor of party identification and candidate preference among white votes in the United States—more powerful in many elections than characteristics traditionally associated with party affiliation and voting behavior such as social class and union membership."[54]

It is important to recognize that this pattern is especially true for Protestants. Just about every denomination—from the United Church of Christ to the Lutheran Church Missouri Synod—falls fairly clearly along a partisan spectrum. For Catholics it is slightly more complicated. Nationally, Catholics are found on the far left, the far right and every place in between. But as the parish model has broken down, many Catholics, too, select parishes according to the partisan and theological leanings. And everybody in town knows which churches are which. For Latinos and blacks, on the other hand, the story is not this simple. Most relevantly, there is no clear cut connection between a congregation's theological and political identity. Nevertheless, for a sizeable and increasing number of Americans, party and religion have become mutually reinforcing aspects of their identity. And for my purposes, the point is that at least part of the explanation for this change is the embrace on both sides of a religion that is no longer prophetic.

My point is that as Christianity has become more profane, many Christian congregations and congregants have naturally become more partisan. Churches that are more segregated and polarized become a means by which each member is pushed to a heightened level of self-assurance and self-righteousness. The members of these congregations are just that much more likely to act like Children of Light. In Niebuhr's words, "Insofar as our congregations are merely religious communities in which an uncritical piety is nourished, they also do no more than to mix patriotic self-congratulation with the worship of God."[55] Self-congratulation is antipathic to what makes religion profound, and therefore to what religion ought to help us remember. What is more, such profane believers are more likely to strive to elect representatives who, in turn, reinforce their constituent's stridency and self-righteousness. The politics we currently witness reflect the impact of this mutually-reinforcing spiral.

WHAT TO DO?

Niebuhr had no illusions about the dangers associated with bringing religion together with politics. It is all too easy for a religion to become profane, and for the faithful to use God as a means for advancing their own objectives. The early fundamentalists certainly saw this danger, as well, and since they held no hope for a fallen world anyway, many chose to abandon the world of politics. But for Niebuhr, withdrawal—ignoring the world of politics and concentrating simply on saving souls—is no less irresponsible and no less unChristian. "The one wrong answer is to find no relevance at all between our faith and our political actions. This answer is wrong because it denies the seriousness of our political decisions and obscures our Christian responsibilities for the good order and justice of our civil community."[56] Despite all the dangers, there is no responsible choice but to engage. Christians must therefore take part in the most egotistical and vain and prideful enterprises on this earth, yet do so with an honest and abiding sense of their own fallenness. They will fail, of course. But Christians must strive to walk the tightrope as best they can, knowing that just as their God is not indifferent to injustice, they cannot be either. If they are to undertake that effort, Christians, and for that matter all Americans, could do with a different example—one that engages the political arena yet preserves religion's profound dimension.

POLITICAL AND PROFOUND: KING'S LETTER FROM THE BIRMINGHAM JAIL

In 1963, as part of a non-violent campaign against segregation, Martin Luther King Jr. was in Birmingham along with other civil rights leaders. After several days of marches and sit-ins, the state of Alabama brought a suit against the campaign, claiming that "the demonstrations were a threat to the peace." In a blanket injunction, circuit judge W. A. Jenkins Jr. ruled illegal "every imaginable form of demonstrations."[57] King and the other leaders insisted that the demonstrations continue despite the ruling. So they did. And on April 12, he was arrested and held in the Birmingham Jail.

King wrote his letter in response to a public statement from the Birmingham religious community. Issued while King was in jail, the brief statement was signed by local religious leaders (all of them white) representing Jews, Roman Catholics, Methodists, Presbyterians, Baptists, and Episcopalians. Published on Good Friday, the open letter argued that the struggle for civil rights should be pursued in the courts, not the streets, and that the rulings of the courts must be obeyed. The clergymen appreciated the "natural impatience" that the Negro community was feeling, but they argued that demonstrations were being led by "outsiders" and were "unwise and untimely."[58]

King responded to the letter by describing his philosophy of nonviolence. King argued that laws should be obeyed only if they were just, if they conformed to the law of God. But one had a moral obligation to disobey laws that were unjust. Nonviolent resistance therefore showed the utmost respect for the law. Nonviolent resisters break the law "lovingly," King wrote.

He also addressed the clergymen's call to wait, responding that the African American community was no longer willing to wait for justice. He recounted the feeling of "nobodiness" that all African Americans lived with throughout their lives. He recounted the story of how his daughter had seen a commercial for an amusement park, Funland, and how he had had to tell her that she could not go because she was black.

King references Niebuhr in the text. And when he writes that he should have realized that "few members of the oppressor race can understand the deep groans and passionate yearnings of the oppressed race," King closely reflects Niebuhr's understanding of the self-righteousness that flows naturally from groups. But King also presented a conception of the relationship between politics and religion that was likewise very Niebuhrian. King famously said, "We must speak with all the humility that is appropriate to our limited vision, but we must speak."[59] And it is clear that in this letter, as well, he is striving to emulate that prophetic balance.

In the opening paragraph (and throughout the text), he addresses his opponents not as enemies or benighted fools, but as "fellow clergymen," "brothers," and "friends." His words reflect a sense of equality that is born of their common vocation, but also as men of faith, and children of God. What's more, King makes clear that this equality extends to common sinfulness. King sees segregation as a sign of the world's sinful core, but he does not place himself above that sin. He decries both "the hateful words and actions of the bad people" and "the appalling silence of the good people." But he places the blame for this on everyone, including himself: "We . . . in this generation . . . will have to repent." Similarly, King laments over "the laxity of the church," of those who "have remained silent behind the anesthetizing security of stained glass windows." But he acknowledges his own role in creating this state of affairs, too. "How we have blemished and scarred that body [the church] through social neglect and through fear of being nonconformists." In closing, King admits his own limited perspective: "If I have said anything in this letter that overstates the truth and indicates an unreasonable impatience, I beg you to forgive me. If I have said anything that understates the truth and indicates my having a patience that allows me to settle for anything less than brotherhood, I beg God to forgive me." Throughout the letter, King assumes a common good will, and a shared commitment to justice; words that would reflect self-righteousness or certainty are notably absent. King is able to enter the realm of politics, insist on the rightness of his cause, and do so in a way that affirms both God's transcendent sovereignty and his own fallenness.[60]

Of course, not all of King's writing or speeches were similarly unassuming. King was an astute politician, and he would appropriate different rhetorical styles based on the audience and his objectives. So it is possible that King's rhetoric here is more for effect than genuine. But it is worth noting that King was in jail for nonviolent protest. And that lends strong credence to the idea that his words were both strategic *and* genuine. King's commitment to nonviolence was born of his effort to emulate the words and actions of Jesus and the spiritual strategy of Gandhi: "The Christian doctrine of love operating through the Gandhian method of nonviolence was one of the most potent weapons available to oppressed people in their struggle for freedom."[61] For a Christian, King believed, the willingness to suffer violence without responding in kind was to emulate Christ himself. And to treat one's opponents, the very one committing that violence against you, with "friendship and understanding," was to see that person as Christ saw him. Thus, King's commitment was born of the same Christian principles of equality and humility outlined above. As for Gandhi, the connection between humility and nonviolence was likewise explicit and essential. "The first step in nonviolence is that we cultivate in our daily life, as between ourselves, truthfulness, humility, tolerance and loving kindness."[62] My point is not to laud King's commitment to nonviolence, it is simply to show that there was more than words behind King's humility. Given that King's own commitment extended to his willingness to be cursed at, jailed, stoned, and ultimately murdered, I think it is fair to say that, rhetoric aside, his words in this letter are reflective of both his actions, and his inner convictions.

Jerry Falwell used to frequently say that Fundamentalists are Evangelicals who are angry about something. To update the point, maybe a member of the Tea Party can best be described as a Republican who is angry about something. And certainly there are many members of the Tea Party movement (including many of those Republican elected officials recounted above) who would also call themselves members of the Religious Right. These angry people might contest that their fear for their country and their freedom is appropriate, and that therefore their anger is righteous; it would be foolhardy to be humble in the face of such a horrible fate, and such vile enemies. But this makes King's example all the more relevant. In the first place, it is surely important to note that this letter was not only prophetic, it was effective. His witness made for a better, more moral America. For those concerned about the condition of our country, that fact ought to give them pause. Indeed, King's exemplifies the words of E. J. Dionne.

> The doubt and humility promoted by religion is not a form of weakness, but rather represents faith's greatest potential contribution to public life. The forms of religious engagement in public life that are rooted in doubt and humility are far more likely to be effective—and far more apt to be just—than approaches rooted in utter assurance and arrogance in the total identification of a human political agenda with the cause of God.[63]

But the more important point is that anger, righteous or not, only cuts so much ice. King was angry too. Indeed, it fairly drips from the pages of his letter. He was angry to be sitting in that jail cell because of an injunction that he knew to be rankly unconstitutional. He was angry to live in a society in which he was regarded as inescapably less worthy than those who had white skin. He was angry to have witnessed murderers and thugs routinely released from an abjectly racist judicial system. He was angry to have to explain to his daughter that she was not welcome at Funland. King's anger was real and it was surely righteous. Indeed, it would require a shattering lack of perspective for any Tea Party member to think that he or she has more right to anger than King did. And yet, in the midst of all that anger, Martin Luther King Jr. still managed to embrace a generosity, an evenhandedness, and a humility that was born of his deepest religious commitments. King shows that while such humility is not easy, while all of us are sinful and deluded, anger does not excuse the burdens of Christian witness.

REDISCOVERING PROFUNDITY

Humility simply is a Christian virtue, instituted by the very one Christians claim to worship. If Christians cannot practice it, if they have grown unable to do more than simply ape the rank partisanization that suffuses the rest of the culture, if they are unable to even suggest that they might have something deeper and more profound to offer, something that transcends the boundaries of partisanship, something that unites all believers in both confession and gratitude, then what difference does it make whether one has a Christian point of view or not, and why should anyone care what they have to say?

If Christians on the right and left were willing to reconsider how they might best serve their country (not to mention their faith and their God), they would do well to keep in mind Niebuhr's call for a prophetic religion, and King's singular example thereof. They might remind themselves that their faith supersedes any partisan outcome. "The urgency of the struggle" must be

> subordinated to a sense of awe before the vastness of the historical drama in which we are jointly involved; to a sense of modesty about the virtue, wisdom and power available to us for the resolution of its perplexities; to a sense of contrition about the common human frailties and foibles which lie at the foundation of both the enemy's demonry and our vanities; and to a sense of gratitude for the divine mercies which are promised to those who humble themselves.[64]

To be sure, King sets a high bar for American Christians. Maybe a little too high. But there are ways to move things in the right direction. For starters, Christian pastors should make it clear that neither sin nor mercy is the province only of some of us. Likewise, Christian individuals should reject any religious talk, of any stripe, that fails to affirm the ground on which religious humility and toleration rests. The First Amendment surely means that any politician or pundit has the right to celebrate the righteousness of their group and to diminish the humanity of those outside. But it ought to give any Christian pause when that celebration simultaneously affirms a faith that demands otherwise. If patriotism is the last refuge of a scoundrel, Christianity isn't far behind. In sum, talk is cheap. It is worth remembering that "not all who say 'Lord, Lord' will enter the kingdom."[65]

Beyond these meager steps, if they were really committed to recapturing a faith that transcends mere partisanship, Christians might start talking with each other about more fundamental questions. As theologian Jennifer McBride puts it,

> Fundamentalists, evangelicals and mainline Protestants all display some confusion about the public role of Christian faith in a pluralistic society. We haven't reflected enough on some basic questions of Christian faith, such as: What exactly is the content of the good news that Christians are to proclaim? What is the relationship between the church and "the world"? What claims should Christians be making about Jesus through our social and political engagement?[66]

Questions like these should come before any question about any specific political issue. They are not likely questions about which all Christians will agree, but if Christians were to engage in honest conversation with those on the other side of the partisan fence, they might recommit themselves to the more fundamental notion that there is a yawning and unbridgeable chasm between the real and the transcendent, between God and human beings, and between God's will and our partisan objectives. They might also come to see themselves as being part of the same community, with the same beliefs and commitments. At minimum, they might come to see themselves less as soldiers in a holy war and more, in Niebuhr's term, as "sinners fighting each other." That would be a significant improvement. The condition of our democracy, to say nothing of their souls, would be much improved.

NOTES

1. Hawkins, "Reinhold Niebuhr's One Scripture Passage."
2. CLCD, 94.
3. CLCD, 135.
4. In what follows, I have not parsed out niceties within different Christian denominations. This account is certainly more Protestant in tone, though Evangelicals and strict Calvinists will find points of dispute. Roman Catholics would accept the basics. Eastern Orthodox probably not. These distinctions are important, of course, but they are not germane to my objective here.
5. Spadaro, S. J., "A Big Heart Open to God."

6. Quoted in Brown and Forst, *The Power of Tolerance: A Debate*, 95.

7. ICE, 139.

8. CLCD, 134.

9. RNOP, 188.

10. See 1 Corinthians 13:12.

11. CLCD, 135.

12. CLCD, 151.

13. ICE, 144.

14. IAH, 173.

15. Schlesinger, "Reinhold Niebuhr's Role in Political Thought," 149.

16. RNOP, 203.

17. "The Social Creed of the Churches," Adopted by the Federal Council of Churches on December 4, 1908. Just to reinforce the connection I go on to make between this document and the present day National Council of Churches, note that this document is found on the NCC's website.

18. Dorrien, *Social Ethics in the Making*, 98.

19. MMIS, 78, 79.

20. ICE, 9.

21. RNOP, 196.

22. Evans, *Apathy, Apostasy and Apostles*, 114.

23. Murch, *The Protestant Revolt*, 31.

24. Ibid., 30.

25. Evans, *Apathy, Apostasy and Apostles*, 94.

26. Lomperis and Wisdom, *Strange Yokefellows*, 55.

27. Ibid., 16.

28. Putnam and Campbell, *American Grace*, 426-429.

29. Wallis, *On God's Side*, 30-31.

30. Here again, for my purposes, distinctions between Pentecostals, Fundamentalists, Evangelicals, Post- and Pre-millennials, and the like are not germane. I therefore define the Religious Right broadly as those Christians who are both theologically and politically conservative. These two have not and do not always go together, but it is fair to say that they do for those referenced here.

31. Williams, *God's Own Party*, 58.

32. Balmer, *Thy Kingdom Come*, 16. I will go on to note that Falwell changed his mind about civil rights. But when he said this, he was explicitly opposed to integration policies.

33. There are many who dispute the comparative relevance of these many rulings. Many contend that abortion was not nearly as important an issue to the movement as was the state threatening a school's tax exempt status. The issue is surely important, but it is not germane to my argument. See *Thy Kingdom Come*, 13-18.

34. Wuthnow, *The Restructuring of American Religion*, 202.

35. The other five were Robert Billings, Ed McAteer, Richard Viguerie, Howard Phillips and Paul Weyrich. See Winters, *God's Right Hand*, 116.

36. Ibid., 9.

37. Falwell denied ever making such a claim. He said that he would pay $5,000 to anyone who could prove he had. In court, Jerry Sloan, a former student, produced a videotape of this sermon. In 1999, ten years after the closing of the Moral Majority, Falwell apologized that he and his ministries had not shown that they love homosexuals "no matter what we think of their behavior." See *God's Right Hand*, 279, 378.

38. Ibid., 81, 245.

39. Ibid., 246.

40. Balmer, *The Kingdom Come*, 170.

41. Ibid., 168.

42. Jesse Helms frequently saw a connection between the will of God, and the Republican Party's political agenda. In his book *When Free Men Shall Stand* (Zondervan Publishing House, 1976), he argued that raising the minimum wage and national health insurance were ploys designed to diminish the status of human beings as children of God.

43. James Dobson Radio, May 21, 2013. See http://www.realclearpolitics.com/video/2013/05/22/bachmann_god_is_going_to_answer_our_prayers_and_free_us_from_obamacare.html.

44. *Congressional Record*, January 7, 2011, H133.

45. Speech to Ministry Students, Wasilla Assembly of God, Wasilla, Alaska, June, 2008. See http://usatoday30.usatoday.com/news/politics/2008-09-03-1664664500_x.htm.

46. Voice of Christian Youth America's radio program "Crosstalk with Vic Eliason," March 7, 2012. See: http://www.rightwingwatch.org/content/james-inhofe-says-bible-refutes-climate-change#sthash.xQht4QxA.dpuf.

47. Remarks, U.S. House Subcommittee on Energy and Environment, March 25, 2009. See http://www.dailymail.co.uk/news/article-1328366/John-Shimkus-Global-warming-wont-destroy-planet-God-promised-Noah.html.

48. *Congressional Record*, November 13, 2013, H7048.

49. Chaves, Anderson, and Byassee, "American Congregations at the Beginning of the 21st Century," 6.

50. Quoted in Bishop, *The Big Sort*, 176.

51. Putnam and Campbell, *American Grace*, 42.

52. See page 79.

53. Putnam and Campbell, *American Grace*, 437.

54. Abramowitz, *The Polarized Public*, 65.

55. RNOP, 280.

56. RNOP, 193.

57. "Negroes to Defy Ban," *Tuscaloosa News*, April 11, 1963, 21. See http://news.google.com/newspapers?id=YREdAAAAIBAJ&sjid=8poEAAAAIBAJ&pg=7376%2C1391871.

58. C. C. J. Carpenter, et al., "A Call to Unity."

59. These words were delivered at Riverside Church, New York City (Niebuhr's home church) on April 4th, 1967.

60. All quotations from King, "Letter From the Birmingham Jail."

61. King, *Stride Toward Freedom*, 79.

62. Ibid.

63. Dionne, *Our Divided Political Heart*, 186.

64. IAH, 174.

65. Matthew 7:21-23.

66. Heim, "The Witness of Sinners.

Chapter Nine

"Guardians of Democracy": Building Humility through Civic Education

The objective of the last chapter was to show that profane Christianity under-mines our democracy. When religion is profound, it constantly reminds us of how we truly are: deluded and sinful. We therefore feel obliged to adopt an abiding attitude of humility. Our nation would be better off if believers and religious leaders were to recommit themselves to the profound dimensions of their faith.

But no such recommitment will solve our problems. Any question of the profound or profane condition of Christianity is only germane, only address-able, for Christians. While profane Christianity is no doubt part of the prob-lem, it is hardly a sufficient strategy for repairing our current state of affairs. Religion might be a touchstone for democratic humility, even essential there-to, but we need to find ways to develop the humility that democracy requires that are not directly religious.

As I have noted, Niebuhr thinks that democracy must use all the means at its disposal to constrain our inclination to become Children of Light. Govern-ment and religion are two ways that we have considered. The third and final way is education. Throughout his uncannily large corpus, Niebuhr does not say much about education. But here is a key quote:

> A democratic society must use every stratagem of education and every re-source of religion to generate appreciation of the virtues and good intentions of minority groups, which diverge from the types of the majority, and to prompt humility and charity in the life of the majority. [1]

Niebuhr thus sees education, like religion, as a means for generating humility and charity. And that is to say, he sees education is an essential means for sustaining a democracy.

In general terms, this last thought is not a novel one. Throughout American history, from Thomas Jefferson to Horace Mann to John Dewey, educators and politicians have worried about the demands of democratic citizenship, and they have looked to schools to develop the necessary habits and dispositions.[2] In our immigrant society, classrooms have long been and still are one essential place for children to learn what it means to be an American. What is more, for this reason and others, schools are uniquely diverse. Even in the most cohesive private school, students are likely to find more diversity of experiences and opinion than they do around their kitchen table. Therefore one essential part of democratic education is learning to accept and engage that diversity. In a 2011 report published by the Civic Mission of Schools, Kathleen Hall Jamieson argues that "the well-being of our body politic is best served by an informed, engaged citizenry."[3] Education, the authors agree, is an indispensable means to that end. Schools therefore are, in the report's title, "Guardians of Democracy." And while this notion has roots that go back to the nation's founding, it remains operative in just about every state in the union. "All states have standards for social studies . . . that includes civics/government along with other disciplines such as history and geography." As well, "the theme of civic ideals and practices is found in every state's standard except Missouri's."[4]

Now to be sure, this unanimity doesn't go much farther. The question of what specific facts, values, and dispositions children most need to learn is a profoundly contentious one. So too are questions about how many courses should be required, what teaching styles are most effective and appropriate, and whether there should be assessments for civic knowledge (as there are, say, for math and reading). Like just about every other dimension of our contemporary society, division regarding these questions reflect a deep and unproductive contention. Nevertheless, just about everyone agrees that our democratic society is better off if children learn *something* about how to be part of one.

Throughout this book, I have argued that Niebuhr's theologically-informed view of how we human beings operate finds significant support in contemporary science. In Niebuhr's Christian language, we are all prideful sinners. In the language of science, we are all guilty of bias and motivated reasoning. But for my purposes the operative point is essentially the same: we are all Children of Light, with inordinately high opinions of ourselves and our groups, and virtually incapable of evaluating the world objectively. In this chapter, I want to argue that this condition ought to be part of that *something,* part of the debate about what our children need to learn about democratic society and their place in it. Our society needs to help students learn how their brain works and how that operation impacts, and for that matter undermines, our ability to maintain a democratic society. More, I want to ask whether education can help us retrain our brains, so that we are better able to understand and evaluate our own values, choices, and behaviors, and those of our groups, as well as those with whom we disagree. Ideally, I would want to help students learn enough that they are able to develop humility toward themselves, and toleration toward their political opponents.

From what has come before, it is clear that that is a tall proposition. Indeed, it is fair to ask how such an enterprise might even be possible. Even if one were to set aside the political difficulties for the moment, there are daunting obstacles that obtain just because of how our brains operate. We know that we cannot consciously evaluate any argument until *after* our brain has already assessed its emotional significance. And we know that when the brain does perceive a threat, that is, if a given statement runs counter to our belief system, it works hard to come up with a way to discount its veracity and value. And we know that all of this is happening at a level that we can neither perceive nor turn off. So how can we even talk about using education to overcome our motivated reasoning? How can we learn how to overcome our own brains?

Evidence shows that we *can* learn to influence our brains, if not quite overcome them. Speaking in broad terms, we can—with difficulty—employ the more evolved, more rational features of our brain to moderate, temper or at least coordinate with those that are older, more reactive, and more emotional.

INFLUENCING OUR BRAINS

Let's start with a very old and important aspect of our brains: the sex drive. In 2001, two European researchers published results of an experiment in which they viewed the fMRI images of the brains of ten young men (ages 20-42) as they were watching pornographic images and films. Employing language that only a scientist could love, the researchers selected images that were especially effective at bringing about "rapidly and automatically a marked positive change in the subjective emotional experience of healthy male subjects."[5] Viewing these selected images, the brains of these healthy males operated much the way nature intended. Accordingly, their fMRIs lit up in regions that will no doubt sound familiar: namely, limbic parts of the brain such as "the right amygdala, right anterior temporal pole, and hypothalamus."[6] In fact, the researchers conclude that their findings "fit with the various lines of evidence suggesting that the amygdala plays a pivotal role in the evaluation of the emotional significance of stimuli."[7]

But then the researchers asked the men to try to "down regulate" or diminish the intensity of their arousal. Down regulation has a number of specific scientific meanings, but in this sense, it simply conveys the general idea of reducing or suppressing the response to a stimulus. They suggested that the subjects try "to distance themselves from these stimuli, that is, to become a detached observer."[8] Most of the time, the subjects were able to achieve this down regulation, but as they made the effort, different parts of the brain showed activation, including the prefrontal cortex and anterior cingulate cortex. The limbic system, including the hippocampus and the amygdala, were quiet. For reasons that we have addressed above, we can only deduce so much from this kind of data. But they do tell us something. They demonstrate that at least with respect to this kind of arousal, "humans have the capacity to influence the electrochemical dynamics of their brains, by voluntarily changing the nature of the mind processes unfolding in the psychological space."[9]

In another experiment, this time involving all women, researchers again examined the subject's fMRIs while they were trying to regulate their emotions. But this time, some subjects were told to try to diminish their reaction *and* others were asked to increase it—to down *and* up regulate. The subjects were shown images that were sad (e.g., a person lying in a hospital bed), and they were asked to try to make themselves try to feel more or less sad. The researchers wanted to see if these efforts to influence emotional response in opposite directions showed similar activation patterns in the brain.

They also wanted to see if different strategies for self-regulation showed different levels of effectiveness and/or patterns of activation. Therefore, before the test, subjects were trained in two different techniques. The "self-focused" group was instructed to think about the image in terms of their own personal relevance. If they were trying to up-regulate, they were told to imagine that the person they were viewing was someone they know, or even themselves. If they wanted to diminish the emotional effect, they were told (like the men watching pornography) to view the events "from a detached, third-person perspective."[10] The other group was given the technique of "situation-focus." They were told to imagine that the events in the picture were going to get worse or better, depending on if they were up or down-regulating.

The brains of both groups were scanned as they viewed the images and employed their techniques. Those scans showed that both groups were indeed able to decrease or increase negative emotion. As well, they showed that both strategies (the self-focus and the situation focus) were equally effective. The only difference, and it is surely a relevant one, is that subjects found it easier to up regulate than down. That is, they found it easier to enhance a negative emotion that was already present—to fan the flames—than it was to stem and even reverse those feelings—to put out the fire. The specifics of the fMRI scans need not deter us, but it is worth pointing out the researcher's conclusion that, here too, their findings "are consistent with the hypothesis that reappraisal involves interactions between prefrontal systems that implement cognitive control processes and systems that appraise the affective properties of stimuli, such as the amygdala."[11] In this experiment, as well, brain scans demonstrate that with sufficient discipline, humans can use their brains to regulate the natural workings of their brains. In the researcher's language, through "the active mental transformation of the meaning of an event" we can use "cognitive control to maintain, if not necessarily transform, an emotional response."[12]

If all this is true, then it would appear to be at least possible if by no means easy to teach students how the brain works, and how they, like all of us, are inclined to bias and motivated reasoning. If down-regulation of emotion is possible, then perhaps it is likewise possible to control or moderate these actions as well. In other words, perhaps these same techniques can help students learn how to control those negative effects—to challenge their own beliefs and their emotional reaction to the beliefs of others.

Now in the first place, it bears repeating that it is impossible to do anything but diminish the impact of emotion on our thoughts and beliefs. But it also needs to be said that even if we could do more, even if we could eliminate emotion from our thinking, that would not be a good thing. The work of Antonio Damasio and others have made it abundantly clear that while emotions can overwhelm our reason, we cannot reason without them. People who have lost the emotional processing part of their brain appear laudably evenhanded in their ability to consider both sides of a question, but they are also unable to come to a decision, or even to judge the importance of the question.[13] The stories Damasio tells of patients incapacitated by their inability to decide which pen to use, or which way to drive to an appointment, are heartbreaking. In the concluding chapter I will speak to the indispensable role of emotion in politics. But the more fundamental point here is that emotion is indispensable to reason itself.

But there is another issue. Notice that in both experiments outlined above, the subjects were focused on a rather specific task. Both the men and women were trying to control their emotional reaction to one kind of image (one sad, the other erotic). It was not easy, but both subjects were able to achieve some measure of control. We might therefore conclude that once this ability was mastered, we'd have solved the problem. After all, once you learn how to swim, you don't need to learn it again. And swimming in a pool is not significantly different from swimming in a lake. Unfortunately, it appears that down regulation is not like that. That is to say, someone who is very good at down regulating their emotional reaction to a sad image, for example, may not be any better at being aware of, let alone regulating, their racial and ethnic biases. In short, our efforts to constrain the reactions of our limbic system, to the degree that they are successful at all, are tied up with the subject that is being thought about.

The reason for this is that our brains are not designed to think generally. Daniel Willingham recounts an experiment in which students were given four problems and told how to solve them: namely by finding the least common multiple. Then they were given a different math problem about a marching band. Even though they had just been told how to solve this kind of problem, less than one in five students were actually able to do so. Why? Because as the students read about the marching band, their brains began recalling images and experiences of high school: football games, cool autumn evenings, sweaty polyester uniforms, emptying spit valves, and on and on. All these images came easily; the idea that there was some structural similarity between this problem and the one they had just been told how to solve, did not. [14]

Willingham doesn't say so, but this condition as well is explained by natural selection. Just as your brain evaluates an image with respect to its emotional significance, it will also automatically focus on the specific circumstances of a problem. Consider once again your ancestor on the savannah from chapter 3. If you see a snake, your brain instantly calls up all it can remembers about snakes: (Is a triangle-shaped head good or bad? Which bands of color are bad? How far can a rattlesnake strike?) But more general information is not useful. The only thing that matters is avoiding that snake, right there and then. The idea that it might be prudent to develop some strategy for avoiding threatening animals, say, is beyond the capacity of your amygdala, and more importantly, is dangerously beside the point. As we have noted, there is a trade-off here. Because we focus on the specific, our comprehension—and thus reaction—"proceeds faster and more smoothly." That is a good thing. Because of it, we are more likely to live another day. But "the cost is that the deep structure of the problem is harder to recognize." [15]

So if this deep structure is so elusive, and if this elusiveness is endemic to our brains, what does that mean for education? Well, for one thing, it means that there is no one strategy that can help students learn how to challenge their own thinking on every occasion. While there are general rules that can help students think more deliberately, the most effective strategy is to develop skills for each specific task. To that end, Willingham suggests a four part process: 1. Identify deep structure; 2. Use metacognitive strategies; 3. Learn the important background information; and 4. Practice. Let us take these parts in turn.

FOUR STEPS FOR DEVELOPING SPECIFIC SKILLS

If the brain does not comprehend this deep structure naturally, then the educator's objective should be to develop knowledge about what that structure is and how to recognize it. In the problem about the marching band, for example, Willingham notes that the teacher could alert the students that that problem was similar to others they had been working on. "Yes, this is a problem about a marching band, but what about the numbers? What really is the problem we want to solve?" Similarly, teachers remind students who are dealing with a difficult text that what is being communicated often lies beneath the basic facts of the story. In *The Great Gatsby*, for example, the green light at the end of Daisy's dock is not just a place to tie up boats. The teacher's job is to help the student understand that such deep structure is in the text, and help them develop the means for discovering and understanding it.

How does the student do that? The teacher helps the student develop one or more "metacognitive strategies"—ways to think about thinking—that they can employ to help them improve their comprehension. These strategies are meant to be simple and memorable. They are often understood as rules of thumb that students can readily recall to keep their focus where it belongs. Again, some simply help a student develop a process for thinking through any problem: "Plan how to accomplish the task" and "Check in on your comprehension." But more useful strategies need to be more specific. "What are the variables?" "What is behind this problem?" "Why did the author use this image?" "What do I predict will happen next?" These and similar little reminders can help students remember to look past the specifics to find the crux of the matter.

Third, students have to learn the circumstances, the "background knowledge," that surrounds the problem. It is very difficult to solve math problems unless you have seen enough similar problems that you can recognize the underlying structure. Similarly, you can't choose the right variables without knowing something about the phenomenon in question. Willingham notes that someone who knows little about automobiles would assume—quite reasonably—that there is no relationship between speeding and the car's color.[16] But someone who has that knowledge—perhaps the owner of that '67 Mustang—would recognize that a candy apple red finish might well make it more difficult to keep your foot off the gas. Just so, students trying to tease out the dynamics between the main characters in *The Great Gatsby* would benefit from learning about American society during the 1920s: the Great Depression, Prohibition, and the loosening of sexual mores.

Finally, the student needs opportunities to practice. The more word problems you do, the better you are at recognizing the deep structure, and the more likely you will employ the correct metacognitive strategy. The more you read, the better you are at identifying when you are not comprehending the text and the better you are able to get yourself back on task. And so on.

With all these pieces in place: deep structure, metacognitive strategies, background knowledge, and practice, students can learn to think more critically about a specific question. They will never entirely overcome the innate bias in their brains, but they can get better at doing so. And the more they practice, naturally, the better they will get.

So for my purposes, this trail reveals that the question about how do we train our brain needs to be more specific. We need to ask whether and how we can teach students to down regulate their emotions when they are confronted with specifically political stimuli. If we want to use education to constrain students' natural tendencies to behave like Children of Light, then we want to teach them how to identify when those natural tendencies are being activated, and then how they might, through practice, reduce their effect. Thus, in Willingham's terms, we need a civic education curriculum that addresses deep structure, suggests metacognitive strategies, provides the relevant background information, and offers opportunities for practice, all so that students can improve their abilities to recognize their political biases and down regulate their reaction to emotional stimuli.

DEEP STRUCTURE: CIVIC EDUCATION ON THE BRAIN

By this point, enough has been said about deep structure. As part of their civic education, as part of our effort to help students learn to behave like democrats, they need to know how their brain operates and how that operation impacts their political behavior. Students need to know about our inescapable inclination to think we are more important, smarter, and more moral than others. They need to know about how difficult it is for us to assess honestly an opinion, belief, or argument—whether we agree with it or not. They need to know the power of group identity, how pleasant it is for us to be part of the in group, how painful it is to be out, and the lengths we will go to make sure we remain in the right one. And then they need to know how all these realities manifest themselves in politics.

To that end, students might learn how their amygdala works, why we need it and how it leads us inexorably and unconsciously to bias. Educators could recount some of the experiments examined in this book. They could be made aware of the Robber's Cave experiment, for example, and discuss how these inclinations play out in their own school. They might thereby come to understand better high school social dynamics at work, as well as their own emotional reactions to being in or out of some group. Finally, they might show students how these realities play out in the political realm. They might discuss Weston's examination of the fMRI scans of Republicans and Democrats when confronted with evidence of inconsistency (see page 56). They might then demonstrate how partisan infotainment exploits these workings of our brains. They could review presentations of Fox News and MSNBC and talk about how both examples feed our innate and unconscious desire to hear our beliefs reinforced, to be told that we are in the good group and that those who disagree with us are out. Such an effort might also compare them with presentations or discussions on *The PBS NewsHour,* say.

THREE METACOGNITIVE STRATEGIES

Kunda has written that in order to reduce bias, "it is crucial that subjects possess more appropriate reasoning strategies, view these as superior to other strategies, and be capable of accessing them at will."[17] Just so, the next step in developing a more meaningful and effective civic education would be to outline metacognitive strategies whereby students might deal with these difficult realities. Here are three ideas,

1. *"Fly on the Wall."* Politics can make you angry. And again, just about every politician (and many, many representatives of the new media) go out of their way to exploit this emotion. They know that making you angry is a good way to get and keep your attention, to get you to vote, and to write a check. So they are quite inclined to identify the enemy and raise the rhetoric. The effect also works the opposite way. If you are not in the appropriate partisan demographic, hearing your group referred to as stupid or as something less than a true Christian, patriot, or American can make you angry, too. So when either of these sorts of sentiments are expressed at a party or at some other casual setting, the resulting conflict can escalate into a shouting match, replete with bruised feelings and worse. Such a condition can also undermine much hope for compromise. It can also make humility impossible.

Everyone has heard the advice from Thomas Jefferson: "When angry count to ten before you speak. If very angry, count to one hundred." The fact is that science supports this advice, at least in part. Counting to ten allows time for your prefrontal cortex time to kick in, thereby moderating if not overcoming the initial reaction of your amygdala. In fact, most researchers will claim that six seconds is enough. Taking a deep breath in and out can be enough time to get past your initial emotional reaction. However, we also know that when it comes to down regulation, it is not simply a matter of time. It is also quite possible that waiting six seconds only serves to up regulate our emotions. If, while we are counting to ten, we focus on what is happening, reflect on the injustice or unfairness of the situation, we can often end up angrier than we were when we started. Just counting, to whatever number, is not enough.

The objective therefore is not simply to count, but to take that time to change one's perspective. The experiments recounted above demonstrate that the best regulative strategy is to use those seconds to try to take yourself out of the situation. Viewing a situation "from a detached, third-person perspective," as if one were a fly on the wall, is far more likely to diminish our emotional investment and allow us to engage our opponent in a manner that is more realistic and productive. Giving students the opportunity to practice democratic discussion (as I discuss below) will almost undoubtedly lead to circumstances in which emotion takes over. Allowing the class to understand what is happening in their brains and how things might appear differently from a fly on the wall perspective can help them learn how to get some control over their emotion and see the event in a more realistic perspective, and thereby allow for a more constructive discussion.

2. *"Consider the Opposite."* We have seen that our biases are beyond our consciousness, and that they are confronted only with difficulty. When we are considering some stimuli we are inescapably inclined to evaluate it in terms of our own beliefs and values. Thus, in politics, any argument, speech, or research finding that we care about is seen as either confirmation of our superiority or a threat thereto. And in the latter case, our brains come up with good reasons for us to render it suspect at best and contemptible nonsense at worst. Thomas Gilovich says that these features of our brain are so deep that it is not enough simply to try to be open minded. Rather, our biases require a "compensatory mental habit" for moderating their effect on our unconscious thinking.[18]

Recall the Taber and Lodge experiment recounted in chapter 3. Despite the researcher's efforts to promote the subject's evenhanded assessment of the issues of affirmative action and gun control, they found "consistent evidence of . . . confirmation bias—with a substantial attitude polarization as a result."[19] That is to say, people found the arguments that supported their opinions more compelling than those against. What's more, at the end of this process, respondents held more extreme opinions than they did before they started. And the more extreme their opinions were when they started, the more pronounced this effect.

Taber and Lodge note with some discomfort that people who were unsophisticated about political issues were less likely to have these biased reactions. Of course, given that the roots of bias lie in the unconscious assessment of threat, this outcome is quite predictable. Those who don't know much about politics don't have much emotional investment in the outcome. But that does not mean that the only solution to hyper-partisanship is cultivated ignorance. James N. Druckman argues that Taber and Lodge overstate the power of bias because they focus on issues where emotional investment is particularly strong.[20] He therefore had his subjects review papers on a less volatile political issue, namely, energy policy. Druckman also argued that

Taber and Lodge's instructions were insufficient. To be sure, Taber and Lodge told subjects to be evenhanded and told them that they would have to explain the controversy to other students. Druckman did the same. But Druckman raised the bar and offered his subjects a metacognitive strategy. In effect, he gave them the opportunity to develop "compensatory mental habits." He told a subset of subjects to think about the argument from the other side, "to consider alternative perspectives."[21] He found that when both changes were made—when subjects were given a less emotional topic and given this specific instruction—motivated reasoning "disappeared."[22]

Again, conclusions must be tentative. For one thing, it is not clear how much of this disappearance is due to the fact that the researchers chose different issues and how much comes from offering a metacognitive strategy. Regardless, there is enough evidence to advocate that such a strategy be part of an education in democratic citizenship. Again, students could learn about the "amygdala hijack," they could be shown examples of strong negative reaction to some political stimulus, and then they could be asked the question: "How would someone who does not believe the way this person does explain this result?"[23] When students are given the opportunity to practice debate themselves (see below), the teacher would likely have the opportunity to address both the phenomenon and the compensatory strategy in real time. Helping students ask this question at the very moment of their reaction can show them how they can effectively mitigate the effects of our biases. The imagination required to consider another's perspective diverts attention from the amygdala, and engages other parts of your brain. It also makes the other appear immediately less irrational. Finally, it can help us identify deficiencies with our own perspective and make it at least possible for us to uncover an insight or a potential argument that we could not have appreciated otherwise.

3. *"Our group values self-criticism."* We know that people are inclined to confirmation bias, that they are more likely to affirm arguments that support their political point of view and reject those that contradict it. More, we know that the more deeply felt a person's point of view is—the more associated it is with their identity—the stronger the bias. We know how the group's values become intimately associated with our individual identity and how pleasure and pain is likewise associated with our membership: If we are in, we feel good. If we are out, we feel bad. Indeed, this drive is so strong that we are inclined to manifest more of whatever the group values. That is, the power of groups push us to polarization: to a stronger and more extreme point of view, as well as an inordinately high opinion of our group.

If all this is true, then it ought to be possible to develop a metacognitive strategy that uses these innate features of human behavior as a way to change the evaluation of threat and self-interest. To that end, a civics classroom could try to create a group identity where differences are both respected and circumscribed by affection, where genuine objectivity is acknowledged as impossible but nevertheless seen as a valuable and approachable goal, where hard questions are valued as opportunities for learning, and where self-criticism is seen as a sign of intelligence, self-discipline, and most importantly, being a member in good standing. As I showed above, Druckman argues that motivated reasoning can be influenced by context. He even suggests that it is worth thinking about how to change the context in relevant ways. He concludes that "the role of social expectations in prompting accuracy seems to be a particularly fruitful area in need of more study."[24] A classroom could strive to create a culture that modified social expectations in just this way.

What Diana Hess calls a "political classroom" gives students the opportunity to engage in meaningful and authentic deliberation. That discussion focus on important issues of the day, or it might raise issues specific to the school (open campus policies, say). It gives students a chance to learn about the issues, reflect on their own experience, determine their own opinion, and then engage in discussion with their fellow students. In a political classroom, then, teachers "teach with and for discussion."[25] The teacher directs but does not dominate this discussion. Indeed, the goal should be for the teacher's role to diminish progressively as the students' skills develop. Instead, the teacher's primary job is to create a class culture in which such discussion can take place. Such a climate sees disagreement as both inevitable and potentially valuable, and models engagement that is fair and respectful. This climate seeks to find and celebrate points of commonality that transcend differences, to find reasons why disagreement need not be the final or only word. Indeed, according to Michael Shermer, this kind of climate is likely the best way for any of us to change our minds at all.

> The main way that we change our minds on moral issues is by interacting with other people. We are terrible at seeking evidence that challenges our own beliefs, but other people do us this favor, just as we are quite good at finding errors in other people's beliefs. When discussions are hostile, the odds of change are slight. . . . But if there is affection, admiration or a desire to please the other person, then . . . that person . . . tries to find the truth in the other person's argument.[26]

A teacher may not be able to create affection, but he or she could remind students of their common identity as "Eagles," "Panthers," or what have you, the history many of them share growing up together, their common interests as students, and even their common commitment to working together and getting things right.

What's more, this kind of group culture need not be limited strictly to the classroom. The report "Guardian of Democracy" affirms that as part of their civic mission, schools should do more than simply teach civics, they should create a culture throughout the school in which the democratic norms are learned and practiced. From the report:

> As a matter of definition, a school with a positive climate is one that promotes norms, values and expectations that support people feeling socially, emotionally, and physically safe; supports a sense of unity and cohesion in the school as a community; promotes a culture of respect and encourages students to consider themselves stakeholders in the school's success. [27]

In their article, "Classroom Deliberation in an Era of Political Polarization" McAvoy and Hess refer to "Adams High" as "the gold standard" for deliberative democracy, and for creating this kind of climate. In this unidentified high school, teachers have designed "an inclusive, mandatory activity that engages all seniors (not just those in the honor classes) in high-level policy discussions that move from the classroom to the hallways, the volleyball bus, and the dinner table." [28] Students do research on the issues they identify, learn firsthand about legislative procedure, and practice rules for civil discourse. Twice a year, the students present bills to the entire school in "general session." Students love the experience, look forward to their turn as seniors, and take ownership of the process. For my purposes, this school-wide commitment might be expanded to include the study of bias in science class. About 30 percent of graduating high school students take a psychology class and the number taking the test for AP Psychology is experiencing "astonishing growth." [29] There should therefore be exciting opportunities to bring knowledge about bias and the brain to bear on these political opportunities. Similarly, selected examples of self-criticism and tolerance and the opposite—taken from both history and literature—might make for interesting discussions. Regardless, the objective is clear: to create an enduring culture that encourages students to reflect on and question their own views, respect those who disagree with them, and to engage them in ways that confirm their common identity as members of the same school and their common objective to make it a better place.

BACKGROUND INFORMATION

I noted in chapter 4 that none of us knows, nor can know, everything we need to make a truly informed political choice. Nobody can know all the history, all the comparative data, all the economic theory, etc., that might inform any one political debate. Far less are we going to possess sufficient knowledge for every conceivable issue. We all have lives and other interests that preclude the possibility or desire to learn everything we need to know and there will always be some information that is simply unavailable. As I noted in chapter 6, this inescapable ignorance is one reason why we frequently appeal to our party identification to help us fill in the formidable holes that all of us have in what we know: If my party says that such and such policy is a good idea given such and such conditions, that is usually going to be good enough for me.

Awareness of this inevitable ignorance ought to moderate our high opinions about ourselves and our opinions. But it should not immobilize us. It is very Niebuhrian to say that we cannot know everything we need to know and that we must nevertheless make a decision. Any good democrat ought to both understand this reality, and learn for themselves what constitutes a workable balance, that is, how much we need to know in order to take part in a constructive debate. If such learning were part of civic education, it might spurn partisan infotainment because their presentation of background information supports a foreordained conclusion. Alternatively, it could include them, but it would present both sides, and seek to separate fact from falsehood or half-truths. It would also seek out accounts that strive to present all the relevant facts. McAvoy and Hess note that a political classroom typically asks students to do some preparatory work before the discussion, things like "completing a set of readings, watching a video, or doing a writing assignment."[30] A classroom discussion about fracking, for example, might show presentations from the energy industry and environmental groups, using the debate to identify bias and spin, straw men and half-truths, as well as to help students identify the facts within each presentation. It would include information about the positive effects of these new energy extraction techniques on the economy of states like North Dakota. It might also consider how dependency on foreign energy sources has influenced American foreign policy. It could explore the impact these new techniques have and could have on environmental issues like ground water contamination as well as potential positive effects on climate change by burning natural gas instead of coal.

PRACTICE

When I coached soccer for very young kids, my compatriot and I quickly found that drills were a waste of time. The children didn't find them fun and even when they did them correctly, which was infrequently, they didn't apply them to the game. After a while, we decided that to a point, we would mostly just let the kids play. As they did, we would stand close by, and when we saw a teachable moment we would blow a whistle. The kids knew at that point to stop and listen. We might talk together about what had happened. We might reposition the players differently, or suggest an alternative idea to a player and then start the sequence over. In other words, any coaching we did would be in response to what was happening as the kids practiced. This kind of learning through the activity worked well for the Rockets. They enjoyed practice more and seemed to learn more about what to do and they started to win some games. This notion of coaching through playing is not far off from the idea of teaching "with and for discussion."

In such a classroom, teachers would try to achieve a vigorous exchange, in which everyone is encouraged (and when appropriate, strongly encouraged) to present their opinion. In the beginning, for example, the teacher might ask to hear from someone who has not yet spoken, or make sure that everyone takes a turn. But at the same time, teachers should also make sure that students feel safe to risk doing so. That effort is likewise fraught with difficulties. A safe discussion space does not mean the classroom becomes a support group. In a political classroom "safe" means that opinions are both respected and subject to challenge, and that personal attacks are unacceptable. High school being what it is, such safety may not transcend the bounds of the classroom. But demanding respect, and defending conversational outliers, needs to be one of the teacher's primary responsibilities. A safe discussion also means that students should feel comfortable referencing their personal experiences when making arguments. Teachers can talk about the relative value of anecdotes vs. data, but as part of a broader discussion, such experiences offer students a chance to make a contribution that can be both instructive and persuasive. For example, in a discussion about the Affordable Care Act, if a student has an uncle with a pre-existing condition, or if he knows his aunt is worried about keeping employees because of rising health care costs, then such information is surely relevant.

Similarly, teachers should try to develop a firm but limited leadership role. And again, over time, that role should diminish. If these specific skills are to carry over to real life conversations, teachers should try to encourage an open debate, one in which students engage each other, rather than one that regularly pivots through the teacher. On the other hand, making sure that the space is safe for fragile egos means making sure that standards for discussion are enforced. They should see their classrooms as "regulated deliberative spaces" and explicitly teach and enforce appropriate behavior.[31] In this kind of practice, the time when a discussion begins to fall apart becomes an excellent teachable moment. The teacher could stop the discussion—blow the whistle, as it were—and ask the students to consider the debate from a fly-on-the-wall perspective. He can ask questions to the class and the instigators. "You got pretty emotional there, can you tell us about your thinking? Was there something that you were reacting to? What would have been a good strategy for him to use there? How do we get things back on track? OK, let's try it again." Making a discussion that is both vigorous and safe is not easy, and it requires practice for the teacher, as well. It also requires support from school leadership so that the teacher, too, feels safe to discuss issues that are controversial. But the effort could produce students ready, and at any rate more ready, to take on the challenge of democratic citizenship.

WOULD IT WORK?

The idea that a civics class ought to offer the opportunity to practice these democratic skills might seem self-evident. Students do not already know how to hold a civil and constructive discussion. And it is certainly not easy to know when one is being "spun." Indeed, the operation of the brain makes it very difficult to master these skills, and the marketplace for the new media offers precious few models of what such behavior even looks like. If it is good for students to learn how to be democrats, opportunities for this kind of practice would therefore seem to be implied. But neither politicians, nor teachers, nor the broader public see it that way.

A policy brief published in June of 2011 by the American Enterprise Institute presented survey analysis which shows that the American public is skeptical about the quality of civic education. Almost half believe that "too many social studies teachers use their classes as a 'soap box' for their personal point of view." There are notable differences between Democrats and Republicans, but majorities of both parties believe that teachers should forego points of controversy and instead focus on "instilling good work habits." On the other hand, less than one in five Americans (both Republicans and Democrats) see "Promoting Civic Behaviors" as a priority for civic education. [32]

For their part, civics teachers are eager to celebrate the virtues of classroom discussion. The AEI brief notes a prior survey which shows that teachers "are almost unanimous in preferring to use [controversial topics] as teaching moments." [33] Such professions are easily made, of course. But McAvoy and Hess quote a 2011 study which demonstrates that they do not necessarily correspond to action. The study of 106 middle and high school classes concluded that "despite considerable lip service among teachers to 'discussion,' we found little discussion in any classes." [34] No doubt the public's skepticism about teachers and their motivation helps to account for teacher reluctance. In our current hyper-partisan environment, distrust is high and apparently ubiquitous. Even if a teacher scrupulously tries to avoid influencing a conversation, it is quite easy for a teacher's motivations to be misconstrued. It is surely easier to forego the whole idea. What is more, lectures about facts are easier. Leading productive and civil discussions about controversial issues, especially with so much teenage angst and hormones in play, is not for the faint of heart.

To compound the problem, changes in the content and structure of civic education is no less daunting a task than it is for government or religion. In the current climate, Democrats and Republicans don't agree about the color of the sky, but apparently neither wants civics teachers to focus on developing democratic dispositions. Partisanship has evaporated trust, and as I have noted, every potential legislative change, no matter how prima facie benign, is assumed to have an unacceptable partisan effect. Students may not be voters yet, but they will be soon enough and therefore anything more than a presentation of the barest facts is too great a risk. Let them learn about the three branches of the legislature, the pocket veto, and call it a day. I obviously don't agree. The facts about the brain recounted here obtain for both sides of the partisan fence; any change is therefore sauce for the goose. But I don't see how anyone could be sanguine about overcoming that distrust.

So if politicians don't trust it, the public doesn't want it, and teachers don't really practice it anyway, what is left to say? Simply this: as it stands, we are missing a rare and comparatively benign opportunity to improve our democracy. Our current political and media environment is saturated with examples of unproductive and uncivil discussions. Even with practice, it presents a strong current to swim against. Indeed, without such opportunities for practice, it is extremely unlikely that students will learn how to engage in fair, honest, and constructive debate. Most would say that our democracy could use more of that kind of debate. But if that is really what we believe, it would be imprudent and shortsighted to forego such an important opportunity to develop it. As part of becoming a democrat, students ought to have the opportunity to learn through discussion, to learn both about the issue at hand, and also how to express their point and engage those with whom they disagree.

Of course, one must be realistic about what such an education might achieve. Just as no Christian believes that anybody can stop sinning, anyone who knows anything about the brain knows that the underlying causes of bias and motivated reasoning cannot be eliminated. Nevertheless, there are good reasons to believe that this kind of model for civic education would have a positive impact on the quality of our democracy. When students have the opportunity to engage in discussion with those who think and believe differently from themselves, data show that they are likely to learn about politics and about the issues under discussion, and to become more aware and tolerant of opposing views. For McAvoy and Hess, "engaging students in classroom deliberation is important for developing democratic dispositions in which people see each other as political equals, value other points of view, weigh evidence, and become more informed about the political issues they will confront in the public sphere."[35]

Even knowledge alone makes a difference, and for reasons that have nothing to do with politics. I knew an umpire (I coached baseball and softball for many years, too) who as part of his training had been taught about the amygdala hijack and how he might avoid it and keep his cool. Brokers also know that confirmation bias can lead them to stick with a stock long after they should have sold off. To counteract this problem, many learn a metacognitive strategy in which they try to consider the opposite.[36] Why should such knowledge not be presented to future umpires, stockbrokers, and citizens? Would they, too, not be better off?

But knowledge alone might have political implications, as well. Niebuhr says that simply reminding believers that they are not God leads them to humility and thus to tolerance. Just so, simply knowing about our biases can diminish their power over us. Fine notes that women who were taking a math test were told that any anxiety they might be feeling "could be the result of these negative stereotypes that are widely known in society and have nothing to do with your actual ability to do well on the test."[37] Those women did better on the test than those who did not receive that timely reminder. Just teaching students the facts about how we inevitably misperceive the world could cause us to be more humble about our own beliefs and more tolerant about those of others. Knowledge alone could thus have a felicitous impact on our democracy.

Finally, I am hopeful that such an effort has a chance because local control of education means that a one size fits all strategy is neither possible nor necessary. It should therefore be possible for more schools like Adams High to try different strategies and then test their effectiveness. Some of these tests could involve traditional data gathering methods: teacher and parent surveys, pre and post testing, tracking students' behavior over time and so on. Results that have research behind them would be in a better position to scale up such efforts. But since this behavior is also rooted in neuroscience, why not consider more direct research? In other words, why not develop fMRI tests for civic tolerance? Recall Westen's experiment that showed that partisans are looking for reasons to reject unpleasant information, and will show signs of relief when they do so. Why not test the effectiveness of various strategies for down regulation of those kinds of emotional reactions? Why not use scientific technologies to assess the efficacy of a more scientifically-informed civics education?

I can see no reason why not. Indeed, in light of the current condition of our democracy, I would argue that such an enterprise ought to evoke a sense of urgency. But there is a more fundamental and Niebuhrian point. Again, our reasoning skills are and will always be suspect. But it is one thing to say that we cannot fully overcome our failures. It is quite another to say that we cannot recognize them as failures—failures that are common to us all, regardless of our partisan point of view. Again, as Fine notes, simply knowing about our biases can impact their power over us. "Mental events that manipulate our brains—emotions, moods, schemas, stereotypes and so on—lose some of their effect when we are aware of their potential to influence us."[38] Knowing that we are all Children of Light ought to make us better able to treat ourselves and our positions with slightly more humility and those of our opponents with slightly more tolerance and generosity. If we can do no more than that, future citizens would be, in very Niebuhrian terms, better prepared to be democrats. In his words,

> Without a sense of the universality of an egocentric corruption, the passion for a universal humanizing quality degenerates into hatred for those who express their egotism in some ways, different from our own. The force of humility and pity no longer operates to bind men together despite their differing interests and convictions.[39]

Civics education can help remind all of us that there is scientific support to this idea of egocentric corruption, and thereby help restore some of our democracy's requisite humility.

NOTES

1. CLCD, 143.
2. By referencing the role of schools in civic education, it might already be clear that in what follows, I am referring primarily to high school students. I have no doubt that the model recounted here could be adapted for use by college students or even adults, but I do not address those questions here.
3. Jamieson, "Message from Campaign Partner," 4.
4. Godsay, Henderson, Levine, and Littenberg-Tobias, "State Civic Education Requirements," 1.
5. Beauregard, Lévesque, and Bourgouin, "Neural correlates of conscious self-regulation of emotion," 2.
6. Ibid., 3.
7. Ibid.
8. Ibid., 2.
9. Ibid., 5.
10. Ochsner, et al., "For Better or For Worse," 484.
11. Ibid., 495.
12. Ibid., 496.
13. Damasio, *Descartes Error*, 193.
14. Willingham, "Critical thinking: Why is it so hard to teach?"
15. Ibid., 10.
16. Ibid., 16.
17. Kunda, "The Case for Motivated Reasoning," 482.
18. Gilovich, *How We Know What Isn't So*, 186.
19. Taber and Lodge, "Motivated Skepticism in the Evaluation of Political Beliefs."
20. Druckman, "The Politics of Motivation," 199-216.
21. Ibid., 205.
22. Ibid.
23. Gilovich, *How We Know What Isn't So*, 188.
24. Druckman, "The Politics of Motivation," 206.
25. Parker and Hess, "Teaching with and for Discussion," 273-289.
26. Shermer, *The Believing Brain*, 68.
27. Gould, et al., "Guardian of Democracy: The Civic Mission of Schools," 23.
28. McAvoy and Hess, "Classroom Deliberation in an Era of Political Polarization," 23.
29. American Psychological Association, Enrollment Data. See http://www.apa.org/ed/precollege/about/enrollment.aspx.
30. McAvoy and Hess, "Classroom Deliberation in an Era of Political Polarization," 21.
31. McAvoy and Hess, "Classroom Deliberation in an Era of Political Polarization," 23.

32. Kelly, Miller, and Lautzenheiser, Contested Curriculum," 4. What exactly is meant by "work habits," and how such habits would correspond specifically to a class on civics, is not clear.

33. Ibid.

34. McAvoy and Hess, "Classroom Deliberation in an Era of Political Polarization," 21. The study they quote is Nystrand, Martin, Wu, Lawrence L., Gamoran, Adam, Zeiser, Susie and Long, Daniel A., "Questions in Time: Investigating the Structure and

Dynamics of Unfolding Classroom Discourse," *Discourse Processes*, 35:2 (2003), 135-198.

35. McAvoy and Hess, "Classroom Deliberation in an Era of Political Polarization," 19.

36. Zweig, "How to Ignore the Yes-Man in Your Head."

37. Fine, *A Mind of Its Own*, 190.

38. Fine, *A Mind of Its Own*, 207.

39. Niebuhr, *Christian Realism and Political Problems*, 13.

Conclusion

Democratic Humility

In the previous chapter, I made the fairly pedestrian assertion that politicians and pundits try to appeal to emotion, especially anger, because they know that it's a good way to get and keep your attention, to get you to vote, and to write a check. Indeed, anger is so effective in this regard, that it has never been, nor will it ever be, otherwise. Politicians need all three; they cannot hope to succeed without them. Therefore, they will always make emotional appeals, telling anyone who will listen that the stakes are high, the enemy is united and powerful, and good people must mobilize to defeat them.

The idea that humility is a good thing, even a necessary thing for a healthy democracy, runs counter to this reality. Really counter. Humility is perhaps the most un-political virtue there is. Humility doesn't incline you to think you of all people should be the new mayor, senator, or what have you; it doesn't get your side out to the polls, and it does not get you the votes you need to pass your bill into law.

Of course, Niebuhr knows this as well.

> Contending factions in a social struggle require morale; and morale is created by the right dogmas, symbols and emotionally potent oversimplifications. These are at least as necessary as the scientific spirit of tentativity. . . . They will have to believe rather more firmly in the justice and in the probable triumph of their case, than any impartial science would give them the right to believe, if they are to have enough energy to contest the power of the strong.[1]

On the one hand, Niebuhr believes humility is essential for democracy. It gives us a perspective that is closer to the truth. It causes us to moderate our inflated opinions about ourselves and our political objectives. And it enables us to tolerate those whom we live with and ardently oppose. But success in politics requires that we be immoderate, that we up regulate our emotion, that we grow more committed to our cause than the facts may warrant, and that we see the opposition as worse than they probably really are. Humility undermines all of this: it causes us to second guess ourselves and our belief and it enervates the will. It would appear that in politics, humility is both necessary and a recipe for inevitable failure.

This dilemma is brought to light in the work of political scientist Diana Mutz. Mutz studied what she called "cross cutting" political discussions— informal conversations/arguments between people who do not agree. Mutz shows that these kinds of conversations can have positive results. People who take part in these kinds of conversations are more likely to recognize that viewpoints different from our own are nevertheless legitimate, and we are more likely to tolerate those who you happen to disagree with.

But that is not the end of the story. In the first place, Mutz notes that conversations like this are rare. When and if people do have them, they are most likely to do so at work. But in their neighborhoods and churches— places where people are better able to sort themselves into a cadre of mutual reinforcement—cross cutting conversations are not that likely to occur. Mutz's finding thus supports the idea that we all like to surround ourselves with people, news, and entertainment that confirms our view of the world.

More importantly, these kinds of conversations have negative results, as well. They can lead to "a kind of paralysis with respect to political action."[2] Again, it is easier to vote, to organize, and to give money when your relationships, your politicians and your chosen media all support your inescapable inclination to think that you are right and they are wrong. The more opportunities one has to hear other perspectives and inconvenient facts, the more one develops tolerance and even respect for alternative points of view. And the more toleration, the more likely one will experience ambivalence rather than action. Thus, those who develop greater toleration are also less likely to be politically engaged.

Mutz's work thus reinforces the notion that these essential features of democratic life are in irresolvable tension: to foster one is to risk undermining the other. And if both are essential to a healthy democratic life, then what is to be done?

For Niebuhr this contradiction is simply another manifestation of the human dialectic. We are free yet constrained, creative yet creatures. We cannot not sin, but we are not incorrigible. We are capable of genuine good, but never without some measure of evil. The best human arrangements recognize and accommodate both sides of this dilemma. Especially so in the political sphere.

In the quotation above, Niebuhr doesn't say that morale trumps "tentativity," or renders the latter illegitimate. Politics requires emotion, but that requirement does not mean we are free to spurn humility. He says rather that both are necessary if politics are to be successful. Working out this dialectic is yet another balancing act that we humans must endeavor to achieve, even though we are doomed to some measure of failure.

For Niebuhr this effort starts by putting things in perspective. Combining humility and "morale" means that we must act immoderately, but we must do so with the notion that at the very bottom, it is really something of an act. "The respective parties are bound to contest elections as if the future of the nation depended upon their victory, but they must nevertheless have a reserve conviction that this is not true, that the nation will be safe in the keeping of either party."[3] Niebuhr believes that this kind of dialectical thinking, or duplicity if you prefer, is indispensable. Indeed, without this "reserve conviction" our democracy is in mortal danger. In the same piece, he says that "whenever the followers of one political party persuade themselves that the future of the nation is not safe with the opposition in power, it becomes fairly certain that the nation's future is not safe, no matter which party rules. For such political acrimony endangers the nation's health more than any specific political policies."[4]

Of course most times we think Niebuhr is right. We know that all the metaphors that surround politics—battles, campaigns, war rooms, attack ads, and so on—are only metaphors. And as bad as we want to win, as much as we think our city, state or nation will be better off if we do, we will not fear for our future if we lose. We reasonably expect that things will go on largely the way they did before. We also know that if one cannot accept this measure of equanimity, if we cannot overcome or constrain our political acrimony, the prospects for our nation's well-being diminish accordingly.

But at the same time, we also know that a reserve conviction can sometimes be both unwise and illegitimate. Sometimes the future is *not* safe. Sometimes politics *is* the only thing that stands between us and a moral outrage, a rank injustice, or a national disaster. And at times like these, neither duplicity nor humility are warranted. At that moment, politics as war becomes the only and perhaps the last alternative to war itself. In 1831, William Lloyd Garrison started his abolitionist newspaper *The Liberator*. In the first issue, he made it clear that he possessed nothing like Niebuhr's "reserve conviction:"

> I am aware that many object to the severity of my language; but is there not cause for severity? I will be as harsh as truth, and as uncompromising as justice. On this subject, I do not wish to think, or to speak, or write, with moderation. No! no! Tell a man whose house is on fire to give a moderate alarm; tell him to moderately rescue his wife from the hands of the ravisher; tell the mother to gradually extricate her babe from the fire into which it has fallen;—but urge me not to use moderation in a cause like the present. I am in

earnest—I will not equivocate—I will not excuse—I will not retreat a single inch—AND I WILL BE HEARD.[5]

The fact is not simply that Garrison was on the right side of history, but that he was right to reject moderation, to reject the idea that he had his own biases, to reject the idea that humility was more commensurate with the facts. Confronted with the abject realities of one human owning another, humility and all its accompanying effects were not only inappropriate, they served to accommodate a moral scandal. Garrison is a heroic figure for precisely these reasons. Our nation is better off for his moral certainty, his passion, and his utter lack of humility. If we had been there, confronted with the same rank injustice, we all hope that we would have had both the insight and courage that Garrison showed. Just so, we hope that if it ever happens that we find ourselves combatting a similarly grave danger or injustice, that we will have the courage of our convictions, and will not hamstring ourselves with second guesses about our biases, questions about the moral rectitude about our group, wonderings about some unknown fact, and so on.

Some would argue that now is precisely one of those times. For these Americans, the easy assumptions about the future are precisely what are at issue, and therefore the battle lines must be drawn. We are, whether all of us know it or not, in a state of politics as war. After Obama was re-elected in November of 2012, Michael Needham, Executive Director of the Heritage Action Fund, put out a video to his supporters. Over dramatic visuals and music, Needham laid out the organization's vision for the next four years. "We are in a war. We are in a war to save this nation. And abandoning our post will condemn it to a future of managed decline." At the end of the piece, the voice of Ronald Reagan brings home the point: "You and I have a rendezvous with destiny. If we lose freedom here, there is no place to escape to. This is the last stand on earth."[6]

Clearly Needham is responding to the 2012 election in a way that will rally the troops, and get them to recommit their time and (especially) re-sources to the causes he identifies. Perhaps that is all that he is doing. Per-haps his war rhetoric is merely that. But if Needham possesses a "reserve conviction," he is hiding it very well, indeed. Heritage Action was a central player in the shutdown and debt limit impasse in 2013 and was among the most vocal opponents of the deal which ended the crisis. In that instance, he and his organization certainly acted as if his reference to war was not merely rhetorical. But leaving aside the question of where Needham himself truly comes down, there is no denying that his is a fairly common refrain. A sizeable minority on the right insist that things are so dire, and our future so precarious, that politics as war is not only justified, it is a moral imperative. The stakes are just that high.

Obviously I don't think these people are right. I think on the contrary that Needham and those who think likewise are acting as Children of Light, with too high an opinion of themselves, too biased a view of the facts, and too low an opinion of their opponents. But the point is that such expressions are virtually inevitable. That is how our brains are designed. And that means that without some form of societal constraint, without some abiding internal awareness that we don't and can't have it all figured out, all of us democrats are naturally inclined to push beyond any reserve conviction, to turn our campaign rhetoric into vitriol, our emotional investment into self-righteousness, and everyday politics into politics as war. Consider again Niebuhr's words. He says that we risk our democracy whenever the followers of one political party *persuade themselves* that the opposition cannot be left in power. This capacity for self-delusion is democracy's internal peril, for we are all liable to become Children of Light, all liable to persuade ourselves that we alone are on God's side, we alone are able to appreciate the stakes of the current circumstance, we alone are able to stand up to the folly of our opponents. This is for Niebuhr an inescapable problem for our democracy, one we must strive to constrain and if possible ameliorate if that democracy is to survive. And I have argued that the condition of our media has left us less equipped to achieve that constraint than we have been for generations.

I am hopeful that politicians can develop rituals that might rebuild a sense of common purpose, that Christians can restore a religion that is more profound than profane, and that all Americans can work to refashion a civic education that teaches students the skills and dispositions they need to be good democrats. I am hopeful, perhaps merely hopeful, because it is not clear to me how else to develop the cultivated sense of humility that democracy requires. We need that humility not in order to preserve decorum or moderation, not in order to make sure we are nicer to each other, but in order to develop a politics that reflects a more accurate understanding of ourselves and our shared condition. We need humility in order to constrain our innate impulses, and thereby make political judgments that are more reliable and more prudent. Finally, we need humility in order for us to better determine those very few times when we must abandon humility. Without it, we are too likely to make the wrong choice, and imperil our democracy far more than any present contest might. Humility is indispensable if we are to sustain what Lincoln called the last, best hope on earth.

A democracy without humility is a democracy in peril. Whatever else we can say about our current state of affairs, Niebuhr and neuroscience show this to be so. Any effort to restore our nation's politics must start here.

NOTES

1. MMIS, xxvii.

2. Mutz, *Hearing the Other Side*, 93.
3. Niebuhr, *Love and Justice*, 67.
4. Ibid.
5. Garrison, *The Liberator*, 224-226.
6. See http://www.washingtonpost.com/blogs/thinktanked/wp/2012/11/07/obama-win-not-a-decisive-defeat-says-heritage-action/.

Selected Bibliography

Works by Reinhold Niebuhr that are frequently cited are identified in the notes by the following abbreviations:

MMIS, *Moral Man and Immoral Society: A Study in Ethics and Politics*. Introduction by Langdon B. Gilkey. Louisville, KY: Westminster John Knox Press, 2001. First published in 1932.

ICE, *An Interpretation of Christian Ethics*. New York: The Seabury Press, 1979. First published in 1935.

NDM1, *The Nature and Destiny of Man, Volume 1: Human Nature*. New York: Charles Scribner's Sons, 1941.

NDM2, *The Nature and Destiny of Man, Volume 2: Human Destiny*. New York: Charles Scribner's Sons, 1943.

CLCD, *Children of Light and Children of Darkness: A Vindication of Democracy and a Critique of its Traditional Defense*. New York: Charles Scribner's Sons, 1944.

IAH, *The Irony of American History*. New York: Charles Scribner's Sons, 1952.

RNOP, *Reinhold Niebuhr on Politics: His Political Philosophy and Its Application to Our Age as Expressed in His Writings*. Edited by Harry R. Davis and Robert C. Good. New York: Charles Scribner's Sons, 1960.

Abelson, Robert. "Beliefs are Like Possessions," *Journal for the Theory of Social Behavior* 16, 3 (October 1986), 223-250.

Abramowitz, Alan. *The Disappearing Center: Engaged Citizens, Polarization and American Democracy*. New Haven: Yale University Press, 2010.

Abramowitz, Alan. *The Polarized Public: Why American Government Is So Dysfunctional*. Boston: Pearson, 2013.

Ariely, Dan. *The Honest Truth About Dishonesty: How We Lie to Everyone—Especially Ourselves*. New York: HarperCollins, 2012.

Balmer, Randall. *Thy Kingdom Come: How the Religious Right Distorts Faith and Threatens America*. New York: Basic Books, 2007.

Baum, Matthew A. "Red State, Blue State, Flu State: Media Self-Selection and Partisan Gaps in Swine Flu Vaccinations," *Journal of Health Politics, Policy and Law* 36, 6 (December 2011), 1021-1059.

Baum, Matthew A. and Tim Groeling. "New Media and the Polarization of American Political Discourse." *Political Communication* 25 (2008), 345-365.

Bennett, John. "Reinhold Niebuhr's Social Ethics." In *Reinhold Niebuhr; His Religious, Social, and Political Thought*, 45-77. Edited by Charles W. Kegley and Robert W. Bretall. New York: Macillan Company, 1956.

Berreby, David. *Us and Them: The Science of Identity.* University of Chicago Press, 2005.

Beauregard, Mario, Johanne Lévesque, Pierre Bourgouin. "Neural correlates of conscious self-regulation of emotion." *The Journal of Neuroscience,* 21 RC 165 (2001), 4-6.

Bingham, June. *Courage to Change: An Introduction to the Life and Thought of Reinhold Niebuhr.* New York: Scribner's, 1961.

Bishop, Bill with Robert G. Cushing. *The Big Sort.* New York: Houghton Mifflin, 2008.

Boswell, John. "Logos and Biography." In *Theology and Sexuality: Classic and Contemporary Readings,* 356-361. Edited by Eugene F. Rogers Jr., Malden, MA: Blackwell Publishers, 2002.

Brown, Wendy and Rainer Forst. *The Power of Tolerance: A Debate.* Edited by Luca Di Blasi and Christoph F. E. Holzhey. New York: Columbia University Press, 2014.

Brownstein, David. *The Second Civil War: How Extreme Partisanship Has Paralyzed Washington and Polarized America.* New York: Penguin Press, 2007.

Bullas, Jeff. "35 Mind Numbing YouTube Facts, Figures and Statistics—Infographic." http://www.jeffbullas.com/2012/05/23/35-mind-numbing-youtube-facts-figures-and statistics-infographic/.

Carpenter, C. C. J., Joseph A. Durick, Hilton L. Grafman, Paul Hardin, Nolan B. Harmon, George M. Murray, Edward V. Ramage, Earl Stallings. "A Call to Unity," See "Demonstrations Called 'Unwise and Untimely: Church Leaders Say That Extreme Action By Negro Groups Should End,'" *Birmingham Post-Herald,* April 13, 1963. http://bplonline.cdmhost.com/cdm/landingpage/collection/p4017coll2.

Chafets, Zev. "Late-Period Limbaugh." *New York Times Magazine,* July 6, 2008.

Chaves, Mark, Shawna Anderson, and Jason Byassee. "American Congregations at the Beginning of the 21st Century: A Report from the National Congregations Study." 2007.

Churchill, Winston. "Churchill By Himself: The Definitive Collection of Quotations." Edited by Richard Langworth. New York: PublicAffairs, 2008.

Cillizza, Chris. "Worst. Congress. Ever. The case in 7 charts." The Fix, *Washington Post* October 31, 2013. http://www.washingtonpost.com/blogs/the-fix/wp/2013/10/31/worst-congress-ever-the-case-in-7-charts/.

Cohen, Geoffrey. "Party Over Policy: The Dominating Impact of Group Influence on Political Beliefs." *Journal of Personality and Social Psychology* 85, 5 (2003), 808-822.

Costa, Jay. "What's the Cost of a Seat in Congress?" *Maplight: Revealing Money's Influence in Congress,* Mar 10, 2013. http://maplight.org/content/73190.

Crouter, Richard. *Reinhold Niebuhr: On Politics, Religion, and Christian Faith.* New York: Oxford University Press, 2010.

Darley, John M. and Paget H. Gross. "A Hypothesis-Confirming Bias in Labeling Effects." *Journal of Personality and Social Psychology* 44, 1 (Jan 1983), 20-33.

Daschle, Tom and Trent Lott. "Prescriptions for comity in government." *Washington Post,* November 22, 2013. http://www.washingtonpost.com/opinions/tom-daschle-and-trent-lott-prescriptions-for-comity-in-government/2013/11/22/9966ce66-532e-11e3-9fe0-fd2ca728e67c_story.html.

Damasio, Antonio. *Descartes' Error: Emotion, Reason, and the Human Brain.* New York: Penguin Books, 2005.

Dionne, E. J. *Our Divided Political Heart: The Battle for the American Idea in an Age of Discontentment.* New York: Bloomsbury USA, 2012.

Dorrien, Gary. *Social Ethics in the Making: Interpreting an American Tradition.* West Sussex, UK: Wiley-Blackwell, 2010.

Dunning, David. "A Newer Look: Motivated Social Cognition and the Schematic Representation of Social Concepts." *Psychological Inquiry* 10, 1 (1999), 1-11.

Evans, G. Russell. *Apathy, Apostasy and Apostles: A Study of the History and Activities of the National Council of Churches of Christ in the U.S.A. with Sidelights on its Ally, the World Council of Churches.* New York: Vantage Press, 1973.

Federal Communications Commission. "Genachowski Continues Regulatory Reform to Ease Burden on Businesses: Genachowski Announces Elimination of 83 Outdated Media Rules." August 22, 2011. http://www.fcc.gov/document/genachowski-announces-elimination-83-outdated-media-rules.

Federal Communications Commission. "Report of the Commission: Docket No. 8516: In the Matter of Editorializing by Broadcast Licenses, Report Appendix." http://transition.fcc.gov/ ftp/Bureaus/Mass_Media/Databases/documents_collection/490608.pdf.

Federal Council of Churches. "The Social Creed of the Churches." Adopted December 4, 1908. http://nationalcouncilofchurches.us/common-witness/1908/social-creed.php.

Fine, Cordelia. *A Mind of One's Own: How Your Brain Distorts and Deceives.* New York: W. W. Norton & Company, 2006.

Fiorina, Morris P. and Samuel J. Abrams. *Disconnect: The Breakdown of Representation in American Politics.* Norman: University of Oklahoma Press, 2009.

Fox, Richard. *Reinhold Niebuhr: A Biography.* New York: Pantheon Books, 1985.

Gamwell, Franklin I. *Democracy on Purpose: Justice and the Reality of God.* Washington, D.C.: Georgetown University Press, 2002.

Garrison, William Lloyd. Inaugural Editorial, *The Liberator* 1, January 1831. Reprinted in Wendell Phillips Garrison, *William Lloyd Garrison, 1805-1879: The Story of His Life, Told by His Children, Vol. I.* New York: The Century Company, 1885.

Gilovich, Thomas. *How We Know What Isn't So: The Fallibility of Human Reason in Everyday Life.* New York: The Free Press, 1991.

Goldman, Daniel. *Emotional Intelligence: Why It Can Matter More Than IQ.* New York: Bantam Dell, 1995.

Godsay, Surbhi, Whitney Henderson, Peter Levine, and Josh Littenberg-Tobias. "State Civic Education Requirements." Circle Fact Sheet, September, 2012.

Green, Joshua. *Moral Tribes: Emotion, Reason, and the Gap Between Us and Them.* New York: Penguin Press, 2013.

Gutmann, Amy and Dennis Frank Thompson. *The Spirit of Compromise: Why Governing Demands It and Campaigning Undermines It.* Princeton, NJ: Princeton Press, 2012.

Haidt, Jon. *The Righteous Mind: Why Good People Are Divided by Politics and Religion.* New York: Vintage Books, 2012.

Hamilton, James T. "The Market and the Media." In *The Institutions of American Democracy: The Press.* Edited by Geneva Overholser and Kathleen Hall Jamieson. *The Institutions of American Democracy: The Press,* 351-370. New York: Oxford University Press, 2005.

Hawkins, Justin. "Reinhold Niebuhr's One Scripture Passage." *Fare Forward: A Christian Review of Ideas,* March 22, 2013. http://www.patheos.com/blogs/fareforward/2013/03/ reinhold-niebuhrs-one-scripture-passage/.

Heim, David. "The Witness of Sinners: Theologian Jennifer McBride on the Nontriumphal Church." *The Christian Century* 130, 24 (Nov 27, 2013).

Henneberfer, Melinda. "Tom Ricks to MSNBC: You're just like Fox, Only Not as Good at It." She the People, *Washington Post,* November 27, 2012. http://www.washingtonpost.com/ blogs/she-the-people/wp/2012/11/27/tom-ricks-to-msnbc-youre-just-like-fox-only-not-as-good-at-it/.

Jamieson, Kathleen Hall. "Message from Campaign Partner: Leonore Annenberg Institute for Civics at the University of Pennsylvania." In "Guardian of Democracy: The Civic Mission of Schools." Edited by Jonathan Gould. *The Leonore Annenberg Institute for Civics of the Annenberg Public Policy Center at the University of Pennsylvania and the Campaign for the Civic Mission of Schools,* 2011.

Jamieson, Kathleen Hall and Joseph Cappella. *Echo Chamber: Rush Limbaugh and the Conservative Media Establishment.* New York: Oxford University Press, 2008.

Jamieson, Kathleen Hall and Erika Falk. "Civility in the House of Representatives: the 105th Congress." *The Annenberg Public Policy Center of the University of Pennsylvania,* March 1999.

Jones, Dan. "Social evolution: The ritual animal." *Nature* 493, 7433 (January, 23 2013). http:// www.nature.com/news/social-evolution-the-ritual-animal-1.12256.

Kelly, Andrew P., Cheryl Miller, Daniel K. Lautzenheiser. "Contested Curriculum: How Teachers and Citizens View Civics Education." AEI Policy Brief, June 16, 2011.

King, Martin Luther Jr. "Letter From the Birmingham Jail," Christian Century 80 (June 12, 1963).

King, Martin Luther Jr. *Stride to Freedom: The Montgomery Story.* New York: Harper, 1958.

Klein, Ezra. "Good Riddance to Rottenest Congress in History." *Bloomberg View.* January 2, 2013. http://www.bloombergview.com/articles/2013-01-02/good-riddance-to-rottenest-congress-in-history.

Klein, Ezra. "John Boehner's Congress is a Train Wreck." Wonkblog, *Washington Post,* September 20, 2013. http://www.washingtonpost.com/blogs/wonkblog/wp/2013/09/20/john-boehners-congress-is-a-train-wreck/.

Kübler-Ross, Elisabeth. *On Death and Dying.* New York: Simon and Schuster, 1969.

Kunda, Ziva. The Case for Motivated Reasoning. *Psychological Bulletin* 108, 3 (1990), 480-498.

Laugesen, Wayne. "Town Hall: Conservatives Converge on Springs (poll)." *Colorado Springs Gazette,* April 24, 2012. http://www.gazette.com/articles/conservative-137465-home-city.html.

Lazarfeld, Paul, Bernard Berelson, and Hazel Gaudet. *The People's Choice: How the Voter Makes up His Mind in a Presidential Campaign.* New York: Columbia University Press, 1949.

LeDoux, Joseph. *The Emotional Brain: The Mysterious Underpinnings of Emotional Life.* New York: Touchstone, 1996.

Lessig, Lawrence. *Republic, Lost: How Money Corrupts Congress—and a Plan to Stop It.* New York: Hachette Book Group, 2011.

League of Women Voters. "Our Work." http://www.lwv.org/our-work/educating-voters.

Loconte, Joseph. "Obama Contra Niebuhr." *The American: The Online Magazine of the American Enterprise Institute.* January 14, 2010. http://www.american.com/archive/2010/january/obama-contra-niebuhr.

Lomperis, John S. A. and Alan F. H. Wisdom. *Strange Yokefellows: the National Council of Churches and its Growing Non-Church Constituency.* Washington, DC: Institute on Religion & Democracy, 2006.

Lord, Charles, Lee Ross and Mark Lepper. "Biased Assimilation and Attitude Polarization: The Effects of Prior Theories on Subsequently Considered Evidence." *Journal of Personality and Social Psychology* 37, 11 (1979), 2098-2109.

Mahoney, M. J. "Publication Prejudices: An Experimental Study of Confirmatory Bias in the Peer Review System." *Cognitive Therapy and Research* 1, 2 (1977), 161-175.

Mann, Thomas E. and Norman J. Ornstein. *It's Even Worse Than It Looks: How the American Constitutional System Collided With the New Politics of Extremism.* New York: Basic Books, 2013.

Matthews, Laura. "What Would Gov. Chris Christie Change in DC?" *International Business Times,* November 19, 2013. http://www.ibtimes.com/what-would-gov-23chris-christie-change-dc-1475650.

McAvoy, Paula and Diana Hess. "Classroom Deliberation in an Era of Political Polarization." *Curriculum Inquiry* 43, 1 (January 2013) 14–47.

Mooney, Chris. *The Republican Brain: The Science of Why They Deny Science—and Reality.* Hoboken, NJ: John Wiley and Sons, 2012.

Munro, G. D., T. P. Lasane, and S. P. Leary. "Political Partisan Prejudice: Selective Distortion and Weighting of Evaluative Categories in College Admissions Applications." *Journal of Applied Social Psychology* 40, 9 (September 2010), 2434-2462.

Murch, James DeForest. *The Protestant Revolt; Road to Freedom for American Churches.* Foreword by Edmund A. Opitz. Arlington, VA: *Crestwood Books, 1967.*

Mutz, Diana. *Hearing the Other Side: Deliberative versus Participatory Democracy,* New York: Cambridge University Press, 2006.

Niebuhr, Reinhold. *Does Civilization Need Religion? A Study in the Social Resources and Limitations of Religion in Modern Life.* New York: MacMillan, 1928.

Niebuhr, Reinhold. *Leaves from the Notebook of a Tamed Cynic.* Forword by Martin E. Marty. Louisville, KY: Westminster John Knox Press, 1990. First published in 1929.

Niebuhr, Reinhold. "Ten Years that Shook My World." *Christian Century* 56 (April 26, 1939).

Niebuhr, Reinhold. *Christian Realism and Political Problems.* New York: Charles Scribner's Sons, 1953.

Niebuhr, Reinhold. *The Essential Reinhold Niebuhr: Selected Essays and Addresses.* Edited by Robert McAfee Brown. New Haven: Yale University Press, 1987.

Niebuhr, Reinhold. *Love and Justice: Selections from the Shorter Writings of Reinhold Niebuhr.* Edited by D. B. Robertson. Louisville, KY: Westminster John Knox Press, 1992.

Niebuhr, Reinhold and Paul E. Sigmund. *The Democratic Experience.* New York: Frederick A. Praeger Publishers, 1969.

Niebuhr, Reinhold. *Reinhold Niebuhr: Theologian of Public Life.* Edited by Larry Rasmussen. San Francisco: Harper and Row, 1989.

Ochsner, K. N., R. D. Ray, J. C. Cooper, E. R. Robertson, S. Chopra, J. D. Gabrielli, J. J. Gross. "For Better or For Worse: Neural Systems Supporting the Cognitive Down- and Up-Regulation of Negative Emotion." *NeuroImage* 23, 2 (October, 2004), 483-499.

Ornstein, Norman J. "Ending the Permanent Campaign." *Boston Review*, May/June 2011. http://new.bostonreview.net/BR36.3/ndf_norman_ornstein_fixing_congress.php.

Packer, George. "The Empty Chamber: Just how broken is the Senate?" *The New Yorker*, August 9, 2010. http://www.newyorker.com/magazine/2010/08/09/the-empty-chamber.

Parker, Walker and Diana Hess, "Teaching with and for Discussion," *Teaching and Teacher Education* 17 (2001), 273-289.

Pew Research Center for the People and the Press. "Partisan Polarization Surges in Bush, Obama Years: Trends in American Values: 1987-2012," June 4, 2012. http://www.people-press.org/2012/06/04/partisan-polarization-surges-in-bush-obama-years/.

Pew Research Center for the People and the Press. "Growing Support for Gay Marriage: Changed Minds and Changing Demographics," March 20, 2013. http://www.people-press.org/2013/03/20/growing-support-for-gay-marriage-changed-minds-and-changing-demographics/.

Pew Research Center's Journalism Project Staff. "The Invisible Primary—Invisible No Longer." *Pew Research Journalism Project*, October 29, 2007. http://www.journalism.org/2007/10/29/the-media-sectors, "The Invisible Primary—Invisible No Longer," http://www.journalism.org/2007/10/29/the-media-sectors.

Pronin, Emily, Thomas Gilovich and Lee Ross. "Objectivity in the Eye of the Beholder: Divergent Perceptions of Bias in Self versus Others," *Psychological Review*, 111, 3 (2004), 781-799.

Public Policy Polling. "Congress Less Popular than Cockroaches, Traffic." News Release, January 8th, 2013. http://www.publicpolicypolling.com/pdf/2011/PPP_Release_Natl_010813_.pdf.

Putnam, Robert D. and David E. Campbell. *American Grace: How Religion Divides and Unites Us.* New York: Simon and Schuster, 2010.

Rauschenbusch, Walter. *Christianity and the Social Crisis.* Forward by Douglas Ottati. Louisville, KY: Westminster John Knox Press, 1990. First published in 1907.

Robinson, Marilynne. *When I Was A Child I Read Books: Essays.* New York: Farrar, Straus and Giroux, 2012.

Ross, L., and A. Ward. "Naive Realism in Everyday Life: Implications for Social Conflict and Misunderstanding." In *Values and Knowledge,* 103-135. Edited by T. Brown, E. S. Reed & E. Turiel. Mahwah, NJ: Erlbaum (1996).

Rudman, Chelsea. "On Fox, Journalist Tom Ricks Accuses The Network Of Operating As A Wing Of The Republican Party." *Media Matters for America*, November 26, 2012. http://mediamatters.org/blog/2012/11/26/foreign-policys-tom-ricks-appears-on-fox-news-t/191509.

Schlesinger, Arthur. "Reinhold Niebuhr's Role in Political Thought." In *Reinhold Niebuhr; His Religious, Social, and Political Thought,* 125-150. Edited by Charles W. Kegley and Robert W. Bretall. New York: Macmillan Company, 1956.

Schudson, Michael. *Discovering the News: A Social History of American Newspapers.* New York: Basic Books, 1981.

Schudson, Michael and Susan Tifft, "American Journalism in Historical Perspective." Edited by Geneva Overholser and Kathleen Hall Jamieson. *The Institutions of American Democracy: The Press,* 17-47. New York: Oxford University Press, 2005.

Schultz, Kathryn. *Being Wrong: Adventures in the Margin of Error.* New York: Ecco, 2010.

Shapiro, Rebecca "Tom-Ricks: Fox News Statement about My Apology Is 'Horseshit.'" *Huffington Post*, November 28, 2012. http://www.huffingtonpost.com/2012/11/28/tom-ricks-fox-news-statement-apology-horseshit_n_2205430.html.

Sherif, Muzafer, O. J. Harvey, B. Jack White, William R. Hood, Carolyn W. Sherif. *Intergroup Conflict and Cooperation: The Robbers Cave Experiment*. Norman: Institute of Group Relations, The University of Oklahoma, 1961.

Shermer, Michael. *The Believing Brain: From Ghosts and Gods to Politics and Conspiracies— How We Construct Beliefs and Reinforce Them as Truths*. New York: Henry Holt, 2011.

Sobeiraj, Sarah and Jeffrey M. Berry. "From Incivility to Outrage: Political Discourse in Blogs, Talk Radio and Cable News." *Political Communication* 28, 1, 19-41.

Solomon, Norman. "Don't Vent, Organize—And 'Primary' a Democrat Near You." *Fire DogLake*. Wednesday May 1, 2013. http://my.firedoglake.com/nsolomon/2013/05/01/dont-vent-organize-and-primary-a-democrat-near-you/.

Solomon, Sheldon, Jeff Greenberg, and Tom Pyszczynski. "A terror management theory of social behavior: The psychological functions of self-esteem and cultural worldviews." *Advances in Experimental Social Psychology* 24, 93 (1991), 93-159.

Spadaro, Antonio, S. J. "A Big Heart Open to God: The exclusive interview with Pope Francis." *America* 209, 8 (September 30, 2013).

Streitmatter, Rodger. *Mightier than the Sword: How the News Media Have Shaped American History*. Boulder, CO: Westview Press, 2009.

Stroud, Natalie Jomini. *Niche News: The Politics of News Choice*. New York: Oxford University Press, 2011.

Sullivan, Andrew. "Here Comes the Groom: A (Conservative) Case for Gay Marriage." *The New Republic*, August 28, 1989. http://www.newrepublic.com/article/79054/here-comes-the-groom.

Sunstein, Cass. *Going to Extremes: How Like Minds Unite and Divide*. New York: Oxford University Press, 2011.

Sunstein, Cass. *Republic.com 2.0*. Princeton, NJ: Princeton University Press, 2002.

Taber, Charles S. and Milton Lodge. "Motivated Skepticism in the Evaluation of Political Beliefs." *American Journal of Political Science* 50, 3 (July, 2006), 755-769.

On Being with Krista Tippett, "Moral Man and Immoral Society: Rediscovering Reinhold Niebuhr: Advanced Learning Guide for Educators and Students," October 25, 2007. http://www.onbeing.org/program/moral-man-and-immoral-society-rediscovering-reinhold-niebuhr/feature/advanced-learning-guide#main_content.

Tuschman, Avi. *Our Political Nature: The Evolutionary Origins of What Divides Us*. New York: Prometheus Books, 2013.

Tyson, Peter. "Are We Still Evolving?" *Inquiry: An Occasional Column*. December 14, 2009. http://www.pbs.org/wgbh/nova/evolution/are-we-still-evolving.html.

Vicuña, Dan. "Common Cause New York Comments on Redistricting Report," October 9, 2014. http://www.commoncause.org.

Wallis, Jim. *On God's Side: What Religion Forgets and Politics Hasn't Learned about Serving the Common Good*. Grand Rapids, MI: Brazos Press, 2013.

Wason, P. E. "On the Failure to Eliminate Hypotheses in a Conceptual Task." *Quarterly Journal of Experimental Psychology* 12 (1960).

Westen, Drew, Pavel S. Blagov, Keith Harenski, Clint Kilts, Stephan Haman. "Neural Bases of Motivated Reasoning: An fMRI Study of Emotional Constraints on Partisan Political Judgment in the 2004 US Presidential Election." *Journal of Cognitive Neuroscience* 18, 11 (November 2006), 1947-1958.

Whitworth, William. "Chet Huntley and David Brinkley: An Accident of Casting." In *Television News Anchors: An Anthology of Profiles of the Major Figures and Issues in United States Network Reporting*, 36-64. Edited by Thomas Fench. Jefferson, NC: McFarland and Co., 1993.

Williams, Daniel K. *God's Own Party: The Making of the Christian Right*. New York: Oxford University Press, 2010.

Willingham, D. T. "Critical thinking: Why is it So Hard to Teach?" *American Educator* 31, 2 (Summer, 2007), 8-19.

Wilson, Timothy D. *Strangers to Ourselves: Discovering the Adaptive Unconscious.* Cambridge, MA: Belknap Press, 2002.

Winters, Michael Sean. *God's Right Hand: How Jerry Falwell Made God a Republican and Baptized the American Right.* New York: HarperOne, 2012.

Wuthnow, Robert. *The Restructuring of American Religion.* Princeton, NJ: Princeton University Press, 1988.

Zweig, Jason. "How to Ignore the Yes-Man in Your Head." *Wall Street Journal*, November 19, 2009. http://online.wsj.com/articles/SB10001424052748703811604574533680037778184.

Index

Abelson, Robert, 36, 45, 89n9
Abramowitz, Alan, 86, 100, 105n16, 105n25
ACLU (American Civil Liberties Union), 53
AEI (American Enterprise Institute), 148
Affordable Care Act, 69, 147. *See also* Obamacare
amygdala, 31–32, 41, 47n4, 53; hijack by, 32–33, 60, 143, 149
An Interpretation of Christian Ethics, Reinhold Niebuhr, 114
anxiety: in Niebuhr, xiv, 6–9, 11–12, 14n18, 18–19, 24; groups as a way of combatting, 51–52, 56, 80, 84
Ariely, Dan, 10, 12
Associated Press, 66

Bachman, Michelle, 122
Balmer, Randall, 121
Baum, Matthew, 66–67
Bennett, John, 19
Benghazi, Libya, 63
St. Bernard of Clairvoux, xvi, 91, 109
Berreby, David, 51, 71
Berry, Jeffrey M., 70, 85
bias, 37, 38, 40, 42–43, 47n21, 59, 150; beyond our awareness, 34, 39, 42; in partisan media, 68, 70, 82–84; strategies for reducing impact of, 45, 141, 142–143. *See also* confirmation bias

Birmingham, Alabama. *See* King, Martin Luther Jr., Letter from the Birmingham Jail
Bishop, Bill, 74n13, 86
Bob Jones University, 118
Brinkley, David, 65
Brownstein, David, 101
Bryan, William Jennings, 117–118
Bush, George H. W., 53
Bush, George W., xi, 58

cable television, xv, 65, 67, 69, 85, 94. *See also* Fox News; MSNBC
Campbell, David, 116, 124
Cappella, Joseph, 74n22
Carter, Jimmy, 118
Catholics, Roman, 119, 125, 130n4
Chesterton, G. K., view on toleration, 111
Children of Darkness, xiv–xv, 24–27, 87
Children of Light, xiv–xv, 23–24, 25–27, 91, 112, 115, 125; moving beyond Niebuhr's concept of, 31, 46, 61; background in Scripture, 23; distinctively American failure, 27–28; in partisan infotainment, 86–88; in Republican politics, 117, 123, 157
The Children of Light and the Children of Darkness, Reinhold Niebuhr, xiv, 7, 22
Christianity, 109–110; makes the most sense of the most facts, xiii, 6, 9, 13,

About the Author

Christopher Beem is the author of *The Necessity of Politics* and *Pluralism and Consensus*. He has also coedited two books: *Welfare Reform and Political Theory* and *Work, Family and Democracy*. He received his PhD from the University of Chicago Divinity School. He lives in Whitefish Bay, Wisconsin.

CPSIA information can be obtained
at www.ICGtesting.com
Printed in the USA
LVHW041756250220
648170LV00003B/394